A Handbook for
Grievance Arbitration

Emerging Issues in Employee Relations
John T. Dunlop and Arnold M. Zack, Editors

Grievance Arbitration
Issues on the Merits in Discipline, Discharge, and Contract Interpretation
Arnold M. Zack

The Management of Labor Unions
Decision Making with Historical Constraints
John T. Dunlop

A Handbook for Grievance Arbitration
Procedural and Ethical Issues
Arnold M. Zack

A Handbook for Grievance Arbitration

Procedural and Ethical Issues

Arnold M. Zack

American Arbitration Association
New York, New York

Lexington Books
An Imprint of Macmillan, Inc.
New York
Maxwell Macmillan Canada
Toronto
Maxwell Macmillan International
New York   Oxford   Singapore   Sydney

Library of Congress Cataloging-in-Publication Data

Zack, Arnold.
   A handbook for grievance arbitration : procedural and ethical
issues / Arnold M. Zack.
      p.   cm.—(Emerging issues in employee relations)
   Includes index.
   ISBN 0-669-27975-7
   1. Grievance procedures—United States.   2. Grievance arbitration—
United States.   I. Title.   II. Series.
KF3544.Z33   1992
347.73'9—dc20
[347.3079]   92-19200
                                                           CIP

Copyright © 1992 by Lexington Books
                  An Imprint of Macmillan, Inc.

Lexington Books
An Imprint of Macmillan, Inc.
866 Third Avenue, New York, N.Y. 10022

Maxwell Macmillan Canada, Inc.
1200 Eglinton Avenue East
Suite 200
Don Mills, Ontario M3C 3N1

Macmillan, Inc. is part of the Maxwell Communication Group of Companies.

Printed in the United States of America

printing number
1   2   3   4   5   6   7   8   9   10

Contents

Foreword

This volume on the full range of procedural questions that arise in the arbitration process is a companion text to the earlier volume by Arnold Zack on substantive issues presented in final and binding labor-management grievance arbitration. These two interdependent volumes are designed for purposes of instruction or for reference, to be used by practitioners as representatives of the parties or as neutrals.

As an experienced craftsman, the author takes us through each process—from preparing for arbitration to the steps in decision making—identifying the concerns of the labor and management parties, any appointing authority, and the arbitrator. The organization of the volume matches the flow of the ordinary grievance arbitration process: preparation, arranging the hearing, problems at the outset of the hearing, arbitrability, the hearing, briefs, subsequent questions, and the procedures of the decisional process. As with the earlier volume, the text is liberally illuminated with cases and questions arising in actual experience, with a seasoned judgment of the appropriate approach of a neutral.

A distinctive feature of this practical guide is the incorporation of complex questions of professional ethics and sensitivity. These are based on the codes of professional responsibility of the appointing authorities and the National Academy of Arbitrators, in which the author has served as a member and sometimes officer for thirty years. The discussion is also alert to the various points in the arbitration process in which the "shadow of the law," to use Professor Mnookin's phrase, exerts an influence on procedures and rulings, should they be reviewed in the courts or government tribunals on grounds of process or public policy considerations.

A theme that permeates the discussion of procedural matters is the numerous subtle ways in which process questions may shape or distort substantive presentations and even arbitral decisions. This observation no doubt helps to explain why these procedural matters are often so controversial, particularly when their consequences may not be fully understood or evaluated by the separate parties. The potential consequences of process also underscore the importance of neutrals resolving these questions, at an appropriate time, in a firm and experienced course.

These procedural issues, it needs to be observed, vary in significance with the industrial relations system and its arbitration form and role. In general, an *ad hoc* arbitration arrangement, with different arbitrators handling each case, is likely to place greater emphasis on these procedural issues than is an umpire arrangement under which a single arbitrator works with the parties over a period of years, particularly where the relationship encourages the counseling and mediation of many disputes. A tripartite form of arbitration may also affect the contentious quality of procedural questions.

Arnold Zack has provided a pair of practical guides to labor and management representatives, to their agents in negotiations and dispute resolution and to neutrals that cover the full range of substantive and procedural issues they are likely to experience in private dispute resolution. The judgments, sometimes in a controversial and bitter setting, may not always command unqualified support, but they are always based on a wealth of experience, tutored by a professional code of ethics and good sense.

John T. Dunlop
Faculty Advisory Committee
Harvard Trade Union Program
Member 1942–1992

Prologue

Zack is back. The author of *Cases on the Merits* has written this companion handbook on the procedural problems, explaining how to obtain winning awards from labor arbitrators.

This handbook should be in every advocate's briefcase because, step by step, it offers invaluable insights.

Don't know how to handle a particular procedural problem? Don't panic! Request an adjournment. Take a breather in the corridor. Look up the appropriate section. This handbook will provide instant relief.

Arnold Zack is a popular arbitrator. He has analyzed why some advocates win while others lose, and has been willing to share his knowledge with other arbitrators and with advocates on both sides of the table. He has launched educational programs within the National Academy of Arbitrators, the American Arbitration Association, and the Society of Professionals in Dispute Resolution, encouraging these organizations to do more, to be all they can be in providing professional training.

In the sixties, Arnold Zack was the director of the Labor Management Institute of the American Arbitration Association, studying the expansion of collective bargaining into the public sector. He watched teachers and other government employees form unions, taking their employers to the bargaining table. He helped devise fair processes for resolving impasses in that controversial environment, and shared in the intellectual excitement of those dramatic times. But Arnie Zack was too energetic to be a researcher. He wanted a more active role, as an arbitrator, deciding the raw human controversies that arise in the workplace. With the AAA's encouragement, he joined the profession, and, since then, has heard and decided thousands of labor grievances and impasses.

In recent years, Zack has provided training and advice to labor management practitioners in Africa, Central Europe, and Russia. He has become an authority on international labor relations, able to resolve the transcultural misunderstandings that often arise between participants in adversarial proceedings.

An advocate learns that verbal communications are suspect. Arbitrationhearings seem to provide a rational format for weighing arguments and the testimony of witnesses, but all is for naught if the arbitrator is inattentive or suffering from some undisclosed prejudice. Only a thorough understanding of arbitration will insure that an advocate has plunged his case, like a harpoon, deeply into the arbitrator's decision process. Zack shows how that can be accomplished.

This is a good book—a practical and useful handbook. Arnold Zack is an education-minded arbitrator who cares deeply about his chosen profession.

Robert Coulson, President
American Arbitration Association

Preface

This volume is a handbook for union and management practitioners in the preparation and presentation of their cases in arbitration, and for the arbitrators to whom they present their cases. Regardless of how long or how often an arbitrator writes decisions, new issues or twists on old issues continuously challenge the profession. I hope the book will help such professionals to these new dimensions.

In format and title, this book is similar to my 1989 volume, also published by Lexington Books and the American Arbitration Association, *Grievance Arbitration: Cases on the Merits in Discipline Discharge and Contract Interpretation*, which deals with the substantive problems confronted by the parties in labor–management arbitration. This volume turns to procedural matters, evidentiary problems, and issues of professional responsibility and ethics. The issues confronted by the parties are presented chronologically, as they would occur in handling a case. As in the earlier volume, the hypothetical case studies arise from actual cases and show how they might be argued by the parties and decided by the arbitrator. The case studies are followed by examination of related matters that might arise in an actual case preparation or presentation.

Other texts and volumes may better guide the reader on issues of court enforcement and how other arbitrators decide similar cases, but this volume tries to provide a sense of prevailing industrial jurisprudence and insight into how most arbitrators would deal with the issues covered. The material present here grew out of a series of training programs conducted for Andrew Levy and Associates in South Africa.

I wish to express my appreciation to Professor John Dunlop, who initiated the idea of this series and who, as he has over the last three decades, set me straight on some of the underlying dynamics of industrial relations structure. My thanks, too, to my assistant Kim Falvey for her unending cooperation and good humor in developing and producing the manuscript. I also want to thank Arbitrator James Litton and American Arbitration Association Editor Earl Baderschneider for their diligence in suggesting changes to an earlier draft of the manuscript.

Of course, my greatest thanks are to my wife Norma for her help and cooperation while I worked on the text, and to our children Jonathan and Rachel, who supplied the names of the case study dramatis personnae, as well as their own ideas of what justice required in many of the cases.

1
Preparing For (or Avoiding) Arbitration

T he United States and Canada are unique in their development of the system of grievance arbitration to resolve disputes over the interpretation and application of the parties' collective bargaining agreement, such matters as the just cause for discipline or discharge, and whether the employer's actions in operating the enterprise are permitted by the terms of the negotiated agreement. Most other industrialized nations of the world lack such a negotiated fail-safe machinery. Unresolved disputes over matters as mundane as a disciplinary suspension of a single employee get varying treatment. If the issue has union membership appeal and the employee has enough popularity, the dispute can trigger work stoppages in entire enterprises—as any tourist hoping to ride on a dependable European transit system can attest. Disputes that fail to arouse such worker outrage in some cases may achieve redress by being shunted off to the government's industrial court for resolution in that forum.

The parties to collective bargaining in the United States and Canada have had the unique benefit of crafting their own private judicial machinery, which emphasizes joint resolution through several levels of appeal to ever higher levels of authority. Final resort of unresolved conflicts goes to a mutually selected and agreed-upon neutral whom the parties entrust with the authority to issue a final and binding arbitration award. The strength of that arbitration award comes from the fact that U.S. unions, unlike those in many other countries, are certified by the government as the sole and exclusive representatives of the workers in their particular bargaining unit. These unions are empowered to enter into collective agreements that are enforceable through the court system. The resulting final and binding arbitration award, however, is not the goal of the grievance procedure. It is a fail-safe, a guarantee of the end to a dispute in the event the parties fail to resolve the dispute on their own. The true strength of the dispute settlement machinery in collective bargaining is its emphasis on the joint resolution of a dispute at the earlier steps of the grievance procedure to avoid the risk of an adverse arbitration award.

This chapter covers the various procedures that may be employed by the parties prior to proceeding with an arbitration case.

Obviously, the preferred course of action is for the parties to resolve the dispute on their own prior to arbitration. This resolution may come at any stage of the grievance procedure—either during the formal grievance steps

1

or even at the courthouse steps. The parties frequently lose sight of the fact that settling the case on their own terms is better than the risk of submitting it to arbitration, where an arbitrator may decide strongly in favor of one side or worse, issue a decision that neither side can live with—one that is worse for both than something they might have settled for on their own.

But if the parties are unable to settle the case between themselves, arbitration is still avoidable. Grievance mediation has become increasingly popular as a step that the parties may invoke to avoid submitting a dispute to arbitration. Whether it be because of failed communication between the parties or because entrenched positions have clouded the parties' perspective on how their dispute might be resolved, or whether it is out of dread that the arbitrator may impose an untenable result, resort to an outside grievance mediator is always available to help the parties reach accord and extricate themselves from the risk of arbitration. By selecting a mediator themselves, or with the assistance of an outside agency, or even by asking their designated arbitrator to serve as mediator, the parties retain control over a negotiated settlement, which would otherwise be surrendered by resort to arbitration. The mediator may reactivate communications between the parties or may come up with new ideas for a settlement that might not have occurred to either or both of the parties as a feasible resolution of their problem. If the mediation fails, the parties may ask the mediator to serve as arbitrator, or if either side so opts, they may turn to a different arbitrator to decide the unresolved issue.

Another procedure that may be undertaken is expedited arbitration. While perhaps not well suited to every dispute, the parties may find this procedure useful to expedite the processing of cases that have remained too long in the grievance and arbitration channels. Expedited arbitration is usually developed by the parties as a system to which they routinely refer certain classes of cases, but it also can have value as an ad hoc process for expediting the resolution of any case.

If the parties are unsuccessful in resolving their dispute, if their resort to grievance mediation is unavailing, and if they are unable or unwilling to agree to an expedited processing of the case, then it becomes incumbent upon them to confront the reality of proceeding to arbitration.

A number of administrative tasks must be confronted and achieved for the arbitration to proceed smoothly. Some are tasks that must be done by the parties separately, such as examining the available evidence and preparing the parties' case. But other tasks should be done jointly by the parties themselves prior to the hearing to help reduce the level of animus at the hearing and to save the time and money that would be added to the bill if the arbitrator were asked to help the parties perform their housekeeping tasks.

Such matters as joint preparation of the exhibits, the stipulated facts, the time and venue of the hearing, and even agreement on the issue to be arbitrated will require discussions by the spokespersons of the opposing parties. This extra joint session to resolve the administrative matters provides yet another opportunity for the parties to resolve the bigger issues that placed them on the road to arbitration. If used effectively, that joint housekeeping meeting provides yet another opportunity for the parties to attempt to resolve their underlying dispute. If they are successful, then the parties have achieved the true goal of the negotiating process—the avoidance of the need for arbitration.

Settling the Dispute

Although this book concentrates on procedural issues that arise in arbitration, it is important to recognize that the objective of the system is to avoid, rather than rely upon, the final step of arbitration. This point must be kept in mind for the effective processing of grievances. Too often, it is faster, easier, and more convenient to rubber-stamp the position taken at the lower steps in the grievance appeal or in the grievance answer and pass the buck upward to the arbitrator. Such deferral entails additional cost and delay and opens up the possibility that the arbitrator may decide the case adversely. This ready deferral to arbitration abdicates the responsibility that is inherent in negotiating the earlier steps—the responsibility to endeavor to resolve the grievance between the two disputing parties before it escalates into intransigence on both sides.

The parties on the shop floor, or those replacing them at the next step of the grievance procedure, are best equipped to preclude the escalation of hostility. It is far better for both parties' future relationship to work out an accommodation over a grievance from which both sides can salvage something. Why risk an arbitration decision by an outsider who is bound by the cold terms of the parties' agreement, who is free to walk away from the case without knowledge of or responsibility for its ramifications, who lacks the range of settlement alternatives known only to the parties, and who usually lacks the authority to fashion the kind of compromise that only the parties themselves can develop?

A conscientious effort at settlement should commence at the first step, when the dispute between the grievant and the immediate supervisor is still fresh. If either or both, at that point, have the self-restraint and willingness to step back from their insistence on their rights, then the need for an appeal will be minimized and resolution more likely. And, indeed, the great majority of grievances are resolved at the lowest level; accommodation is reached and the procedure achieves its asserted goal of early resolution in part because of the availability (and risk) of appeal.

But even if rigidity of position (or personality) precludes such a first step settlement, hope is not lost. Multiple appeal steps are the tradition in the grievance procedure precisely because they provide for the input of new participants—presumably with fresh perspectives and greater objectivity—and for a more acute sense of the risk inherent in appealing to outsider arbitration. The involvement of higher officials on both sides certainly doesn't guarantee settlement, any more than discussions at the shop floor, but it exposes the conflict to scrutiny by more senior, more detached, and (one would expect) more experienced, experts in the process and relationship. By virtue of their greater responsibility, experience, and a relationship arising from prior negotiations and arbitrations, they may be able to fashion a resolution that is more palatable than one considered at lower levels. Their additional responsibility for resolution, and perhaps for the cost of further appeal, and their additional objectivity in assessing the range of decisions that might evolve from further appeal, might be sufficient to stimulate a settlement that might not otherwise be considered. For these reasons in particular, it is essential that the parties fully utilize all the specific steps of their negotiated grievance procedure instead of bypassing them for immediate appeal to arbitration. The intensity of the hostility on some issues might lead the parties to conclude that arduous adherence to several steps is only a meaningless exercise, but forced reexamination of those positions at interim steps can provide new opportunities for innovative resolution that would be lost through shortcuts to arbitration.

Although some issues do involve crises that dictate rapid escalation up the grievance procedure to arbitration, utilization of the several contractual appeal steps—while perhaps appearing to be a useless gesture—nonetheless provides additional opportunities for settlement that would otherwise be lost.

The practicality and preferability of settlement should remain in the forefront of the parties' consideration throughout the grievance appeal. Even when the formal steps of the grievance procedure have been exhausted and the case is finally set for arbitration, there is still time for settlement. Indeed, the threshold of the arbitration hearing may be the most fruitful time for settlement. At this point there may be fresh advocates, who are perhaps more objective in their assessment than the protagonists who have been carrying the torch through the earlier steps. New advocates may have a more realistic or even cynical view of the arbitration process and of the risk that each side runs of losing everything. That risk, the expenses of the arbitrator, and the lost opportunity costs of presenting their witnesses, might prompt new advocates, more than their predecessors in the case, to critically reexamine the likelihood of arbitral victory and the benefits of a negotiated settlement. An added incentive for that settlement is the fact that at arbitration, unlike at the earlier steps, the union usually replaces the grievant as the "owner" of the grievance, and the decision as to whether or not to appeal to arbitration is relegated to the union. Thus, empowered with the contractual authority to decide whether to arbitrate, the union, which might have been haunted at the lower steps by the militancy and litigiousness of the grievant, may at last be insulated from fears of a Duty of Fair Representation suit and settle rather than risk an adverse decision in arbitration.

In addition, the parties may fear that any settlement as the case winds its way to arbitration could create an adverse precedent for processing future cases. That jaundiced view misses the point that the grievance procedure, rather than arbitration, is the preferred final resting place of grievances. There is always fear that the last-minute settlement offers may be used in future cases as evidence that the conceding party was less than zealous in pursuit of its claim or at least recognized the weakness. But that portent can be vitiated by a mutual understanding that any settlement should not be taken as a precedent. Thus, the agreement will not come back to haunt the parties in the future or provoke them to arbitration merely to save face. The concept of settlement without creating a precedent is equally valid to avoid adverse repercussions from settling disputes at lower steps. This device is useful to protect the parties at whatever stage of the grievance procedure they opt to settle.

One technique that many parties use in determining whether to pursue the grievance to arbitration—a decision each party must make independently—is in effect a cost–benefit analysis. Clearly, such assessment of the risk of winning or losing involves a number of judgments. Does the economic cost of processing, preparing, and presenting the case through arbitration (including the possible reliance on attorney, transcript, and brief) outweigh the economic cost of the case at stake? Is there a cost of losing the case in terms of the risk of an adverse decision with repercussions for similar pending situations? Is the increased status or power resulting from a win worth the time and cost involved? Conversely, is so much at stake in terms of depletion of status or power resulting from a loss that the side can't afford *not* to appeal the case to arbitration? Could the union, and perhaps the employer, be sued for breach of the Duty of Fair Representation if the case is not pursued through arbitration, or if a settlement is reached at a level less than the grievant might have thought attainable through arbitration? Is long-term status at stake from a favorable or an adverse arbitration decision, or is this a case that will not set a precedent either way? Would a settlement of the grievance be viewed as an admission of weakness, or would it enhance the parties' relationship? What are the relative benefits or risks of agreeing to a settlement at the earlier stages compared to waiting until later, or even until the eve of the arbitration hearing?

These questions obviously have different answers for the employer and the union involved in any particular case, but they must be asked and answered. The outcome of arbitration is not certain. One factor affecting the parties' choice of an arbitrator is that different arbitrators may decide the same case differently. Arbitration is always a risk since it places the decision beyond the control of the parties. Settlement, on the other hand, is always within the parties' control, although the decision to settle must be made with an awareness of the risks and benefits attached to that choice as well.

Grievance Mediation

At the second meeting of the National Academy of Arbitrators, Professor George W. Taylor of the Wharton School of the University of Pennsylvania and Nobel Braden, vice-president of the American Arbitration Association, debated the preferred format for arbitration.[1] Should arbitration be a problem-solving procedure in which the arbitrator primarily seeks to mediate the dispute with the decision reflecting an outcome by consensus, or should the arbitrator refrain from the mediatory role, and conduct the hearing as an adjudicatory process basing the decision solely on the objective data submitted by the parties during the hearing?

The latter viewpoint, advocated by Nobel Braden, prevailed in the evolution of the new procedure of arbitration and has become the universally accepted format. Richard Mittenthal, in a thoughtful paper presented to the 1991 meeting of the National Academy of Arbitrators, pointed out that the adversarial approach has reigned triumphant in the intervening years since that debate occurred.[2] The prescription against mediation as a foreign element in the arbitration hearing has even been recognized in the Code of Professional Responsibility.[3]

Despite the tendency to embrace Braden's view of arbitration as an adversarial process, there has long been a parallel—although perhaps less common—practice for some parties to embrace mediation by arbitrators. However, if a mediator is defined as one who meets separately, and in private, with each party to urge them closer to settlement, the arbitrator who calls both advocates to the hall to encourage them to try to settle a grievance cannot be considered a mediator. The arbitrator in this case has not met with either party separately, has not become privy to any confidential information from one side out of the hearing of the other side, and has had no input from either side that might compromise neutrality or jeopardize the decision-making authority.

Even if one were to exclude such hall caucuses from the definition of mediation, it is clear that some arbitrators go beyond that joint discussion with the parties. They undertake the mediatory role at the request of the two parties and, presumably, surrender or at least defer their authority to render an arbitration decision in that case. In so doing, they don the hat of the problem-solver, extolled by Taylor and so common to the "Impartial Industry Chairman" in the earlier days of the process. The ethical standards for undertaking such a role are spelled out in section 2 of the code:

1. When the parties wish at the outset to give an arbitrator authority to both mediate and to decide or submit recommendations regarding residual issues, if any, they should so advise the arbitrator prior to appointment. If the appointment is accepted, the arbitrator must perform a mediation role consistent with the circumstances of the case.

2. When a request to mediate is first made after appointment, the arbitrator may either accept or decline a mediation role.

c. . . . An arbitrator is not precluded from making a suggestion that he or she mediate. To avoid the possibility of improper pressure, the arbitrator should not so suggest unless it can be discerned that both parties are likely to be receptive. In any event, the arbitrator's suggestion should not be pursued unless both parties readily agree.

Over the years, numerous companies and unions have called upon their arbitrators to help them resolve their disputes as mediators. Examples of that practice are found throughout the post war era. But beyond asking the arbitrator to mediate in resolving a case scheduled for arbitration, a practice of grievance mediation has also evolved in which the case is scheduled solely for mediation, not arbitration (although that step may still be involved if the mediation fails to resolve the dispute). In such instances, the neutral is hired not as an arbitrator, but as a mediator, with authority limited to mediating rather than arbitrating the cases on the docket for that date.

Resort to the scheduled mediation of grievances awaiting arbitration has increased, as parties often feel beleaguered by blocked grievance procedures and backed up arbitration dockets—particularly as contract renegotiation time draws nearer—and seek to clear the decks of pending unresolved cases. The practice has come into even greater vogue recently as a device to reduce the volume, cost, and delay that has come to be associated with arbitration.

Advantages of Grievance Mediation

Cost Savings. Successful mediation at the end of the grievance appeal has the benefit of avoiding the extra costs associated with transcripts, griefs, multiday hearings, and arbitrators' "think time" for writing decisions. It also saves money by encouraging multiple cases to be mediated in a single day, compared to the plodding one issue per day, or longer, that characterizes conventional grievance arbitration. In addition, the time taken to issue an arbitration award may result in the employer having to give substantial backpay or, at least, in lengthy uncertainty as to the employee's status.

Time Savings. Just as avoiding the arbitration formalities saves costs, time is saved as well by foregoing the delays for provision of transcript and brief submission and the arbitrators' delays in issuing the award. Mediation of multiple cases in a day also means more rapid resolution of disputes, compared to the lethargic tradition of one case arbitrated every few weeks. Even though the mediation doesn't occur until the end of the grievance appeal, with its attendant costs and time expenditure, the prospect of mediation may stimulate a more expeditious processing of the cases prior to it. This may be particularly true if their resolution is part of clearing a backlog before contract negotiations.

Equity. There is no challenge to the preferability of the parties settling cases on their own, even with the help of a mediator, in lieu of having a decision imposed upon them by an outside arbitrator. Regardless of whether or not the mediator pressures the parties to settlement, the final choice is theirs and thus, is more consistent with the objectives and ideology of the grievance appeals process. Thus, by definition, if the parties agree to a result, it will be more fair than the one imposed upon them on the basis of a dry recital and perhaps of an unfair, unreliable, or untrue recitation of facts from a lineup of employer and union witnesses. The certainty of an acceptable, or at least a tolerable, outcome contrasted to the risk of a loss in arbitration is another asset of the system.

Disadvantages of Grievance Mediation

Despite the desirability of grievance mediation, it still carries certain risks.

Proforma Appeals to Mediation. In the traditional utilization of the grievance appeal, the union must decide on its own whether to appeal to arbitration, withdraw, or settle the grievance. The recognition that this decision must be made is a strong inducement to the parties to settle their dispute before the deadline for appeal to arbitration. The introduction of the mediation step relieves the parties of the need to attempt settlement during earlier grievance steps. They know there will be a mediator with just that goal, and so it becomes easier for them to rubber stamp positions taken below to get the case to that formalized mediation level. As a result, the parties are less likely to direct their energies toward settlement than they would be without the mediation step. At the same time, the regular involvement of the mediator might push the union to compromise in a case in mediation, which, if appeal to arbitration, might have resulted in total union victory.

Duty of Fair Representation Risks. To the extent that mediation is only invoked for a portion of the pending grievances, the union runs a risk. A disgruntled grievant, particularly one who has been goaded into accepting a compromise or informed by the union that it has wrongly compromised the claim, may claim a violation of the Duty of Fair Representation for being shunted onto the mediation track or for being pressured into a settlement instead of being afforded the full contractual right of access given to other employees in the arbitration appeal.

Dilution of Arbitration Victories. Throughout the grievance appeal, the employer retains the final authority (except for the arbitrator) to determine whether or not a grievance is to be wholly or partly granted. The employer, perhaps less politically sensitive within its ranks, may be less likely to compromise a case that it strongly believes it can win in arbitration. The union, on the other hand, may not be as willing to take that risk, and may be induced to accept a mediator's compromise rather than gamble on gaining more through arbitration. As a consequence, the employer may, if it has the option, withhold from the mediation stage those cases that it is convinced are winnable in arbitration. The result may be settlement of those cases the employer felt would run a risk in arbitration, but a holdout for arbitration for those cases the employer felt it would surely win. Employees may very well be troubled about the value of an arbitration system that tilts to the employer in this way. Although perhaps not fatal to the continuation of the contractual grievance and arbitration system, this bias may create some political problems for the union trying to explain why it compromised its strong cases in mediation and lost so many of the cases that went on to formal arbitration.

Selecting Cases for Mediation

The role of grievance mediation in the formal grievance procedure is a matter for the parties' negotiation. In most relationships, the collective bargaining agreement is silent on the subject, and the parties employ grievance mediation on an ad hoc basis: when they believe it may help dispose of deadlocked cases—such as a backlog—when a periodic grievance review draws near, or prior to negotiations for a successor agreement. But in most cases where it is regularly utilized, the parties' collective bargaining agreement establishes the conditions for its use. Some agreements call for all cases to be submitted to, or at least scrutinized for submission to, a routine mediation step. Others establish a procedure for grievance mediation when only one of the parties invokes its utilization. The agreement provisions should specify which types of cases are to be mediated, the criteria for either party to propose or reject mediation, the format for the mediation, participation, location, timing and the number of cases to be heard at a sitting.

Selecting Neutrals

Some collective bargaining agreements specify the name of the individual who will serve as grievance mediator throughout the term of the parties' agreement. Some establish panels from which the parties will select a mediator for a particular series of cases. Others are silent on specific mediators but expect the parties to agree on the mediator, or absent agreement, turn to the American Arbitration Association for the designation of a grievance mediator, much as they would for the designation of an arbitrator.

Most neutrals and partisans identify mediation as a higher and more demanding art than arbitration because it requires, beyond the substantive knowledge of the field and the dispute, the abilities to communicate with the parties, think quickly enough to challenge and recast proposals, relay messages exactly, and retain the acceptability of often-hostile adversaries throughout the mediation. At the same time, the mediator must attempt to cajole the parties to mutually resolve their dispute. Many arbitrators have those skills innately or have picked them up during their careers, but many do not and their expertise is best confined to sitting as a hearing officer, followed by the issuance of an arbitration award.

In selecting a grievance mediator, the parties are best advised to talk to their counterparts on the other side to determine which neutrals would be the most compatible in that role. Compatibility and level of comfort are far more important than how a series of cases was resolved in some other adversarial relationship, because in mediation, by definition, the parties need only agree to resolutions with which they feel comfortable.

Mediation or More

The mediator's objective is to bring the parties to agreement. If able to do so, the purpose of the mediation is fulfilled. But at times the parties are not so pliant or willing to settle. If the parties' agreement or procedure is limited to mediation, then the failure of mediation would presumably return the unresolved dispute to the docket of cases pending arbitration to be decided by another arbitrator according to the terms of the parties' agreement. But the failure of mediation need not bring that result. As in the mediation of interest disputes, parties unable to reach agreement may seek further guidance from the mediator. This move does not mean the mediator assumes the role of arbitrator to impose a decision, but it might mean that the parties could solicit the mediator's help in other ways. One of the ways in which grievance mediators frequently go beyond their mediatory role is to project how the parties' case might be resolved if appealed to arbitration. Thus, mediators who are unable to achieve agreement might be asked to provide an off-the-record assessment of how the case might be decided if appealed to arbitration. Armed with that advisory opinion, the parties might then have a further inducement to settle. That opinion is, of course, not binding and not admissible in the arbitration hearing, but it might encourage the party at greater risk in the arbitration to try to salvage more in a mediated settlement.

Single Versus Multiple Cases

If the agreed-upon mediation process involves a single grievance, then the end of that case, whether settled or not, is the end of the mediator's responsibility. But if the task involves more than one case, then the mediator has the additional task of packaging the case's resolution. Those that are successfully mediated, one by one, present no problem. For cases that are not settled, and in which the mediator goes beyond strict mediation to providing advisory opinions of how the grievance might be arbitrated to encourage further discussion about settlement, the mediator may opt to provide individual advisory opinions on a case-by-case basis or wait until the conclusions of the docket provide a recommended resolution as a package proposal for settling all cases. In some situations, the parties might agree that rejection of the total proposal by either side would immediately catapult all the cases to arbitration. With such a formula, each side runs the risk that failing to accept a single unfavorable recommendation might cause it to lose favorable recommendations that are adverse to the other side. But in other situations, the parties might choose to settle or trade off some of the cases in order to reach agreement, thus resolving some cases and returning others to the arbitration backlog. Such procedures, and the resultant appeal rights, are properly the subject of collective bargaining negotiations for inclusion in the parties' agreement.

Clearly, the objective of the mediation step is to encourage the parties to resolve their disputes through traditional mediation or through following the mediator's advisory opinions on how the case might be ruled on by an arbitrator. But in either situation, the resolution is the parties' own and, as such, if successful, is preferable to an appeal to arbitration. If unsuccessful, the right of appeal to arbitration remains.

Expedited Arbitration

At the start of its popularity, around World War II, arbitration was expedited. One of its initial appeals was that it was speedy. The parties more conscientiously endeavored to resolve their disputes before arbitration; they even utilized the arbitration step differently. Lawyers were seldom used; instead, the spokespersons were likely to be in-house union and management personnel, who were more attuned to the consequences of the issue on the employer, the employees, and the workplace, than to merely winning or losing. These personnel relied, too, on arbitrators who shared their viewpoints and orientation, usually permanent umpires long experienced with the parties and dedicated to the maintenance of stability in the workplace. At that time there was also greater employee reliance upon the union for guidance and less challenge to leadership or risk of law suits over breaches of Duty of Fair Representation. Similarly, on the employer's side, there was less fear of an employee resorting to external legal or administrative appeal and less need to worry about the legal ramifications of the arbitrator's decision beyond its impact at the workplace.

But arbitration changed. Union members became more educated and more sophisticated about their legal rights and alternative remedies. Unions became more concerned about potential challenges to their authority by outspoken members and by employers. Employers became more concerned about the proclaimed finality of the arbitrator's decision. The courts became more likely to assert independent judgment on legal issues arising from what had earlier been accepted as an internal labor–management forum, with unchallenged and largely unchallengeable results. Throughout this process, the legal ramifications and consequences of the cases tended to increase the prospects of their escalating to arbitration. The result was an increasing volume of formalized arbitration, with greater reliance on outside union and management attorneys. At the same time, arbitration spread to the public sector and spawned a greater demand for a new generation of neutrals, as many of the original arbitrators—the veterans of the War Labor Board—died, retired, or reduced their workload to cases closer to home. The new arbitrators were less likely to have their roots in the collective bargaining process, and more likely to be comfortable in the more formalistic rituals of adjudicatory arbitration.

The consequence of all these changes has been delay in processing cases to the arbitration step, delay in utilizing the services of overbooked union and management attorneys, and delay in finding dates on which all advocates and arbitrators can attend. Although blame for most of the delay in case processing is often placed at the feet of overscheduled advocates, the arbitrators, too, must bear responsibility for delay. They often schedule hearings for all their free days and thus ignore their responsibility to leave enough days available for writing so that decisions can be issued in the requisite thirty or even sixty days provided by the parties' agreement or the American Arbitration Association (AAA) or Federal Mediation and Conciliation Service (FMCS). The parties' reliance on the same stable of arbitrators they've used in the past, with whom they feel most comfortable, keeps the schedules of these arbitrators overbooked, leads to delay in decision writing and issuance of awards, and increases the problem of delay. The irony of that arrangement, particularly in an era of economic malaise and declining union membership, is that more and more fully competent journeymen arbitrators are available on shorter notice, while the parties continue to direct ninety percent of the cases to ten percent of the arbitrators, thus exacerbating the delay problem.

For all these reasons, it is only logical that parties seek ways to make the system more expeditious. Certainly, expedited arbitration streamlines the process by assuring employees of more rapid resolution of their grievances while saving the parties time and money that would otherwise be devoted to the costly and time-consuming processing of cases through regular arbitration. But there are cases, perhaps the majority of arbitrations, in which the parties may be sensitive to a grievant's feelings or the threat of a suit over failure to accord the full rights of the normal arbitration procedure, or in which the parties are unable to agree on the procedures or cases to be submitted to expedited arbitration, or in which one or both of the parties seeks to develop a clear case record for any possible legal appeal from the arbitration step. The American Arbitration Association has developed a special set of rules for expedited arbitration.

Expedited arbitration has taken different forms. In some systems, it entails shortening the grievance appeal process, with briefer contractual time periods for appeals and answers or the bypassing of one or more appeal steps. The down side of that expedition is that it deprives the parties of the full range of opportunities for settling grievances and may result in the arbitration of cases that might have been settled had they been given full access to all of the contractual steps and appeal times.

Other systems shorten the time between agreement to arbitrate and the holding of the arbitration hearing. Success with this type of expedition is illusory if the parties insist on using outside counsel and the busiest arbitrators, all of whom contribute to the increasing delays of the present system. Delays in scheduling hearing dates would be dramatically reduced and the arbitration system would be restored to much of its earlier efficiency if the parties were courageous enough to forego reliance on outside attorneys and use some of the less well-known, and, thus, less busy arbitrators. The chances are that the most highly experienced arbitrators and the journeymen who are not quite as busy would resolve the dispute the same way—regardless of whether the parties were represented by top advocates or in-house counsel. More rapid scheduling of hearings is attainable even without risking submission of the case to a more readily available, but less busy, arbitrator.

Most often, alacrity is sought from the arbitrator alone, by requiring that the decision be rendered rapidly after the hearing—perhaps within a five day period—or that decision be rendered at the close of the hearing, or within twenty-four hours, with the written opinion to follow. Under this system, the procedure would operate as usual up to the arbitration step, but then pressure the arbitrator as a way to minimize delays that are usually endemic throughout the system.

In the light of the foregoing drawbacks, it is difficult to establish a typography of the perfect expedited arbitration system. Ideally, it would be a system that reduces the delays through the entire process: in the appeals of arbitration, in the quest for an arbitration date, in the time allocated for the arbitrator to render the award, and perhaps in the form of the award itself. The improvements that would result from such rapid processing of arbitration cases could be applied to all cases or could be ascribed to a portion of the arbitration caseload.

Only when the revision in procedures is applied to handling a portion of the cases does it apparently earn the term "expedited system," implying that the routine, more ponderous system is to be reserved for the remainder—the bulk of cases. If the parties can't agree to make their whole grievance and arbitration system expeditious, what then are the components of the ideal "expedited system"?

The American Arbitration Association has established a set of Expedited Labor Arbitration Rules that the parties may agree to abide by either in their collective bargaining agreement or whenever they undertake expedited arbitration. The parties may agree to abide by all or only a portion of the AAA rules. If they are able to reach agreement on some of the procedural issues, they can exempt those elements from the AAA rule coverage. Among the items covered by the AAA rules are appointment by the AAA of the neutral arbitrator, the initiation of the procedures, determination of the hearing time and place, representation at the hearing, adjournments, ex parte proceedings, rules of evidence, and form of the award, and so on.

Obviously, it is preferable for the parties to negotiate their own procedures for the expedited arbitrations. Let us turn to some of the components of such a system that must be addressed.

Covered Cases

If the parties opt to apply the system to only a portion of the cases, which cases should they be? Clearly, discipline and discharge have the most visibility, and may arouse a great deal of emotion and attention, so that both the employee and the employer benefit from a rapid processing of such cases. In the case of a termination, a quick decision in the employer's favor permits the employee to seek employment elsewhere without having to reveal the possibility of leaving the new job to reclaim the former job in the case of a victorious award. If the employee wins, a quick decision brings a more rapid return of the job and reduces the employer's backpay burden. In those increasingly frequent cases of reinstatement without backpay, often imposed by arbitrators to placate both parties, a more rapid decision reduces the loss of pay to the employee by a quicker return to productive employment.

Some parties apply expedited arbitration only to terminations, others to discipline short of discharge, while others apply it solely to contractual issues. The choice depends on the goals of the parties. The objective may be to reduce time delays, to lower the costs of appeals to arbitration, or to avoid the complications of trying to implement tardy awards. The parties to such a system must determine which category of cases are eligible for expedited treatment and, within that category, how the cases are to be selected. Are they to be chosen from the backlog, or from special categories? Are they to be appealed by seniority, with the oldest cases being heard first, or with one of the parties having the authority to choose the cases for arbitration? Or are only certain categories of cases to be heard by the expedited process as they arise?

Time Limits in Processing

Are the contractual time limits for grievance appeals and answers to be shortened? Are steps to be bypassed? Is there to be a reduced window of time to appeal to arbitration? Although special treatment for certain types of cases or certain grievances might arouse the resentment of other employees, a rational reformation of processing steps and appeal times would probably withstand legal challenge as long as not deemed discriminatory.

Selecting the Arbitrator

If the parties' feel that the greatest delay in case processing is in awaiting the arbitrator's decision, there are numerous ways of shortening that period. New or less busy arbitrators with shorter waiting periods could be designated to hear the cases selected for the expedited system. Another device would be to select the busiest arbitrators well enough in advance so that dates can be scheduled periodically throughout the year and be readily available for the hearing of grievances when they are still fresh, instead of scheduling the arbitration date only after the case has been appealed to arbitration. In some expedited systems, arbitrators are asked to reserve dates each month in the expectation that some case will be ripe for arbitration, with an arrangement to cancel the dates should no cases be available for hearing on that month's expedited agenda.

Probably the most expeditious way of securing the ready availability of the top arbitrators is an agreement by the parties suddenly facing arbitration to set dates immediately, through agreement on available date, and then turn to the AAA or other neutral agencies to appoint an arbitrator available for one of those specific dates or to create a shortlist of arbitrators available on the agreed-upon dates from which the parties could select. That practice would permit the parties to hear cases with only a few days' notice, thus taking advantage of cancellations that frequently plague the schedules of busy arbitrators.

Expedited Hearing

Shortening the hearing is another way of expediting the process, particularly if it leads to holding more than one case per day. Some expedited procedures require stipulated facts and lists of exhibits to be exchanged in advance. Other systems bar witnesses, or allow only the grievant, or have arrangements for "offers of proof" of what witnesses would testify if called. There is no question that if the parties have prepared and communicated adequately prior to the hearing, they can achieve substantial time savings. Witnesses might be necessary only to help the arbitrator resolve issues of credibility. Of course, time could also be saved at and after the hearing by eliminating transcripts and briefs. Some say that the presence of a court reporter stimulates more posturing and speech-making than would otherwise occur.

In many expedited arrangements, the parties plan for the arbitrator to hear multiple cases within a single day—for example, as many cases as can be heard between 10 A.M. and 5:00 P.M. The arbitrator is, of course, expected to issue decisions on all those cases on an expedited basis as well. Shortening hearings to permit multiple presentations in a single day requires sacrifice and commitment by both parties and agreement by the grievants. To achieve such ends, the parties may contract with the arbitrator for the requisite hours of service and stipulate that the arbitrators should stay for as long as is necessary to complete the presented cases.

Expedited Decision

In order to reduce cost and delay in the preparation and issuance of awards, expedited procedures often call for quicker decisions without opinions, or with abbreviated opinions, and limited to one to two pages; or, as noted earlier, they may call for immediate issuance of the decision with the opinion to follow. The requirement of shorter and much more rapidly issued decisions or of decisions without opinions raises questions about the decisions' value as precedents when contrasted to those issued in normal arbitrations with greater time for more thoughtful and better prepared opinions. For that reason, most expedited systems expect their decisions to be non-precedential.

Assurance of expedited decision writing and issuance is within the parties' control. It may be achieved by requiring as a condition of employment that the arbitrator announce bench decisions or that the arbitrator issue the decision within a specified number of days. The parties could even make the arbitrator's payment conditional on decisions being issued by the agreed-upon deadline.

Even without such conditions, expedited decisions are likely to be issued quickly because they are short and because, in many cases, the opinions and decisions do not give rise to any additional compensation, beyond the expedited "day." Furthermore, arbitrators, under the Code, are required to abide by such agreements on expedited awards or risk being called to task for violating the code.

Section 5E of the NAA Code of Professional Responsibility provides as follows:

> 1. When an arbitrator understands, prior to acceptance of appointment, that a bench decision is expected at the conclusion of the hearing, the arbitrator must comply with the understanding, unless both parties agree otherwise.
> 2. When an arbitrator understands, prior to acceptance of appointment, that a concise written award is expected within a period after the hearing, the arbitrator must comply with the understanding, unless both parties agree otherwise.

The fact that the parties find it necessary to resort to expedited systems is testimony to the malaise of delay that currently permeates arbitration. While expedited systems may solve the problem for some of the cases, for some of the parties they raise the broader issue of whether arbitration has become so burdensome, so delayed, and so costly that its perceived benefits are overwhelmed. Perhaps attention should be shifted to making arbitration more efficient, more rapid, and less encumbered, thus obviating the need for temporary or partial restructuring for only a favored portion of the grievants and their cases.

Preparing for Arbitration

If the grievance is not readily resolved by the parties at the lower steps of the grievance procedure, it becomes necessary to prepare for appeal to arbitration. Such preparation does not mean that arbitration is inevitable or that settlement of the case is foreclosed. On the contrary, prompt and thorough investigation of the case may even improve chances of settlement by enlightening both parties and leading them to reexamine their rhetoric and their formal stance on the dispute in the light of the fully revealed evidence. The prospect of arbitration may stimulate the parties to reassess their chances of winning or losing if the case is appealed.

Some advocates may take the position that the fruits of their investigation should be concealed from the other party in the hope that relevation at the hearing will catch the other side unaware and, thus, ensure a victorious arbitral decision. Fortunately, that position is not the preferred or preponderant view of most advocates and adherents to the process. Any dispute is a problem between the parties. Self protection and the continued stability of their relationship dictate that their dispute be resolved before it begins to fester. Any disclosure of relevant material that leads the parties to rethink the merits or risks of proceeding with the dispute may prove instrumental in stimulating further discussions to resolve the dispute, while deliberate concealment of crucial evidence until the hearing may deprive the other party of facts which might trigger settlement and may result in its exclusion by the arbitrator.

Investigating the Facts

Rapid and thorough investigation of the facts of a dispute is a crucial element in arbitration preparation. Whether the dispute has arisen over discipline or contract interpretation, certain events transpired, certain people were involved, and certain statements were made. Some or all of these elements may prove conclusive in the arbitrator's determination of the arbitration case. Any resolution, whether through settlement or through arbitration, may depend on mutual acceptance of facts. It is important to find out what occurred and who said what. Certain facts will be undisputed; some will be contested. Supporting data in the form of documents, affidavits, or statements from witnesses may become important in convincing the other side or, ultimately, the arbitrator of the accuracy of one side's reporting of those facts.

In order to secure the most accurate and persuasive recital of what transpired, it is important that all the witnesses of an event be identified and that their recollections be recorded as soon after the event as possible. Witnesses, like everyone, forget more and more of an event as time goes by. Asking the witnesses to write out and sign a list of as many of the details as can be recalled as soon as possible after the event is important.

Such statements can be used in settlement negotiations to demonstrate what witnesses are expected to testify if called in arbitration. They also can prepare the witnesses by reminding them of what transpired when, months later, they are called to the witness stand. These statements may also buttress the witnesses' testimony by being admitted into evidence as contemporaneous accounts of the incident if a witness is challenged on cross-examination or strays in the testimony from what was written on the statement.

Examining the Documents

The issue of whether the employee's action violated the parties' collective bargaining agreement, or the employer's policies or rules, or prior grievance settlements or arbitration awards between these same parties, or even pertinent statutes or court decisions dictates careful scrutiny of such documents. Relying on someone's recollection of the documents can be very misleading—or even wishful thinking. It is important to read thoroughly the allegedly relevant arbitration awards, settlements, court decisions, or statutes to determine whether they are controlling or even relevant. This reading should be done before determining whether or not to pursue a grievance to arbitration. In the case of the collective bargaining agreement and employer's policies and rules, it is also important to examine the documents in full to determine if provisions other than those cited might influence the arbitrator's (or the other side's) view.

In most cases, the relevant documents will be available to both sides. But if one side uncovers supporting documentation that may not be known to the other side, self-interest—not to mention commitment to its settlement objectives—would dictate rapid disclosure to the other side in hope of bringing an end to the conflict and a resolution of the dispute. Prior grievance settlements, reached without precedent on the understanding that they would not be cited in subsequent disputes, would be barred from any submission in any arbitration proceeding. Nevertheless, these settlements could be used in the parties' own settlement negotiations as models for how the present dispute could be resolved—again—without precedent.

Prior arbitration awards between the same two parties may be invoked by one party as binding precedents. Arbitrators are not legally bound by such prior decisions, but unless the precedent is totally repugnant, subsequent arbitrators will usually accept them as precedential to forestall the continual challenges what would result from having two presumably contrary opinions on an issue.

If the cited prior arbitration award arose under a prior agreement and there was no intervening renegotiation of the earlier interpreted language, most arbitrators would conclude that the parties accepted—indeed, endorsed—the earlier award by making no effort to change the contractual language on which that prior arbitration decision was based. The general view is that the parties, in essence, incorporated that prior award into their new agreement as a clarification of the earlier, disputed language.

A different use is made of arbitration awards rendered under contracts between different parties. Arbitrators will receive any offered arbitration opinion, examine them for relevance at a later time, and then decide which, if any, to rely upon. Those decisions may be valuable for enhancing the persuasiveness of the arbitrator's reasoning, but are not binding on other parties to a different dispute. When presented to the other side during the processing of the grievance, such decisions may have the same persuasive impact, by demonstrating what might be persuasive if shown to the arbitrator. Such a demonstration might help to stimulate the prospects of settlement prior to the final step.

Researching Past Practice

Although the parties' collective bargaining agreement may properly be hailed as the controlling standard for arbitrating disputes between the parties, it does not stand in isolation. What might appear to be clear language may be subject to varied interpretations in the light of prior arbitration awards. Its application may also be varied by the prior experience of the parties in living with that agreement. The current collective bargaining agreement and its predecessors serve as the standard against which employee and management actions are to be judged. If actions are taken that are known to the other side and yet appear to be contrary to that standard, the practice serves to modify that "clear" language. Accumulated instances of behavior on any particular issue, whether in discipline or contract interpretation, constitute a "past practice," a wealth of experience in jointly living with the agreement's provisions. While usually developed as consistent with, and therefore an endorsement of, the contract language, the past practice may, in some situations, deviate from strict conformity to the contract language. In such cases, where the past practice has been consistent, known to both parties, and permitted to continue unchallenged, it could constitute evidence of a contract reformation that may override what one would expect to be a single way of interpreting or applying the agreement.

Evidence of a past practice that varied from the contract terms, and evidence of its condonation, would be admissible to support an interpretation at variance with the strict contract terms. The persuasive strength of that past practice would be further enforced by evidence that it existed under prior agreements, that it continued for an extended period, and, most importantly, that it was not contradicted or cancelled by contravening negotiations. Research into such practices, whether or not they favor one side's position on grievance, is important to test the strength of a position that apparently departs from the contract language. When the strengths of that past practice are brought to the attention of the other party, their reliance on the contract per se may be refocused and the quest for settlement may be furthered.

Preparing the Case

After all the relevant facts and documents are assembled, the next step is to develop the case for presentation to the arbitrator.

For evidence to achieve its greatest impact, it is essential that a theory of the case be developed in which the contractual right is initially asserted in the opening statement, with witnesses and evidence then presented to prove that right. In the case of discipline, for example, the employer's theory of the case would be that it had the right to exercise discipline for certain infractions of the rules and that the grievant had breached the rule and was accordingly properly disciplined. The union's theory in that same case might be that the rule was unreasonable. Or that the rule, while reasonable, was not properly communicated to the grievant; or, alternatively, that, while the rule was reasonable and properly known, the grievant was innocent of the charges, so that the discipline should be rescinded.

Whatever theory either party postulates, it must recognize and accept as true what it assumes will be proven by the other side. Therefore, a party's theory should be consistent with accepted facts and its evidence should be concentrated where it is most likely to persuade the arbitrator to its view.

In selecting evidence, it is wise to cull whatever is ancillary to the theory of the case; having it available for rebuttal presentation is perhaps prudent, but it should be withheld from the direct presentation. Thus, in a discipline case involving a charge that a grievant was AWOL on a particular day, evidence that the grievant had meticulous attendance at call ins at all other times or had been hailed as a very good worker, while not essential to the union's theory, might have even more impact on rebuttal if damaging testimony were provided by the employer's witness or on cross-examination of the union's witnesses. Similarly, with exhibits, if the union's case were based on the theory that the grievant had called in on the day in question, exhibits that showed calling in on other days would not prove a call in on the day in question, but might have greater relevance if introduced in response to testimony that the grievant had seldom bothered to call in.

Confining the presentation to the most relevant and the strongest evidence is also true when selecting witnesses. Though there might have been five or ten witnesses to an altercation, it would be unnecessary—and indeed even risky—to have more than one testify. It might be wise to keep the other witnesses in reserve in the event that the employer's witnesses contradict the testimony of the union's witness that there were three to eight other observers of the incident. But to have multiple witnesses testify to the same event risks that the other side might challenge their testimony on a minor aspect of their observation that has elicited different recollections, and thus place their testimony on the crucial observation in jeopardy.

To ensure that the best witness is selected for such testimony, it is wise to test all potential witnesses through mock questioning in order to determine which observer has the best recollection, the best manner in testifying, the best understanding of how that testimony fits into the theory of the case, and the best ability to withstand much cross-examination without erosion of the side's position. A rehearsal of the case is a useful vehicle for testing the merits, style, and form of the parties' entire case. It is best accomplished by having the most competent staff person serve as a mock advocate for the other side and pointedly challenge exhibits and witnesses. Such an exercise can be crucial in disclosing the weaknesses in a presentation, in providing incentive for finding bolstering evidence or stronger witnesses, or in showing the party that the case is weak, likely to lose in the arbitration, and thus more suited to settlement than arbitration.

In preparation for the presentation, it is also important to devise the opening statement to offer at the hearing as well as an outline of a potential closing statement, to be adjusted as the evidence evolves at the hearing. In the case of the opening statement, it is appropriate for the party with the burden of proceeding to spell out a full opening statement for recitation at the hearing. But if the other side is the moving party, then a mere outline of the theory of the case is sufficient to support a response to the other side's opening that accepts its provable assertions as fact and focuses on those areas where the evidence of the two sides is likely to conflict. Slavish adherence to a previously prepared script tends to engender the arbitrator's distrust.

The preparation of a fixed closing statement is risky because advocates tend to become wedded to that script, thus forfeiting the opportunity for a more creative oral response to the evidence presented. Thus, a checklist of the points to be made in proving the theory of the case may be adequate preparation for the closing statement, thereby leaving room for a response to any surprise evidence that may be submitted by the other side.

Joint Preparation for the Hearing

Even if the parties are unsuccessful in settling the grievance prior to the hearing, they can, at least, try to reach agreement on certain procedural matters that will help to minimize procedural wrangles at the hearing and make it go more expeditiously. To the extent that they shorten the length of a potential multiday hearing, such efforts also tend to reduce the cost of the arbitration.

The representatives who arrange the details for the hearing should recognize that their conflict is over a particular issue of contract rights or entitlement and that the dispute can only be settled if the parties are able to resolve the housekeeping matters. It may make one party feel better to win a skirmish or two over "the shape of the table" issues, but such ancillary spats detract from the core dispute they have been wrestling with through the several steps of the grievance procedure. Those grievance discussions were held with the expectation that the dispute would ultimately be heard at arbitration, a goal that can only be reached if the parties act in good faith to control their urge to prevail on subordinate issues. Once both agree on the level playing field, the purpose of their appeal can proceed.

Advance Agreement on the Issue To Be Arbitrated

It is surprising how often parties who have debated a grievance through the several steps of the grievance procedure, knowing full well what is in dispute, are unable to articulate what they wish to submit for resolution by the arbitrator. Too often, they postpone any effort to reach agreement on a common issue until the start of arbitration. This negligence wastes the parties' time, that of the arbitrator, and that of their witnesses as well; it also increases the cost of the arbitration because unproductive witnesses must sit around waiting for the proceedings to begin. If hourly paid advocates are utilized this waste of time becomes even more punitive.

Although the parties may defer agreement on the issue until the hearing in the expectation that the arbitrator may help them reach such agreement, the arbitrator hardly knows the genesis of the dispute or the interests of the parties. He or she is a total stranger to the dispute, and may decline to become involved in that conflict. After all, the parties themselves have tracked the dispute and must reach agreement before the arbitrator gains any jurisdiction in the matter. Because it is essential that they reach agreement for the matter to proceed to arbitration, it makes more sense that they make that attempt early, before they become victims of the pressure and distractions of the arbitration hearing. If the parties are far apart on the issue when the hearing starts, their alienation is bound to adversely affect the arbitrator's evidentiary rulings. Such early efforts at agreement are usually successful and, once achieved, permit the arbitration to commence promptly, without the endless wrangling and posturing that usually is entailed when the parties argue in the presence of the clients and the arbitrator.

Indeed, the effort of meeting to reach agreement on the issue provides another valuable opportunity to settle the dispute. If the parties have avoided the problem of framing the issue, that exercise may disclose new arguments or reliance on contract provisions that may stimulate a rethinking of positions and perhaps a recognition that it might be preferable to settle the dispute than risk defeat in arbitration.

Agreement on Exhibits

Arbitration proceedings should have no surprises. If the grievance procedure is properly used, all the relevant evidence and documentation should be disclosed well before arbitration. A smoother hearing will result if the parties have exchanged and even numbered their exhibits prior to the hearing. Jointly created documents, such as the collective bargaining agreement or memos of understanding or the paper trail of the grievance appeal, are usually marked as joint exhibitions that both parties would rely on in the furtherance of their cases. The employee's attendance record, the position's job description, or a floor plan of the shop, are other examples. Those documents that just one side relies upon are usually marked in a series as employer or union exhibits. Although disputes over relevance, authenticity, and the like may have to be deferred to the arbitration for rulings on admissibility, most exhibits are not surprises, and time can be saved if the parties agree on the admissibility and numbering of exhibits well ahead of the hearing. Each side should recognize that the arbitrator will want to examine such items and that it is usually preferable to agree in advance to their admission than to raise objections that would raise the arbitrator's curiosity and perhaps suspicion as to why one party would seek to prevent examination of that item.

Stipulation of Facts

In some cases, agreement can be reached between the parties as to the facts of the case so that a stipulation of the facts can be developed for presentation to the arbitrator, thereby avoiding the need for testimony on undisputed matters. If the parties had utilized the grievance procedure as intended—as a procedure for establishing the facts of the case—then they should agree on the events surrounding the dispute by the time they get to arbitration. Although some factual matters still may be disputed, for unchallenged matters the development between the parties of a set of stipulated facts will make the hearing go more quickly to the heart of the conflict and provide a smoother and more expeditious hearing that permits the arbitrator to focus attention wholly on the contested matters. Once agreed upon, the stipulated facts could be drawn up as a joint submission to the arbitrator or, by agreement of the parties, could be read into the record by the moving party in its opening statement.

Agreement on Arbitration Time, Place of Hearing, and Transcripts

Even if the parties cannot agree on the foregoing issues, they must discuss and agree upon certain housekeeping matters in order to arrange the hearing that is the prerequisite for implementation of their arbitration agreement. This agreement must be achieved despite any hostility that exists between the parties. Who is to be the arbitrator? When is the hearing to convene? At what location? Will there be a transcript taken of the proceedings? As noted in chapter 2, these questions all require negotiation and accord and must be resolved if the arbitration is to proceed.

Conclusion

Good sense and planning dictate that the parties resolve these administrative details as early as possible to minimize the risk of such mundane matters magnifying into controversy, which may occur if there is delay in their resolution and they become swept into the bigger dispute between the parties.

2
Arranging for the Hearing

If the parties cannot resolve the dispute during the grievance appeal procedure and it proceeds to arbitration, other arrangements must be made concerning the forthcoming hearing. Primary among these is the selection of the arbitrator. Although some collective bargaining relationships rely upon a single arbitrator to resolve all disputes arising during the life of the agreement, most provide the parties with the right to choose among a number of arbitrators for resolution of a particular dispute. The selection procedure depends upon the arbitration structure the parties incorporated in their collective bargaining agreement. But whether the agreement calls for a tripartite board or a single arbitrator, or whether it calls for ad hoc selection or selection from a rotating panel, the parties must follow the contractually mandated steps for arbitrator selection while at the same time endeavoring to select an arbitrator whom each side anticipates will be most sympathetic to its side of the case. But in this process, the ethical constraints against selecting an arbitrator with whom they have had prior personal or business relationships or prior discussions of the case will invariably restrict the acceptable selection to those professional arbitrators with extended experience, untainted prior dealings, and mutually recognized expertise on the subject to be arbitrated.

Once the arbitrator has been selected, the parties must resolve other issues prior to the actual hearing date. Some of these issues might well have been resolved by the parties prior to the selection of the arbitrator and may not require any role for the neutral. As noted in the preceding chapter, such accords may involve joint agreement on exhibits, free exchange of evidence leading to stipulations of fact, agreement on the time and place for the holding of the hearing, and even agreement on the issue to be arbitrated.

But infrequently the relationship between the parties or between the spokespersons precludes agreement on some or all of these matters. On such occasions, the parties may turn to their agreed-upon arbitrator, in advance of the hearing, to resolve issues that, if postponed, might preclude the holding of the hearing. Thus, if one of the parties refuses to voluntarily provide an exhibit requested by the other side or refuses to have a particular witness available at the hearing, the other side might approach the arbitrator to secure a signature on a subpoena requiring the exhibit or witness by present at the hearing.

Appeal to the arbitrator also, on occasion, may be necessary to resolve disputes between the parties as to the date, time, and place for holding the hearing. Usually, the parties are able to resolve such matters on their own.

But if one side objects to meeting at the other's premises, or if one side objects to holding the hearing after working hours, such issues might be submitted to the arbitrator to determine a time and place acceptable to both parties for the hearing.

Occasionally, one of the parties may refuse to participate in the hearing because of unwillingness to adapt to the other side's requirements on locus or venue, disagreement on the subject matter of the dispute, or a perception of flawed procedures. In such situations, the arbitrator may be warned by either or both parties that one of the parties will not appear. That situation may force the arbitrator into the role of a mediator to secure the participation of the recalcitrant party—if only to ensure attendance at a hearing where the refusal to go forward may be argued. But in a few cases, when there is adamant refusal to attend any hearing, the arbitrator has to decide whether to proceed with an ex parte proceeding and the additional problems that such a proceeding entails.

On the other end of the spectrum, the arbitrator may be confronted with parties who get along too well and who have not only reached agreement on the administrative issues, but have also agreed on how the arbitrator should decide the case. The final section of this chapter deals with the problems faced by the arbitrator and the parties when they seek an informed award that the arbitrator is to sign and thereby absolve them of any responsibility for that (agreed upon) outcome.

Selecting the Arbitrator

The structure of the arbitration tribunal is established by the terms of the parties' collective bargaining agreement, as the agreed-upon final step of the grievance procedure.

Well before arbitration was recognized as a field of specialized expertise, early disputants utilized three-person arbitration panels to resolve labor and other types of disputes. In that format, each party would appoint a partisan member of the tripartite panel, and they would agree on the neutral arbitrator to serve as chair. (It was, and is still, rare to have a panel of three neutrals.) In this way, the parties were reassured that their respective positions, if unpersuasively presented in the hearing, would have an advocate during the decision-making, with the partisan "arbitrators" advising the neutral chair. While the tripartite structure may have been essential in an era when the neutral chair was selected because of prestige and community and ethical standing, there is less call for tripartite panels now that a large cadre of experienced labor management neutrals is available for service. Tripartite panels continue to be used in arbitration of other types of disputes in which the requirements of professional expertise have not led to a cadre of recognized specialist arbitrators, and in which the parties distrust the level of expertise of the neutral they have selected as their panel chair.

A number of collective bargaining agreements, such as those in the transportation industry, still call for tripartite panels. Even though they use professional arbitrators as chairs, they deem the executive session input worthwhile to protect their interests and to steer the arbitrator through the intricacies of their procedures, practices, and traditions. They feel these benefits justify the extra time and cost associated with the structure and its requisite executive session prior to rendition of the award.

Thus, whether the parties' agreement calls for three neutrals, partisan arbitrators selecting a neutral chair in tripartite arbitration, or the parties themselves selecting a single arbitrator, that selection is possibly the most crucial role for the parties to exercise in arranging for the forthcoming hearing. Not only is selecting an arbitrator the necessary prerequisite to holding the hearing, it is also crucial because the parties must select the neutral who will ultimately determine the outcome of the dispute.

The parties may follow a number of routes for the selection of their neutral. They may negotiate for a single arbitrator for the duration of their agreement or for a panel of arbitrators from which one neutral is selected for each case. Or they may seek to agree upon a separate arbitrator for each dispute and turn to a designating agency for assistance when they are unable to agree on their selection.

In designating a permanent umpire, the parties agree on an individual as the sole arbitrator of all disputes that arise during the life of the collective bargaining agreement. This, too, is a structure with a purposeful history. When parties initially embraced arbitration as a device to peacefully resolve disputes and assure tranquility in their enterprise or industry, they turned to revered neutrals with recognized expertise in their industry or field and with broader dispute settlement skills than used in formal arbitration now. These neutrals were crowned as industry or impartial chairmen, with a mandate that encompassed a more universal role in resolving disputes between the parties than over a single issue. They often mediated both interest and rights disputes and favored more of a problem-solving approach than the adversarial orientation currently in vogue. Their current progency are the permanent arbitrators. In some cases, the umpire's contract runs for one year; in other cases, it runs for the duration of the contract's multiyear term. In reality, though, tenure of the umpire depends upon that neutral's continued acceptability to both parties. If unacceptable early in the term, the parties may cancel the umpire's contract or buy it out. Or if only one party seeks the umpire's removal, the removal may be postponed until the umpire's personal contract runs out. Umpires effective in maintaining acceptability with both parties presumably have contracts renewed year after year and some have survived for decades as the parties' court of last resort.

In other collective agreements, the parties negotiate a panel of individuals to serve as arbitrators and specify how the cases are to be allocated among the panel members. Sometimes the choice is by rotation, with the arbitrators taken in turn for successive cases. Sometimes it is by alternately striking panel names until a single final arbitrator is agreed for the next pending case. Sometimes the parties take turns selecting the designated panel member.

Most collective agreements do not name arbitrators. Usually the arbitration clause initially provides for the parties to agree upon an arbitrator for a pending dispute. Failing such an agreement, the contract provision for arbitrator designation will be invoked, perhaps by turning the case over to the AAA or FMCS or to one of several state agencies that maintain rosters for the designation of the arbitrator pursuant to their respective rules. The AAA and FMCS maintain rosters of experienced arbitrators from various regions and, when requested, will supply a list of names from that roster as specified in the parties' agreement.

There are certain advantages to the use of ad hoc arbitrators. First, the parties may reuse or abandon an arbitrator after the first case, depending on their satisfaction with the individual. Second, the parties may select the arbitrator best suited to the particular case—for example, time study—by examining the arbitrator's credentials. Third, the parties may try a number of arbitrators until they find one with whom they are satisfied and then continue to use the arbitrator for as long as both find the decisions fair and acceptable.

On the other hand, the use of ad hoc arbitrators requires repeated expenditures of time and money for each case selection. Also, the "highest neutral choice" may not necessarily be the best person available, and use of different arbitrators makes it harder to develop a consistent law of the shop or clear precedent and may lead losing parties to seek to retry issues before a different arbitrator to secure a more favorable precedent. In addition, each new arbitrator must be educated on the parties' practices, the industry condition, and so on, at considerable expenditure of time and money.

The parties may request a list of local or national arbitrators, arbitrators with experience in job evaluation or time study, those who speak Spanish, or even those who are available to hear the case on a particular date. In some cases, the list may contain five, seven, or nine names that the parties strike alternately, leaving the last name as their designated mutual choice of arbitrator. In other cases, an identical list is sent to both parties for preferential ranking and is then returned to the agency, which designates the arbitrator with the lowest numerical score as the parties' highest mutual choice. In the event of disagreement on naming an arbitrator, the rules usually permit the agency to appoint the arbitrator.

Regardless of the selection procedure, the contract with always ensure the designation of an arbitrator from either the parties' own panel or that provided by the designating agency. Each party will select based upon its perception of how each of the nominees would handle the immediate case. The parties often research, as best they can, how the suggested arbitrators have ruled on similar cases by examining their own files, asking other clients and other advocates, and searching the arbitrator's published awards. Most parties are content to find an experienced arbitrator with independent judgment and without a history of tilting to either side, because they recognize that the other side is engaged in similar research and that an arbitrator who seems acceptable because of a ruling on a comparable case probably would be unacceptable to the opposition, which would also discover that ruling. Advocates also look to the arbitrator's reputation for fairness and efficiency in running the hearing, promptness (or tardiness) in issuing awards, and, in a tight economy, the proximity to the locus of the parties, and daily fee and billing practices.

Duty to Disclose

A problem may arise when one of the parties agrees to the selection of an arbitrator because of a special relationship that the party hopes (or expects) will induce the arbitrator to make a favorable decision—perhaps irrespective of the merits of the case. Such a presumption of bias may arise from the fact that the advocate and arbitrator were classmates, former partners, or social friends; or from knowledge of the arbitrator's financial interest or ownership of stock in the enterprise; or from a familial relationship. Usually, the arbitrator is not aware of the expectation of favoritism until he or she learns of the selection or perhaps until the start of the hearing. The Code of Professional Responsibility requires the arbitrator to take specified action when discovering such potential conflicts.

CASE STUDY: *The Case of the Lost Classmate.* The union's international representative, Phil Vilar, calls the arbitrator's office to advise her that the company personnel director and he have agreed upon her to hear a termination case.

The date and place are agreed, and on arrival at the hearing, the arbitrator sees the company is being represented by David Lange, her former classmate in law school.

The arbitrator calls company lawyer Lange and Vilar into the hall, explains the prior relationship, and offers to withdraw from the case. Lange objects on the grounds that he has not had any contact with the arbitrator in the ten years since law school. The Vilar complains to the company lawyer that he should have told the union and that the delay in getting a new arbitrator would be costly and unfair to the grievant seeking reinstatement. At last Vilar reluctantly agrees to continue with the arbitrator and the case. The arbitrator opts to stay in the case.

Section 2B of the Code of Professional Responsibility reads in part as follows:

Required Disclosures

1. Before acceptance of an appointment, an arbitrator must disclose directly or through the administrative agency involved, any current or past managerial, representational, or consultative relationship with any Company or Union involved in a proceeding in which he or she is being considered for appointment or has been tentatively designated to serve. Disclosure must also be made of any pertinent pecuniary interest. . . .

3. An arbitrator must not permit personal relationships to affect decision making.

Prior to acceptance of appointment, an arbitrator must disclose to the parties, or to the administrative agency involved, any close personal relationship or other circumstance, in addition to those specifically mentioned earlier in this section, which might reasonably raise a question as to the arbitrator's impartiality. . . .

4. If the circumstances requiring disclosure are not known to the arbitrator prior to acceptance of appointment, disclosure must be made when such circumstances become known to the arbitrator.

5. The burden of disclosure rests on the arbitrator. After appropriate disclosure, the arbitrator may serve if both parties so desire. If the arbitrator believes or perceives that there is a clear conflict of interest, he or she should withdraw, irrespective of the expressed desires of the parties.

Discussion Question 1:   Did the arbitrator act properly?

If, before designation, the arbitrator has knowledge of a relationship that should be disclosed, it should be revealed then. That discovery might occur when the arbitrator is called by the American Arbitration Association or other tribunal administrators and told of selection for a case. If the arbitrator owns stock in the privately held company, has consulted for the union, has a professional or personal relationship with identifiable individuals in the union or management, this association should be disclosed at that time. But if the arbitrator does not learn of the discloseable relationship until the hearing, as in this case, the disclosure must be made then.

A less clear obligation to disclose arises in relationships that would be less likely to affect the arbitrator's decision. Should the arbitrator disclose ownership of ten shares of stock in a publicly traded company, or possession of municipal or state bonds in a public sector dispute—or the purchase of treasury notes in a federal sector dispute? Should a social relationship with another partner in the advocate's law firm be disclosed or the enrollment of their children in the same nursery school? If the arbitrator had a summer job three decades earlier that required union membership, should that fact be revealed if the union is the same one—or a different one—involved in the present dispute?

The initial issue is not for the arbitrator to decide whether to continue in the case. Rather, the arbitrator must reveal any relationship that might be perceived as resulting in a bias and leave the parties to determine whether, knowing of the relationship, they are comfortable submitting to the arbitrator's decision.

There are three levels of such relationships. The first comprises relationships so tenuous that raising them most likely would create no problems, so that the arbitrator might remain silent about them—for example, having gone to the same university as an advocate but not having met, having seen a witness or counsel in some other case, or having a spouse who owns ten shares of stock in an unrelated subsidiary of the conglomerate company. The second level involves relationships that might raise an issue of bias, such as having been in the same fraternity or sorority, having at one time worked in the same firm, or occasional socializing with a witness, or their spouses being good friends, or owning a few shares of stock in the enterprise. In those first two situations, as in the case example, the arbitrator should fulfill the obligation of disclosure on even what might be considered a trivial relationship and leave that issue to the parties to weigh. It is their case, and they are entitled to a decision that has not been influenced by any questionable relationship. Although the disclosure may cause the arbitrator to "lose" income from the case, failure to disclose prior to the hearing, coupled with a party's discovery of a undisclosed relationship, may appear to be a deliberate suppression and result in a far more embarrassing loss of clients, as well as of reputation. Such a failure might even lead to potential litigation based on suppression. It is certainly much easier to disclose *any* relationship that might be questionable. The parties are generally more alert to the arbitrator's history than the arbitrator thinks, and they have selected the arbitrator with full awareness of some prior entangling alliances. The failure to disclose, rather than the relationships themselves, will raise eyebrows and protest. Indeed, an arbitrator very likely enhances the perception of integrity by such a disclosure of even the most minimal prior relationships. Failure to disclose in timely fashion may result in a motion to vacate or annul the arbitrator's award on the grounds that he or she was sullied by failing to disclose a prior relationship, which, if known, might have precluded the arbitrator's selection.

The third level of relationships concerns those that, even if disclosed, challenge the arbitrator's image of independence and result in suspicion of bias, or actual bias, even though denied by the parties. In the preceding case, despite the acquiescence of the union attorney to the arbitrator's continuing, a question of impartiality lingers. The arbitrator must be mindful, both in terms of professional responsibility and in fear of subsequent legal challenge by the losing party, of whether favoritism toward or bias against a party might impair the arbitrator's responsibility for a neutral judgment. In the preceding case, as a matter of self-interest, the arbitrator should have realized that a decision in favor of either party might be challenged on the grounds of bias. Despite the inconvenience to the parties, and perhaps even at the expense of the delay, the arbitrator might more properly have concluded that perceptions of bias, either at the hearing or (more likely) when issuing the award could justify withdrawal from the case.

In cases administered under the AAA rules, the arbitrator is also bound by Rule 17, which is similar to the preceding requirements of the code:

> Prior to accepting the appointment, the prospective neutral arbitrator shall disclose any circumstances likely to create a presumption of bias or that the arbitrator believes might disqualify him or her as an impartial arbitrator. Upon receipt of such information, the AAA shall immediately disclose it to the parties. If either party declines to waive the presumptive disqualification, the vacancy thus created, shall be filled in accordance with the applicable provisions of these rules.[5]

Discussion Question 2: What should the employer have done to avoid this situation?

Since the employer's advocate knew the arbitrator was a former schoolmate, it was the advocate's responsibility to reveal that relationship to the union, preferably prior to agreement on the arbitrator. Even if not party to the selection process, the advocate should have told the other side when first learning of the arbitrator's selection. Despite the embarrassment of the commotion and charges at the hearing, the employer should have realized if the company won that the decision of the arbitrator might be challenged by the union on the grounds of favoritism; or if the union won, the company might sue to overturn the award on the grounds that the arbitrator had leaned over backwards. In either case, unless the employee's claim was totally granted, both parties would risk a suit by the disgruntled grievant, who could allege violation of the Duty of Fair Representation for using that arbitrator and for having continued after the disclosure.

The employer might have mitigated the union's concerns and fear of suit by offering, off the record, to expedite the selection of a substitute arbitrator, to compensate the employee for the lost wages accrued until a new hearing date, or to absorb any other costs attributable to its earlier failure to disclose the relationship.

Discussion Question 3: What could the union have done to avoid this situation?

The union may have been an innocent party until the hearing if it was unaware of the relationship. If it had known earlier and had no objection to the arbitrator, the union should have agreed with the company to advise the arbitrator, so that she need not have raised the issue at the hearing. Although the union is always subject to the risk of a law suit based upon a charge of failure of the Duty of Fair Representation, the union's sensitivity to the charge may have been stimulated by the kind of outburst that occurred at the hearing—even though the arbitrator sought to control it by meeting with the advocates outside the hearing room.

As the union was willing to proceed, despite the revelation, it would have been wise to secure the grievant's personal acquiescence before announcing agreement to avoid the risk of later litigation based upon some perception of bias.

Of special concern to the union, and sometimes to the employer as well, is the risk of suit arising from cases in which the grievant is represented by an outside counsel who is not a party to the labor–management relationship and who may be suspicious of arbitrators whose economic survival depends on continuing acceptability to both unions and management. This concern might be particularly relevant in an umpireship in which the parties have an ongoing contractual relationship with the single arbitrator. In such cases, it would be to the union's advantage to protect itself from any potential charge of collusion by explaining to the grievant's counsel the relationship of the parties to the arbitrator and permitting the grievant's outside counsel to take part in the arbitrator selection process—including, perhaps, resort to a new arbitrator unencumbered by the luggage of that relationship. Such fears may also have validity in panel or even ad hoc selection of arbitrators, when the grievant's outside counsel—alert to the interdependence of arbitrator, union, and management—might challenge an adverse award as the product of a conspiracy to deprive a dissident employee of contractual or even statutory entitlement to a fair hearing.

The consequence of efforts by either party to gain a favorable result in the case, by tilting the selection of an arbitrator to exploit some personal or professional connection should be obvious. Even if one or both of the parties is tolerant of such impropriety, the arbitrator, because of a professional obligation as well as economic self-interest, should readily reveal these prior relationships. The parties might be better served by selecting an arbitrator without this extra baggage or by making clear disclosure of such relationships. But if they adhere to their choice of arbitrator once any prior relationship is revealed and determined to be nonprejudicial, the parties should be able to proceed with the case.

Specialized Expertise of the Arbitrator

Some cases require an arbitrator with expertise in specialized fields. Generally, in such cases, the parties will seek a group of nominees who have such expertise. The parties may create a contractual panel composed of arbitrators who have the requisite expertise, such as in time and motion study. If they do not have such a negotiated panel, they may ask a designating agency to create one on an ad hoc basis from which to select an arbitrator for a pending dispute.

But the parties during the selection process may not know whether the arbitrator they have chosen has the requisite expertise. Furthermore, the issue of specialized experience may not arise until during the hearing. In such cases, the designated arbitrator may lack the qualification called for to resolve the dispute.

Section 1B of the code specifies that:

> 1. An arbitrator must decline appointment, withdraw, or request technical assistance when he or she decides that a case is beyond is or her competence.

In this instance, it would be improper for an arbitrator to accept an appointment for a case involving time and motion study, if the arbitrator knowingly lacks sufficient competence in that erudite field. But one could argue that the language is sufficiently vague to permit the arbitrator to venture into the area, even if never having done such a case, if "he or she deduces that a case is [within rather than] beyond his or her competence."

But Section 1A of the code requires that:

> Essential personal qualifications of an arbitrator include honesty, integrity, impartiality and general competence in labor relations matter.

It should follow that an arbitrator, at the very least, should disclose lack of experience in that specialized area, offer to withdraw from the case, or request the technical assistance provided for in code provision 1B1.

The revelation that the arbitrator is not omniscient is usually refreshing, if not disarming, to the parties and will lead the arbitrator to secure the information and upgrade the skills necessary to decide the case. It is, after all, the responsibility of the parties to present sufficient data for the arbitrator to intelligently resolve their dispute. An admission by the arbitrator of insufficient expertise in any issue provides the parties with the signal to bring the arbitrator up to the level of skill required in the case. That need may be met by greater explanation by the parties at the hearing, provision of expert testimony, adjustment of the single arbitration system to tripartite panel (so an expert from each side can join the arbitrator and assist in reviewing and deciding the case) or authorization from both sides for the arbitrator to enlist a neutral professional expertise of their or the arbitrator's choice. One area in which the parties very frequently invoke the testimony of outside experts is in disputes over medical issues.

Arbitrators are frequently confronted with the question of whether or not an employee is fit to return to work. The dispute may arise from a grievance filed by an employee who seeks to return from sick leave or from an employee who declines an employer's order to return to work. In either case, both parties are likely to turn to the expert testimony of physicians, psychotherapists, osteopaths, chiropractors, psychiatrists, and so on to support their positions. The arbitrator is often left to resolve such disputes among experts, including questions of the expertise and qualifications of witnesses with training in different disciplines or even different medical fields. Sometimes the arbitrator finds the evidence sufficiently persuasive on one side to support a decision for that party; sometimes the arbitrator feels ill-equipped to render an expert decision. It is perfectly appropriate for the arbitrator to suggest referral of the dispute to a specialist of the parties' choice, or of the arbitrator's choice, to render the final and binding decision, if the parties agree.

It may also be appropriate for an arbitrator to consult an outside expert while rendering the decision on the case, but only if the parties are advised of and agreeable to this action. The arbitrator alone must bear the responsibility for rendering the decision.

The code in section 2.G1 does permit the arbitrators to do independent research as long as it is within the mandate that "An arbitrator must assume full personal responsibility for the decision in each case decided." It is clear that resort to such independent research is, under sec 2.G1a, "dependent primarily on the policies of the parties on these matters, as expressed in the contract, or other agreements, or at the hearing."

It follows that the prudent course for the arbitrator would be to solicit authorization for such independent research and for the parties to make sure that the arbitrator does so only with their acquiescence. To ensure that, it is perfectly appropriate for either party to question whether the arbitrator fully understands the technical issue, whether he or she would want further assistance from the parties' experts, or whether he or she feels the need to consult or research the issue further with the approval of the parties.

Prehearing Contacts with the Arbitrator

The adversarial nature of the arbitration process makes it improper for either party to provide information on the case to the arbitrator without the other party having the opportunity to challenge or at least respond to such input. Thus, there should be no communication with the arbitrator on substantive matters prior to the commencement of the hearing.

In cases where the American Arbitration Association or some other administrative agency makes arrangements with the parties for the hearing, the arbitrator is insulated from any charge of being the recipient of ex parte or one-sided communications. But when no administrative agency is involved and the parties are in direct contact with the arbitrator, there is a greater risk of one or both of the parties taking advantage of discussion over administrative matters to communicate with the arbitrator about the case. In most cases, the parties and the arbitrator are extremely careful to avoid such substantive references, except perhaps to identify the issue as a "termination case," a "promotion case," "a case of layoff with an arbitrability issue," and so on. The failure of either party to adhere to the unspoken rule of not discussing the case would require the arbitrator to report such ex parte communication to the other side and thus live up to the responsibility to disclose such "information" as "might reasonably raise a question as to the arbitrator's impartiality."

Of course, any arrangement to the contrary regarding communication to the arbitrator that is agreeable to both parties is permissible. But such prehearing contact, even when discussed and agreed upon by the parties, is quite limited. If there is any submission at all, it may be the parties' collective bargaining agreement, or agreed-upon exhibits, or, even more rarely, if the parties agree, written opening statements by both. But in accordance with the rule against ex parte submissions, the arbitrator would not be likely to read such documentation unless certain that it is being submitted pursuant to an agreement between the parties.

Aside from the issue of improper submission of information concerning the substance of the case, there is the issue of the perception of impropriety that may arise from the appearance of communication with one or both of the parties. Even when the parties and the arbitrator diligently keep at arm's length, which is most likely to insulate them from charges of impropriety, the risks remain. When dealing with particularly volatile issues of particularly suspicious parties, advocates, grievants, or even witnesses, a chance encounter involving a few words of small-talk in an airport, hotel restaurant, or company parking lot may stimulate suspicion, distrust, and perhaps even an ethical challenge. The risk of such charges might preclude even the most experienced arbitrators and advocates from engaging in what might in other contexts be viewed as enjoyable conviviality, particularly among advocates and arbitrators who may meet with and work with one another repeatedly for years. "The less said, the less to explain."

Subpoenas

In most cases, the parties have fully shared their information and exhibits and explained what witnesses would testify if the case goes to arbitration. But at times one or both of the parties, contrary to their proclaimed intent of resolving the case at the lowest steps of the grievance procedure, may endeavor to guard the evidence or fail to disclose it. There are also times when the parties announce that they will not have present at the hearing witnesses sought by the other side for questioning. As a result, arbitrators are occasionally asked to issue subpoenas to make certain that individuals and/or documents are present at the time and place of the hearing. On the one hand, it may be contrary to the concept of arbitration as an adversarial process to permit one party to contact the arbitrator prior to the hearing to ask for the issuance of a subpoena. But, on the other hand, waiting until the hearing for argument on the issuance of the subpoena risks requiring a second day of hearing for such information or individuals to be present. Joinder on the issuance of a subpoena may also jeopardize the privacy and preparation of one side, which may seek the subpoena to assure the presence at the hearing of a surprise or rebuttal witness.

The problem is further complicated by the question of whether, under law, the arbitrator has the legal authority to issue subpoenas. Some argue that the authority is provided by the U.S. Arbitration Act or the respective state arbitration statutes. Others argue that arbitrators lack such authority. In some states, it is clear that attorneys, as officers of the court, have that authority whether serving as advocates or arbitrators. One could argue that the initial unilateral request by the advocate of one side for the issuance of a subpoena would justify offering the other party the right to respond both on the issue of the arbitrator's authority and on the propriety of the subpoena. But to invite that response from the other side might undermine the preparation, position, and even the case of the party requesting the subpoena. The arbitrator would thus become embroiled in a legal dispute over his or her subpoena authority, more properly an issue for the courts, not a private arbitrator.

Whether or not arbitrators have the legal authority to issue subpoenas, it seems clear that they lack the authority to enforce any subpoena they issue—that is the province of the courts.

Thus, the issuance of the subpoena may be, at best, gratuitous and presumptuous, but it is also, at the very least, a means of encouraging any individual or document that one party wishes present at the hearing to be made available in order to avoid the delay that would result from a discussion at the hearing of the issuance of the subpoena in terms of authority and scope.

Most arbitrators appear to sign and thus issue subpoenas when specific information as to person or document is presented to them by one party in advance of the hearing. Regardless of the arbitrator's authority and the subpoena's enforceability, the subpoena serves as a demand by the arbitrator that the individual or document be provided at the hearing. It does not determine the admissibility of the testimony or documents. At the hearing, both parties are available to argue whether the subpoenaed individual should testify or the subpoenaed document should be admitted into evidence. The rationale for issuance is thus to ensure that the proceeding is conducted expeditiously and without the delay that might be occasioned by a debate between the parties over the arbitrator's authority, a resort to a court to resolve that issue, or simply a delay for another day of hearing to have the requested witness or document available for a discussion of the issue introducing the testimony or evidence.

The subpoena, therefore, is little more than a goad to ensure the requesting party will have, at the hearing, those witnesses and documents necessary to fully present its case in the most expedient form. If the witness or document is not present at the hearing, or if the opposing party objects to the witnesses' testimony or the documents' introduction, the arbitrator, who is by then authorized to decide the submitted issue, will be in a better position to determine whether the testimony or document is necessary or relevant to the case. The arbitrator will also be in a better position to explain that an adverse inference will be drawn from failure to comply with the subpoena. By so doing, the arbitrator is in effect stating that, even though lacking authority to enforce the subpoena, the requesting party's inferences about the failure to respond to the subpoena will be accepted if the objecting party insists on denying access to the testimony of the disputed witness or document.

An ancillary motivation for the subpoena, particularly in collective bargaining agreements that provide witness fees for employees subpoenaed to testify in adversarial proceedings, may be to ensure the contractually provided compensation for such witnesses. Whether such compensation is appropriate in arbitration procedures becomes a separate issue to be resolved in another forum or arbitration proceeding.

It should be emphasized that arbitrators should only be asked to sign subpoenas that are specific about the individual or document(s) requested for presentation at the time and place of the scheduled hearing.

Locus and Time of Hearing

For parties with longstanding practice at arbitration, the location and time of the hearing present little basis for dispute. They usually follow a pattern that both have found acceptable and conducive to the smooth running of hearings. The location, in most cases, would be at the workplace, often in a conference room in the employer's office. Such hearing sites are convenient for ready access to documents and files, for rapid access to witnesses, who need only interrupt their work for brief testimony, and to minimize work interruption. In some cases, the parties may meet at a similar facility in the union's office. Such meeting places in partisan territory are effective only if the parties feel comfortable and secure there, are free from interruption, and are not intimidated by making their presentation in "hostile territory." In many cases, one of the parties may object to meeting on the other side's territory, or there may be a lack of suitable premises, so that the parties meet in neutral territory. In cities where the American Arbitration Association maintains offices, it has hearing room facilities available. In other communities, the usual resort is to use a conference room at a nearby hotel or motel. While such off-site facilities incur additional expense compared to meeting in one of the parties' offices, they do provide isolation from partisan interruption, readily available parking, coffee and meal facilities. However, meeting in such facilities may restrict ready access to supportive documentation or the opportunity to visit the work site for a view of the operation or equipment when requested by either party.

Thus, wherever the parties agree to meet, it may be necessary to adjourn the proceedings to conduct a plant visit or to break the proceedings while documentation for presentation at the hearing is secured by either party.

The issue of hearing time usually presents no problem. Most parties accept the tradition of a 10 A.M. hearing time, which permits the parties to assemble and meet with their witnesses, go over the case and their testimony, and, on occasion, meet with their counterparts from the other side to seek agreement on the issues, discuss the admissibility of exhibits and stipulations of fact, and even the possibility of settling the case. The 10:00 A.M. starting also usually provides time for the arbitrator to travel from home to the hearing on the same day, without the added expense of an overnight hotel bill.

But even the hearing time occasionally raises dispute, when the witnesses may be required to come on their personal time, perhaps after a full night shift of work, or, as in public education, when the employer may insist on a late afternoon starting time to avoid additional payment to substitute teachers while participants attend a hearing during normal school hours.

Arbitrators are sometimes called upon to resolve conflicts between the parties over location or time of the hearing. Since such issues arise prior to the formal hearing, the arbitrator may lack the submission, the formal issue, and thus the authority to impose a decision on the parties. Nonetheless, the disputing parties usually accede to the arbitrator's suggestion as to time and place of hearing. In cases administered by the American Arbitration Association, the parties, by adherence to the AAA rules, grant to the arbitrator the authority to decide issues of hearing time and place. Rule 19 states:

> The arbitrator shall fix the time and place for each hearing. At least five days prior thereto, the AAA shall mail notice of the time and place of hearing to each party, unless the parties otherwise agree.[6]

Sometimes, the arbitrator might try to mediate such a dispute by phone by pointing out the disadvantages or inconvenience of a particular time or place or by recommending an alternative to the two positions.

Ex Parte Hearings

The adjudicatory nature of arbitration dictates that both parties attend the hearing to present their respective cases and cross-examine the other party's witnesses. But, on rare occasions, one of the parties may refuse to take part in the arbitration. The refusal may be due to objection to the arbitrator's jurisdiction, disapproval of the arbitrator's administrative prehearing rulings, or conviction that the case cannot proceed without its willing participation.

Conversely, the other party may be equally insistent on proceeding with the hearing and invoke its right to have the matter resolved as guaranteed by its collective bargaining agreement. The rights to arbitration and to a final and binding arbitrator's decision cannot he denied because the other party refuses to take part in the proceeding. The arbitrator has an obligation to provide the forum for the party that is eager to proceed. But the arbitrator has a counterbalancing obligation to provide the recalcitrant party with clear notice that the hearing will proceed whether or not the objecting party is willing to participate.

Arbitrators usually provide the opportunity for the objecting party to make a "special appearance"—that is, attend a hearing for the limited purpose of arguing why the arbitration proceeding should not go ahead. That party then raises legal or contractual arguments against the arbitrator's going forward to a hearing on the merits. Section 5.C1 of the code requires the arbitrator to hear and consider such arguments before deciding whether to proceed with an ex parte hearing—that is, one without the participation of the objecting party. But unless the arbitrator decides that the case is not arbitrable, or that the objections to proceeding are meritorious, the obligation is to go forward with the presentation of the substantive issues at the hearing.

The question then arises as to whether the hearing should proceed at that time or some future time. Section 5.C2 of the code specifies: "An arbitrator must be certain, before proceeding ex parte, that the party refusing or failing to attend the hearing has been given adequate notice of the time, place, or purposes of the hearing."

Thus, unless the arbitrator is convinced the requisite notice had previously been provided to the recalcitrant party to permit going on with the ex parte hearing that day, arrangements must he made for a subsequent hearing date. Most arbitrators would follow the practice of providing explicit notice to both parties that, at a particular time and place, the hearing will go forward and that in the absence of the objecting party, it will proceed ex parte. The recalcitrant party therefore has specific notice of the consequence of nonappearance and nonparticipation.

A similar standard of notice is set forth in the AAA rules, which then describe the arbitrator's responsibility for the conduct of the ex parte hearing:

2. . . . Arbitration in the absence of a party, unless the law provides to the contrary, the arbitration may proceed in the absence of any party who, after due notice, fails to be present or fails to obtain an adjournment. An award shall not be made solely on the default of a party. The arbitrator shall require the other party to submit such evidence as may be required for the making of an award.[7]

The only opinion on the subject by the NAA Committee on Professional Responsibility and Grievances was issued on June 7, 1986 (Opinion No. 13).[8] It concerned a grievance with an arbitrability challenge on timeliness. The employer advised the union that it would only arbitrate the issue of timeliness and would not be prepared to go forward on the merits issue. The union insisted that both the arbitrability issue and merits be arbitrated at that one hearing.

After the joint presentation on the arbitrability, the arbitrator offered the employer a two-hour adjournment to prepare its case on the merits and said that he would hear the merits as an integral part of a single hearing. The employer protested that the case on the merits could not be prepared in two hours and left. The arbitrator proceeded with an ex parte hearing on the merits. The union won on both issues.

The committee found that the arbitrator had failed in the obligation under part 5.A1 of the code to assure both parties "sufficient opportunity to present their respective evidence and argument" and that the arbitrator should have resolved any doubt over whether two hours was sufficient time to prepare in favor of granting a continuance. "That was the only way he could have complied with his responsibility to assure a fair and adequate hearing." The Committee found the arbitrator had violated Part 5-A-1c by preventing the employer from putting forward its case fairly and adequately."

As to the propriety of the ex parte hearing on the merits, the committee found the arbitrator had violated part 5.C1 and C2:

> The arbitrator did not have to hold an ex parte hearing just because the employer elected to walk out. The failure of the employer to remain did not relieve the arbitrator from the responsibility to follow 5.C1 & 2. The employer, from its perspective, had not been given "adequate notice of the purposes of the hearing." Since there was no joint submission of both issues, the employer was not prepared to go forward on the merits, understanding that its sole responsibility was to prepare for the arbitrability issue, and that fact alone should have persuaded the arbitrator not to have held an ex parte hearing.

An arbitrator who, despite adequate notice, is faced with conducting an ex parte hearing is placed in the position of judging a case that may be only partially disclosed. When an opposing counsel is absent, the arbitrator lacks the traditional posture of an objective listener to who relies on evidence, cross-examination, and objections over the tactics of the other side to fashion an overall picture of the dispute.

In such ex parte proceedings, the arbitrator is likely to exercise a more participatory role, perhaps even to the extent of asking questions or raising interjections that would normally be the sole responsibility of the other side. Despite the one-side participation, the responsibility of the arbitrator is nevertheless to exercise judgment for a fair resolution of the dispute.

In some cases of ex parte hearings, arbitrators have had a transcript taken that is then supplied to the absent party to provide an opportunity for rejoinder or for reopening the hearing (with the other side's consent) for presentation of any additional evidence the other side deems necessary. In such ad hoc arrangements, the party that proceeded at the initial hearing may acquiesce to holding the additional hearing, if only to avoid the litigation that the absent party might otherwise bring.

Stipulated Awards

The ongoing relationship of the parties occasionally places them in a position in which they are able to agree on the resolution of a pending grievance, but potentially face a political or legal problem in signing off on the settlement. They would prefer to have the arbitrator codify or sanctify their "settlement" in the forum of a final and binding arbitration award.

This expectation presents no problem if the parties approach the arbitrator with a request for an award reflecting their prior agreement. As long as the arbitrator's award incorporates that settlement and identifies the outcome as that of the parties, there is no question of a code violation. The award would read something like the following:

> At the hearing on the above-listed case, the parties reached the following agreement: Ann Griffin will be reinstated with full seniority and other rights, but without back pay, effective August 1st.

If the parties are unable to acknowledge their agreement and feel obliged to go forward with the hearing without telling the arbitrator of their preferred result, they might be able to present the case so the arbitrator is led to the result they desire. That strategy may entail some risk, particularly if certain witnesses are not called, or certain questions are not asked. There is no certainty that the arbitrator will not see through the set up, or that crucial questions will remain unasked, or that the arbitrator will deliver the result the two spokespersons had preferred.

A bigger problem is the situation in which the parties approach the arbitrator prior to the hearing and explain the result they seek. Sometimes the parties blatantly make the arbitrator's selection dependent upon the commitment to issue the result they want.

Part 1A of the code reads as follows:

A. General Qualifications

1. Essential personal qualifications of an arbitrator include honesty, integrity, impartiality, and general competence in labor relations matters.

2. An arbitrator must be as ready to rule for one party as for the other on each issue, either in a single case or a group of cases. Compromise by an arbitrator for the sake of attempting to achieve personal acceptability is unprofessional.

Part 2A of the code, Recognition, reads:

A. Recognition of Diversity in Arbitration Arrangements

1. An arbitrator should conscientiously endeavor to understand and observe, to the extent consistent with professional responsibility, the significant principles of governing each arbitrator system in which he or she serves.

2. Such understanding does not relieve an arbitrator from a corollary responsibility to seek to discern and refuse to lend approval or consent to any collusive attempt by the parties to use arbitration for an improper purpose.

In addition to the positive ethical qualifications set forth in part A of the code, when read in the light of the proscription in part 2.A2, the code clearly states that the arbitrator should not agree to be bound to a result irrespective of the evidence presented at the hearing. That obligation is particularly true when acquiescence would codify a collusion by the parties in a result that otherwise would not be the normal outcome of a full hearing. Most arbitrators would decline to serve when their selection depends on a commitment in advance to issue a previously agreed-upon decision.

A more difficult case arises when the parties do not demand a certain decision as a condition of selection, but do express their desires in whole or part concerning the outcome of the case.

The code in part 2 I, Consent Awards, reads as follows:

1. Prior to the issuance of an award, the parties may jointly request the arbitrator to include in the award, certain agreements between them concerning some or all of the issues. If the arbitrator believes that a suggested award is proper, fair, sound, and lawful, it is consistent with professional responsibility to adopt it.

a. Before complying with such a request, an arbitrator must be certain that he or she understands the suggested settlement adequately, in order to be able to appraise its terms. If it appears that pertinent facts on circumstances may not have been disclosed, the arbitrator should take the initiative to assure that all significant aspects of the case are fully understood. To this end, the arbitrator may request additional specific information and may question witnesses at a hearing.

Many arbitrators, when faced with a request for a certain outcome at the conclusion of the hearing, will decline to serve on the grounds that awareness of the result preferred by the parties would provide an unwelcomed tilt toward the "acceptable" result and thereby impede, if not violate, the arbitrator's obligation under part 1.A2 of the code to be as ready to rule for one party as the other.

But despite that prediction, it is acceptable under the code, when approached for a requested result, for the arbitrator to decline to commit to that outcome but to continue in the case with the caveat to the parties that the result of the proceeding will be determined solely by the evidence presented at the hearing. But the arbitrator who continues in the case is under the injunction of part 2.I1a to take the initiative at the hearing "to assure that all significant aspects of the case are fully understood," even if such measures mean requesting additional information and questioning witnesses.

In the end, the arbitrator's professional survival depends upon written opinions and decisions that are internally consistent and sound. It would be short-sighted—not to mention professionally suicidal—for an arbitrator to issue an opinion and decision that complies with a party's request but that is not supported by the evidence or is inconsistent in the light of the rest of the opinion. A short-term gain from meeting the wishes of the parties may result in a long-term disadvantage if the parties circulate the unjustified opinion and decision. But if the arbitrator, by holding a full hearing with the necessary initiative, is able to reach a result that is acceptable to both parties, the long-term satisfaction from a full hearing and well-crafted opinion with a justifiable decision will bolster, rather than detract from, the arbitrator's reputation for competence and integrity.

CASE STUDY: The Case of the Joint Dumping. Rick Avilla has been with his employer for three years as a machinist. He's been active among union dissidents, has sought to overturn its present leadership, and has had a letter of warning and a three-day suspension for insubordination.

One day, at a few minutes before quitting time, Rob Robins, his supervisor, assigned him to some additional work. Avilla refused to do the work and said he had to leave. Robins ordered him to stay. Avilla swore at Robins and allegedly shoved him aside on his way to punch out. Avilla was terminated, and the case was brought to arbitration.

As the arbitrator entered the hearing room, the company personnel director approached him and reported that the case was easy and that both parties would not have brought it to arbitration except that Avilla threatened to sue them for their effort to oust him. The union and the management had agreed that Avilla was a "bad apple" and that the termination should be sustained.

The arbitrator, hearing this, sought the union president and reported what had been said to him. The union president said he was in complete agreement and that the parties expected the arbitrator to sustain the termination.

The arbitrator brought both spokespersons together and stated that he could not guarantee the result of the case but would hear it if they wanted him to, without any promises as to the outcome. He heard the case and sustained the termination.

Discussion Question 1: Did the arbitrator act properly?

When the company representative told him that the union expected to lose the case, the arbitrator was obligated to report that ex parte communication to the other side. In this case, both were in accord, so that the arbitrator had to consider whether to refuse or to proceed with the hearing. The union's expectation that the grievant would be terminated placed the arbitrator in the position of joining in the parties' collusion to remove Avilla.

The arbitrator declined to commit, and stated that he would go forward with the hearing without giving any assurance that he would decide as the parties desired. That option was certainly available to the arbitrator under the terms of the code, although it is obvious that his continued acceptability would be contingent on upholding the removal. As noted earlier, the arbitrator, in proceeding in such a case, has a stronger obligation to make sure that a full record is developed and that all relevant evidence is presented.

Discussion Question 2: Should the arbitrator have told the grievant of the discussions with the representatives?

The arbitration arrangement is between the employer and the union. The latter has the obligation to represent its constituency properly. Even though an arbitrator might resent the burden of collusion, and even though there is a desire to assure the grievant of a just hearing, most arbitrators would find it improper to go behind the union's back to talk to the grievant or any other witness about the proceedings. The opportunity to question the grievant would come at the hearing, and even if the grievant is not called to testify by the union, the arbitrator has the authority, if not the obligation, to call witnesses—particularly under such circumstances.

Discussion Question 3: Should the prospect of Avilla suing the parties affect the arbitrator's undertaking to hear the case?

Most arbitrators are unintimidated by threatened law suits against the parties if the arbitrator has confidence in the propriety of the proceedings and the award. But in this case, the two spokespersons sought a commitment to the outcome and clearly expressed their desires and hopes for a termination award. Under these circumstances, many arbitrators would consider a potential lawsuit as likely to be directed at them, as well. The fear of a charge of collusion involving both parties and the arbitrator is very real. If the arbitrator chooses to remain in the case, it might be wise, for added protection, to arrange for a transcript to establish the thoroughness and impartiality of the arbitrator's hearing, even though the result coincided with the parties' desires.

Discussion Question 4: What if the union had not called the grievant to testify in response to the supervisor's testimony that Avilla had shoved him?

The arbitrator has responsibility to conduct a full and fair hearing, particularly when the union representative has approved of the termination. Although arbitrators are generally reluctant to substitute themselves as the advocate for either party, the arbitrator's concern that the union was not fully representing the grievant, coupled with responsibility under the code, would probably have led the arbitrator to call the grievant to the stand, even if the union had not.

Conclusion

Ideally, by meeting in advance to resolve some of the procedural prerequisites for a smooth hearing, the parties will have eliminated many of the obstacles to the arbitration procedures. Ideally, too, such meetings provide an additional opportunity to discuss the case itself and may lead to a settlement that was unattainable earlier. But if there is no such resolution the dispute must continue on to the hearing.

3
Problems at the Start
of the Hearing

The time, date, and place for the hearing have been agreed upon. The arbitrator appears as scheduled, and the proceedings seem set to run smoothly. But problems can arise. For instance, one of the parties may be missing. If this absence is a deliberate "no show," the arbitrator has to determine whether to go forward with an ex parte hearing then or at a later date, according to the standards described at the end of the preceding chapter. Alternatively, the absence may be tardiness or miscommunication, to which the parties under the arbitrator's guidance should be readily able to accommodate.

But even if both parties are present and ready to proceed, a number of wrangles may still arise before the arbitrator is in a position to hear and decide the case.

The initial question for resolution is the formulation of the issue to be arbitrated. Ideally, the spokespersons for the parties have resolved this matter prior to their arrival at the hearing. However, in most cases, agreement on the issue must be secured at the hearing before the taking of evidence. Usually, the matter will be worked out by the spokespersons, particularly because at that point the arbitrator has had no opportunity to learn about the dispute. But sometimes the arbitrator, despite unfamiliarity with the particular dispute, may nudge the parties toward an agreement on the issue or, at minimum, a procedure for reaching agreement. This chapter presents several alternatives that may be utilized by the parties in reaching such an agreement on the issue and points out the pitfalls of not reaching agreement.

The chapter next deals with the problem of agreement on whether there should be a transcript, who should pay for it, and who should have access to it. The increasingly adversarial nature of the arbitration process has stimulated the use of lawyers as presenters and, therefore, the reliance on transcripts, as well as on post-hearing briefs. At the same time, the increasing cost of arbitration, particularly for unions with decreasing membership, forces the unions to forego reliance on transcripts while at the same time seeking to assure that any transcript provided to the arbitrator is accurate. Procedures for assuring transcript accuracy are also set forth in this chapter.

Numerous other problems are likely to surface for the first time at the start of the hearing, when the parties first confront such issues, particularly if they are represented for the first time in the appeal by outside counsel.

Among such issues are what should be done when one of the parties requests a postponement. Should such last-minute postponements be granted or denied in light of the parties' knowledge that the hearing was scheduled to proceed at the time and date specified? But what if the postponement request arises from the illness or unavoidable absence of a witness? Is it fair to require a party to proceed with alternative, but less persuasive witnesses? Who should bear the cost of the postponement?

Another issue that arises as a consequence of the increasingly adversarial nature of the process, coupled perhaps with the TV-based understanding of what should happen in court, is the increasing frequency with which sequestration of witnesses is requested. Although sequestration serves a purpose in avoiding piggy-backed testimony in cases where credibility is at issue, if employed for other disputes it merely tends to extend the proceedings with minimal benefit to the decision maker.

Finally, this chapter turns to an examination of the problems faced by the parties and the neutral when the tripartite arbitration panel is employed. Aside from the second chance to present views provided by such a format, the idealized concept of a tripartite panel is eroded by the needs of the parties to have their team members play varying, and often conflicting, roles as witness, advocate, and wing person.

The chapter concludes with a consideration of the placement of exhibits into evidence, one of the most controversial and often least understood aspects of the arbitration process. The often-muddled rules of evidence do provide a rational framework for determining what exhibits should be admitted. In some cases, there will be little dispute over admission of exhibits, such as the collective bargaining agreement, the paper trail of documents that led to the filing, denials, and appeals of the case to arbitrator. Admission becomes more muddied when one considers other offered exhibits—for example, a grievant's prior record, statutory or court law, or decisions of ancillary forum. The problems become even murkier when one considers the admissibility of exhibits that were stolen from the other side's files, or exhibits that are unauthenticated, or copies of xeroxed copies, or copied tapes. And if the requested exhibit is not produced, what weight should be given the mere assertion of what it is alleged to contain? And what weight should be attached to an exhibit of drug test results, in which the chain of custody of the substance, the veracity of the test results and the interpretation of those results may be subject to challenge?

These and other issues are likely to arise at the start of an arbitration hearing, when the adversaries have the first forum in which to raise such issues. They may certainly complicate and delay the start of the hearing, but they must be resolved in order to clear the stage for the main presentations—the procedural and substantive issues that brought the case to arbitration.

Agreeing on the Issue

The authority of the arbitrator to decide a particular dispute arises from the submission of an issue for resolution. If there is no agreement on what the issue is or how it is to be determined, the parties cannot be bound by the arbitrator's decision. If the parties do not mutually cede to the arbitrator the right to issue a final binding decision on any agreed-upon issue, the arbitrator has no authority to proceed because no mutually specified dispute has been presented. Ideally, the parties will be able to reach agreement.

In order to frame an issue so that it will lead to a decision that is dispositive of the parties' dispute, the question must be framed in language that is broad enough to cover the position and argument of both parties. Take, for example, a dispute over the rate to be paid to an employee on temporary transfer. The union argues, pursuant to article 2, that the higher rate of the job into which the employee transferred is applicable. The company argues that the controlling language is article 3, which governs compensation on short-term transfers.

The union might frame the threshold question as follows: "Did the company violate article 2 in its payment to the grievant during the period of the transfer?" The company, on the other hand, would be likely to frame the issue with reference to article 3 rather than article 2. Neither formulation would be likely to be acceptable to the other side. The core of such a dispute is the propriety of the company's payment in the context of the parties' collective bargaining agreement. An issued framed in terms broad enough to encompass the arguments of both parties by embracing both articles 2 and 3 would bring an end to the dispute over the issue and grant the arbitrator enough range to embrace both positions. The parties would be more likely to reach agreement on an issue that, when decided, would end their conflict if they frame the issue embracing both articles or the contract as a whole, such as: "Did the company violate article 2 and/or article 3?" Or they might make the submission, "Did the company violate the parties' agreement?"

Some advocates believe they can secure an advantage by insisting on a very narrow, restrictive issue that deprives the other side of a contractual reference on which to base its argument. An example would be "Did the employer violate the contract when it terminated X after he stole the lumber?" But such a tactic merely intensifies the hostility in trying to frame the issue and offers, at best, a temporal advantage. Even if the other party accedes to such a one-side phrasing of the issue, the arbitrator, sensing the tilt during the hearing, might well urge a redrafting of the issue to make it neutral or to permit it to embrace the positions of both sides. Since the intent of arbitration is to resolve the parties' dispute, such interference with the phasing of broad language merely forestalls the achievement of that goal.

When the parties agree to use the entire contract as their reference in assessing whether there has been a violation, there is room for every argument and reliance upon all the contract provisions. Indeed, this format is the simplest for reaching agreement on the issue: It is neutral, and it doesn't create new or irrelevant issues any more than a statement listing specified provisions, but it provides assurance to both parties that the full range of their contract-reliant arguments will be heard without tactical exclusion by fancy footwork on framing the issue. The arbitrator will be the ultimate judge of whether or not the contractual provisions relied upon by the parties are pertinent or controlling in the case.

Some arbitrators refrain from any participation in the parties' exchange in framing the issue. Other arbitrators tend to be more active and may even undertake a mediatory role if desired to help the parties reach agreement on the phrasing of the issue. If that effort is unsuccessful, certain alternatives substitute for an agreed-upon submission.

The Demand for Arbitration as the Issue

In cases that are processed through the procedures of the American Arbitration Association, the union's appeal to arbitration is registered by filling out a Demand for Arbitration form addressed to the employer, which reads in part as follows:

> The undersigned, a party to an arbitration agreement, contained in a written contract dated _____ , providing for arbitration, hereby demands arbitration thereunder.
> Nature of Dispute: _____
> Remedy Sought:_____
> Hearing Locale Requested:_____

Because the Demand for Arbitration usually identifies the alleged contract violation and the remedy sought, it sufficiently defines the dispute to substitute for a jointly stipulated statement of the issue.

Where the parties agree, or their collective bargaining agreement specifies that disputes are to be processed pursuant to the AAA Voluntary Labor Arbitration Rules, the submission of the Demand for Arbitration sets forth the arbitrable claim. As noted in rule 26, Order of Proceedings:

> A hearing shall be opened by . . . the recording of the place, time, and date of the hearing and the presence of the arbitrator, the parties and counsel, if any; and by the receipt of the arbitrator of the Demand and Answer, if any, or the Submission.[7]

Thus, in cases administered under the rules of the American Arbitration Association, the failure to reach a stipulated submission or agreed-upon statement of the issue does not prevent proceeding with the case. In a sense, the commitment to pursue an agreed statement of the issue is reversed. Under the American Arbitration Association rules, the nature of the dispute and remedy sought as set forth in the Demand for Arbitration, substitute as the issue unless the parties, together with the arbitrator, subsequently agree upon a statement of the issue in dispute.

Disposition of the Grievance

If there is no agreement on a stipulated issue, and if there is no AAA Demand for Arbitration negotiated by the parties as a substitute for the issue, the arbitrator still seeks some grant of authority over some issue to be able to arbitrate.

Any claim that been processed as far as the arbitration step has its genesis in a grievance filed pursuant to the grievance procedure of the parties' collective bargaining agreement. Such a grievance filing, usually initiated in writing, but occasionally filed orally and later reduced to writing, is the necessary prerequisite for any claim being appealed up the grievance chain to arbitration. The parties could agree upon the issue to be the disposition of the grievance.

Although employers may initiate grievances, usually the union undertakes the appeal, and it usually is willing to agree to a statement of the issue. The employer is more likely to be unwilling to agree, for several reasons beyond its opposition on the merits to the claimed contract violation.

First, the employer may view the grievance as a one-sided statement of the conflict between the parties. The grievance may be, after all, an allegation of contract violation authored, or even exaggerated by, a rank-and-file employee filled with outrage at what the employee perceives as a violation. The grievance is not written as the dispassionate, balanced statement of a disputed claim that might result from greater contemplation and more careful draftsmanship. If the issue assumes an unproven allegation, the employer may think that, by agreeing, it is admitting that the allegation is true. Take a grievance that reads: "The employer violated the contract when it fired A after he fought off a physical attack by his foreman." The employer may deny that the foreman ever touched the employee and may refuse to agree to a grievance that asserts so.

Second, the employer might object to proceeding on the grievance as the issue if it has procedural objections to the arbitrability of the grievance.

Third, the employer might object that the grievance is different from the one that was the subject of the parties' discussions during the processing of the earlier grievance appeal steps. Despite the language of the foregoing grievance, for example, the parties' appeal discussions might have been focused on the grievant's refusal to follow a supervisor's order immediately preceding the alleged altercation.

Finally, proceeding with the grievance itself as the issue may ignore the issue of remedy that might otherwise be specifically cited if the parties were able to jointly frame an independent issue.

None of the foregoing concerns would be ignored if the parties were to agree to the disposition of the grievance as the issue to be arbitrated. On the contrary, such agreement would recognize that the filing of the grievance began the administrative process that ultimately led to the arbitration and would provide each side with full opportunity to raise any claims they deem appropriate in reciting the chronology of their handling the appeal. By the time those recitations and arguments have been heard, the arbitrator will have had all the input necessary to cull from the presentation the substantive issue in dispute, the procedural or arbitrability objections, and what remedy, if the employee wins, would be appropriate to make the grievant whole.

Leaving the Framing of the Issue to the Arbitrator

Sometimes, the conflict over the framing of the issue becomes so intense that the parties are unable or unwilling to agree on an issue prior to the start of the hearing, even after hours of wrangling. On such occasions, one of the parties might suggest deferring discussion on framing the issue until after the hearing. Such an approach only postpones the conflict; it also tends to make the conflict more intense because, by that time, the full record has been made and an even greater premium must be placed on favorable or biased wording when the stakes are higher and the outcome of the dispute more easily discerned. Postponement also imposes a handicap on the arbitrator, who is thereby deprived of the guidance in making admissibility rulings that would be provided by an agreed-upon statement of the issue prior to the start of the hearing.

Arbitrators are split over the proper course to take when there has been no agreement on the issue. Some take the position that they have no authority to proceed with the hearing without a prior agreement by the parties on the issue that empowers the arbitrator. The purists of this school decline to proceed unless the parties take the requisite action to create such empowerment, although they would probably conduct an ex parte hearing where the missing party has obviously not ceded agreement to the issue proposed by the party present. Most arbitrators, however, are likely to help the parties frame the issue. Despite their unfamiliarity with the case, the jousting of the parties usually provides enough insight to help push the parties to agreement or, at least, to suggest disposition of the demand for arbitration or disposition of the grievance. The arbitrators fail-safe, and one the parties are likely to join, is the proposal that the arbitrator frame the issue based upon the input and alternatives proposed by the parties. The arbitrator may wait until well into, or even through, the hearing to formulate the issue, or may announce the issue as soon as given authority to frame it. Whichever course is taken, empowering the arbitrator to frame the issue ensures finality on an issue and gives the arbitrator jurisdiction to proceed with the case. In some cases, the arbitrator may refrain from articulating a framing of the issue until it appears in the written opinion. Such delayed revelation deprives the parties of the opportunity to assess, and perhaps protest, the fairness of the arbitrator's distillation of the issue. The arbitrator, as well, should be careful to ensure that the issue focuses on the real dispute between the parties and that they acquiesce to the arbitrator's wording.

Framing a Remedy Issue

Regardless of how agreement is reached on the issue, it is important to make sure that appended to it is the question of the remedy to be applied in the event that the grievance is sustained in whole or part. In the absence of agreement on a remedy, the arbitrator may be deprived of any authority to fully compensate the employee for the employers' contractual violation or be unable to provide even a partial remedy, by imposing a lesser penalty on the employee.

In some situations, the parties' agreement prescribes the remedy for a contract violation, so that the arbitrator need not consider the remedy, but most agreements do not. Such contractual remedies may stipulate that, if the arbitrator finds that the imposed discipline was not for just cause, the employee will automatically be reinstated with full back pay.

A similar situation may arise in cases of wild-cat strike actions, in which the arbitrator's authority may be restricted to determining whether or not an employee was engaged in prohibited strike activity. In these instances, a decision on the penalty and any potential remedy is reserved by the employer.

Inclusion of the remedy in the stipulated issue is desirable for both parties. For the union, it ensures that the victorious grievant will be placed in the situation that the employee would have occupied but for the employer's action, and combines the two questions of whether the employer acted wrongly and, if so, how to make up for it. For the employer, its inclusion is vital to bring finality to the dispute. To hold that the employee won the case without providing a remedy to rectify the employer's wrongdoing leaves a frustrated employee and workforce and a festering dispute that the arbitrator was not empowered to bring to its anticipated finality.

Thus, it is critical that the union propose a remedy as part of the issue and that the employer propose it if the union fails to do so. Usually, the arbitrator will raise the issue of a remedy, even if the parties do not, if only to ensure that the parties both agree on whether the remedy issue is to be before the arbitrator.

Arbitrability Challenges as Part of the Issue

The fact that the union exercises its contractual right to appeal a case to the arbitration forum does not mean that the case is arbitrable on its merits. For any number of reasons, the employer may argue that the case is not arbitrable—for example, that the contract bars the arbitrator from deciding the case on the merits because it is not a grievable or arbitrable matter or because procedures were violated while processing the case.

If the employer refuses to agree to the phrasing of the issue because of its conviction that the case is not arbitrable, that arbitrability issue must first be resolved. If it is an issue of substantive arbitrability, then it may even be necessary to secure a court determination of the arbitrator's jurisdiction over the dispute before proceeding with the arbitration.

A much more common procedure is to submit the issue of arbitrability, substantive or procedural, to the arbitrator as a preliminary question. If the arbitrator rules that the case is not arbitrable, there is no need to resolve the substantive issue. If the arbitrator, on the other hand, finds the case to be arbitrable, it is not until that ruling is made that there is authority to proceed to decide the case on its merits. Sometimes the arbitrability issue is raised as a ploy to delay the process. That goal may be the intent of the party that insists on a separate hearing and decision on arbitrability. Although arbitrability challenges are perfectly proper and within the rights of the parties, there is no reason that they should obstruct the smooth flow of the process. The preferable course would be to raise and articulate the arbitrability issue while at the same time proceeding to hear the case on the merits, thus enhancing the cathartic value of the process and leaving the arbitrator to deal with the arbitrability issue and, if arbitrable, the merits issue in the same final opinion.

The framing of the issue in such cases either should proceed with an initial question—"Is the following grievance arbitrable?"—before setting forth the substantive issue, or it should proceed by agreeing on the language of the substantive issue, with the notation that, "The employer (or union) challenges the arbitrability of the foregoing issue."

But whichever approach is taken, the question of arbitrability must be resolved by the arbitrator as the threshold issue prior to resolving the issue on the merits, regardless of the arbitrator's preference to resolve the disputes on the merits.

Once the issue has been formulated, the arbitrator has some sense of the nature of the dispute between the parties. Indeed, among experienced arbitrators, the discussion over the issue may well trigger a sense of déjà vu or, as Yogi Berra is reputed to have said, "Déjà vu all over again."

Is the arbitrator obligated to disclose to the parties at this point, or indeed at any point during the proceedings, that he or she decided a similar or identical case at an earlier time? That issue was raised before the NAA's then Committee on Ethics in 1955 (Opinion 2). An arbitrator had heard an identical case involving the same company but a different union and had issued an unpublished award. Did this previous ruling raise doubts as to the arbitrator's impartiality?

The committee said the past arbitration did not affect the new case because "it is virtually impossible for the arbitrator to know, prior to the actual submission of a case, whether it is, in fact, identical with one he has previously decided . . . each case has some unique, distinguishing feature that requires special consideration." The committee found that the decisive ethical question was not that the issue was similar, but whether the arbitrator "is still open to persuasion either way." It added that if, however, the arbitrator felt bound by a prior decision, that fact should be disclosed.[9]

Transcript

Will There Be a Transcript?

In the early days of arbitration as an internal dispute resolution system, when it was handled by in-house management and union advocates, there was little concern for a word-by-word record of what transpired in the hearing. But the intervening forty years have seen an increasing reliance upon transcripts, so that now there are often disputes at the hearing over the taking of a transcript and the use to which it will be put and/or the access of the participants of the proceeding to that transcript.

The traditional standard that the process belongs to the parties also controls the issue of whether a transcript is to be taken of an arbitration hearing. In most relationships, that issue is resolved long before the initiation of the case. If the parties have had prior experience of arbitrating, it is likely that the issue has arisen before and that parties have resolved it as a matter of practice for future arbitrations.

In other cases, the parties may have agreed upon the issue of having a transcript before the commencement of the present arbitration case. The question of whether or not there will be a transcript in a particular case is sometimes raised at the outset of the arbitration hearing. The employer and the union advocates may have different positions as to whether a transcript should be taken of the proceedings. If the parties have such a conflict, it may become incumbent on the arbitrator to determine whether a transcript should be taken of the proceedings.

The first question to be considered is the right of either party to take a transcript for its own use. Most arbitrators take the view that either party is entitled to take whatever notes of the proceedings it deems desirable for the presentation of the case and, if need be, for its preparation and presentation of a post-hearing brief. Thus, an arbitrator would not interfere with either party taking its own handwritten notes or having a secretary present to take shorthand notes, there should be no objection to either party having a court reporter taking the proceeding down in stenotype or by use of a voice mask.

It should follow that there would be no objection to either spokesperson taking a tape recording of the proceeding for the same use. The reliance on a tape recording, even though allegedly for the client's own use in preparing for a post-hearing brief, may be challenged by the other side and perhaps by the arbitrator as well. The potential problems might be even more glaring if the proceedings were taped by the grievant, a witness, or some interested observer. During the post-Watergate era, the recollection of the eighteen-minute gap in a tape of one of Nixon's conversations raised a number of questions over whether tapes could be doctored. But if the tape is to be kept just for one party's personal use, that issue is not likely to arise. The more difficult question arises if there is a court litigation or administrative appeal—or indeed, a court appeal—pending the outcome of the arbitration case or where the tape might be used to overturn the arbitration award for inaccurate recitation of fact or where statements by witnesses on tape might be produced in the subsequent proceedings.

Some arbitrators have sought to resolve conflicts over the subsequent use of tapes by maintaining personal control over access to the tapes. They limit access to the tapes for the parties on either side to the actual preparation of the parties' brief.

A second question concerning transcripts involves the right of the party that has arranged for the transcript to provide a copy to the arbitrator when the other party objects.

There would be no problem if the party objecting to providing a copy of the transcript to the arbitrator withdrew that objection or if it agreed to pay its share of the cost of the transcripts provided to the arbitrator. With the increasing cost of such transcripts, many parties have tried to save money by providing photocopies to the other side at a much lower cost than if an extra copy is provided by the court stenographer. Transcripts for a one-day hearing can amount to hundreds of dollars.

The greatest problem in this area arises when one party objects to the other side giving a copy of the transcript to the arbitrator or having to bear any joint cost of providing it to the arbitrator. The outcome of that conflict depends, in large measure, upon the attitude of the arbitrator toward having a transcript.

The Arbitrator's Access to a Transcript

Arbitrators have differing needs for transcripts. Many arbitrators are detailed note-takers and have little or no need of transcripts to write their opinions. Some arbitrators are note-takers out of habit, others have developed the practice because of occasional bad experiences with incompetent transcripts. More common may be the arbitrators who take less-detailed notes when transcripts are taken; finally, there are arbitrators who require the transcripts as a condition of proceeding with the case and who utilize excerpts of such transcripts as an integral part of their opinion writing process. Certainly, when an arbitrator requests a transcript for personal use neither party is likely to object and the cost distribution between the parties does not become an issue.

But what should an arbitrator do when one party wishes to provide him or her with the transcript and the other party objects and is unwilling to share any of the costs? Most arbitrators take the position that each party has the right to have a transcript, that the party with the transcript has the right to provide the arbitrator with a copy, and that, just as the other party would have a right to examine any exhibit that was submitted to the arbitrator, the recalcitrant party in the case of the transcript would also have a right to examine the transcript to ascertain whether it is an accurate recitation of the arbitration hearing.

Although the recalcitrant party, usually the union, may be unwilling or unable to bear the cost of a copy of the transcript, it should have the right to examine the transcript provided to the arbitrator to ascertain its accuracy. If the recalcitrant party wished to utilize the transcript for writing its own post-hearing brief, then most arbitrators would take the position that any use of the transcript for that purpose would require purchasing a copy of the transcript because it would be for the party's own use. The argument for that position is that, while either party is expected to bear its own costs in an arbitration proceeding and to share costs of the arbitrator, one side should not have to bear the cost for a benefit accrued to the other side merely because the latter is unwilling to bear its share of the costs for a transcript that it would use equally for development of a post-hearing brief.

Access to the Arbitrator's Copy of the Transcript

When the arbitrator has indicated willingness to receive a copy of the transcript and seeks to provide the other side with an opportunity to review the accuracy of that transcript, how should that access occur? If the case is administered through the American Arbitration Association, then the tribunal administrator handling the case may make the transcript available at the AAA offices so that the other party can verify its accuracy. In the absence of an AAA administration, the arbitrator may permit the examining party to examine the transcript at the arbitrator's office for the same purpose. The question of whether or not the examining party would be able to take the transcript and photocopy it or retain it long enough to develop its own post-hearing brief depends upon the attitude of the party providing the transcript to the arbitrator. If the relationship is antagonistic, the arbitrator would probably strictly administer the examining parties' access to the transcript. If the relationship were more harmonious, then the providing party might even be willing to allow its adversary to utilize the transcript, even for the preparation of its post-hearing brief.

The Cost of the Transcript

It should be obvious that the main issue over access to the transcript is one of cost. Section 21 of *The Voluntary Arbitration Rules of the American Arbitration Association* on the issue of stenographic record provides that:

> Any party wishing a stenographic record shall make arrangements directly with the stenographer and shall notify the other party of such arrangements in advance of the hearing. The requesting party or parties shall pay the cost of the such record. If such transcript is agreed by the parties to be, or in appropriate cases, determined by the arbitrator to be the official records of the proceedings, it must be made available to the arbitrator and the other party for inspection, at a time and place determined by the arbitrator.[10]

Official Record?

As indicated by the foregoing excerpt from the American Arbitration Association Rules, the determination of what is the official record of the proceeding is left to the discretion of the parties. If the parties agree that it is the transcript, the arbitrator, as a creation of the parties' procedure, would be bound by that determination. If the parties dispute whether to take the transcript or the arbitrator's notes as the official transcript, then the arbitrator may have discretion in determining whether personal notes or the transcript will comprise the official record.

The practicality of such determination would, of course, only be tested if there were to be an appellate review of the arbitration proceeding or the arbitrator's award. If a court undertook such a review of the content of the hearing, it might opt to abide by the arbitrator's decision to hold the notes taken by the arbitrator at the hearing as the official record. But the court might opt, instead, to rely upon the ideally accurate transcript as the document governing what was said by anyone at the hearing and then to determine whether the arbitrator's decision was consistent with the evidence presented at the hearing—including whether it drew its essence from the transcript as indication of the four corners of the parties' agreement.

Postponement

The processing of grievances to arbitration is usually quite time-consuming. From the time a grievance is filed until the arbitration hearing may take six months or more, but the processing through the parties' internal grievance procedure takes but a small portion of that time. The greater delay comes from arranging a hearing schedule that is agreeable to the parties, their advocates and attorneys, if they have them, and the arbitrator of their mutual choice. Even when that scheduling is completed and the date is set for the arbitration, there may be additional delays of several weeks or months. Assuming that the parties, their advocates, and the arbitrators act in good faith when they agree upon an arbitration date, there is always the possibility of an unanticipated intervening event, such as an accident to a crucial witness or a suddenly required court appearance by counsel, that may lead to either party requesting a postponement of the scheduled arbitration date. Usually the parties agree to such postponements when the advocates or important witnesses including the grievant, are precluded from attending the hearing. Arbitrators' practice of charging for cancellation fees within certain specified times protects arbitrators against the loss of income from a postponed hearing date, and if the parties agree to the postponement, the arbitrator has no more cause for challenging the parties' mutual postponement than for challenging the parties' agreement to settle the dispute.

A more troublesome problem occurs with a requested postponement by one party close to, or at the commencement of, the arbitration hearing. The other party, which has contacted its witnesses, prepared its evidence, and presented itself at the hearing with the expectation of proceeding with the case, may object to the postponement. Such postponement, if granted, would extend the already elongated period consumed by the processing of the case and would, in addition, require a further day of hearing weeks or months later, with all of the entailed costs.

When there is an objection to the postponement, the arbitrator may be in the position of trying to resolve the issue in a mutually satisfactory manner to avoid the more troublesome decision of whether to grant a request to proceed ex parte by the party present. Some parties arrange to have the postponing party pick up the cost of the arbitrator's fee for the initial hearing day. This agreement would help persuade the other party to agree to the postponement by relieving it of its share of the arbitrator's fee. The second approach might be to determine if the information to be testified to by the missing witness would be agreed to by the other party, thereby obviating the need to reschedule the hearing for the missing witness. If stipulating facts that the missing witness would testify to is not acceptable, the third alternative would be agreement by the parties of an "offer of proof." Under such an arrangement, the parties would agree on what the missing witness would have testified, without agreeing on the accuracy or truth of such testimony. In some cases, this testimony would be rebutted by other witnesses or supported by other witnesses. But when a missing witness's testimony would be crucial, an offer of proof would not resolve the issue of what that witness would have testified. The fourth alternative might be to ask if a substitute witness could be provided who was as aware of the incident as the missing witness and who could testify as credibly in that witness's absence.

If the parties approach the issue of the missing witness in a good faith effort to provide an acceptable substitute for the testimony for the missing witness, then it should be possible to forego postponement and to conclude the full hearing on the day on which it was originally scheduled. There are situations in which a crucial missing witness, for legitimate purposes, may not be able to be present and the parties usually are willing to accommodate those exigencies. In the event of conflict, it is up to the arbitrator to determine whether the testimony or cross-examination of that witness would be so crucial as to justify a continuance until another date.

If such postponement is agreed upon, there remains the question of determining the cost of the initial hearing. Arbitrators, unless given the authority by the parties, have no authority to apportion costs. And most collective bargaining agreements provide for the cost of the arbitration proceedings to be shared equally by the parties, with each party bearing its own cost of counsel. The arbitrator, therefore, would have no authority to impose a full charge on the party requesting the postponement.

In a few situations, a request for postponement is made deliberately to inconvenience the other side, to force an extra day of hearing that might otherwise have been avoided, or to demonstrate disrespect for the goals of the process. In such cases, the arbitrator may determine that a postponement is unwarranted and threaten to proceed ex parte, thereby shifting the burden to the party requesting the postponement to determine whether or not it wishes to proceed with the process or risk having an adverse decision granted against it in its absence.

Third-Party Participation

The conventional expectation, based on the traditions of labor–management arbitration, is that both parties will designate their spokespersons from within their own ranks or that they will hire outside counsel to act on their behalf. That tradition, in the last few years, has given way to increasing reliance by the grievant on outside independent counsel. In some cases, the union is alerted to this preference prior to the hearing and may authorize the outside counsel as its spokesperson at the arbitration hearing. In other cases, the union objects to surrendering its authority over its case to outside counsel, but may be willing to have outside counsel serve as support and as part of the union's team during the arbitration hearing. A more troublesome problem arises when, unannounced, the grievant arrives at the hearing with an independent counsel.

This situation places the union in the awkward position of attempting to exclude the grievant's representative and thus risking a law suit based upon failure to comply with the Duty of Fair Representation. The employer might also be subject to the Duty of Fair Representation suit if the outside attorney is able to convince a court that the company and the union colluded in their proceeding before their chosen arbitrator. Such a claim might be based on the theory that the union and the employer are in collusion with the arbitrator, who is contracted to decide all disputes between them. Under that argument, the arbitrator would have a proclivity to decide for the company or the union without fully appreciating the rights of the individual grievant.

The arrival of outside counsel may reflect a number of factors. First, it may be that the grievant has had a long relationship with the outside counsel as friend or personal attorney and feels more comfortable with such representation than with representation by the union. Second, the outside counsel may arrive on the scene as the grievant's counsel from another, perhaps related, proceeding. Thus it would not be unusual for a grievant who is pursuing an NLRB action or an OSHA action or a workers compensation action to want that same counsel to represent him or her in the contractual spinoff of the external law suit. Third, the outside counsel may be called upon as counsel because of the grievant's fear of unfair treatment by the union or the employer—let alone the arbitrator— in the processing of the case. In such situations, in which there is a potential for a Duty of Fair Representation law suit, the union may take the grievant's counsel as its spokesperson in the processing of the arbitration case.

Fourth, and perhaps most troubling, is the situation in which the grievant has come under the sway of an outside attorney who is not experienced in labor–management relations and who has held out the prospect of a lucrative award to the grievant if given the opportunity to represent him or her in a dispute arising from a grievance. In such situation, all parties are placed at a handicap. The outside counsel, if considering whether to bring an action on the breach of Duty of Fair Representation, may opt not to participate in the case but to sit in as an observer in the proceedings. In such circumstances it is up to the parties—and, if they dispute the matter, up to the arbitrator—to determine what roles such outside observer may take. Clearly, if the parties ask the outside observer to depart, the arbitrator would enforce that agreement and decline to proceed with the outside observer in attendance. The more prudent procedure would be to have the outside counsel serve as a member of the union's team, subject to any negotiated restrictions that the parties may be willing to impose upon that individual and that he or she is willing to subscribe to. One could argue that, as a member of the union team, the advocate could take notes like any other union team participant. If, however, the outsider seeks to have a tape recording or transcript made of the proceeding, then the arbitrator would entertain an objection from either or both parties to preclude such record-keeping as not being consistent with the parties' practice in presenting arbitration hearings. Also, if the outside counsel is to become a member of the union team, arrangements should be made about who examines or cross-examines witnesses to be sure that there is only one questioner from each side for each witness.

In some cases, the grievant's counsel and the union representative might alternate in the questioning of witnesses or one may do the direct questioning, while the other asks all the questions on cross-examination. Still another division would be for the grievant's personal counsel to question and cross-examine on the facts of the case, while the union representative handles questions that relate to the role and responsibility of the union.

Although the division of responsibility may be within the authority of the arbitrator, the usual approach is to secure the employer's acquiescence to any bifurcation of roles. The approval is usually forthcoming as long as there is clearly no doubling up of questioners that would give the union any right to double questioning compared to the employer's questioner.

A related problem may occur in a jurisdictional dispute between unions when a representative of union B seeks to intervene in or observe a case between union A and the employer. The easiest solution, of course, would be to invite both unions to join the process, with full rights to present, examine, and cross-examine witnesses.

Although union A and the employer may have a collective bargaining agreement with an arbitration clause that binds both, and although the arbitrator may properly decide the dispute between union A and the employer, several problems may arise. Union B may seek to testify, or may seek to become an active participant, with rights to present evidence, to call witnesses, and to cross-examine witnesses. The arbitrator, as the creation of union A and the employer, has no authority to expand the proceedings to include union B. Even if excluding union B from participation and even from testifying or observing might lead to greater problems and perhaps even to a lawsuit, the arbitrator is bound to do what union A and the employer determine. Suggestions might be made about the prudence of allowing even limited participation by union B, but the arbitrator is bound by the determinations of union A and the employer.

Sequestration

The increasing resort to legalisms in the field of arbitration and, perhaps, the increasing resort to the use of outside attorneys have brought a growing tendency to follow the radio and television models of courtroom procedure. That trend is most evident in the number of requests for sequestration of witnesses.

While the testimony of one witness certainly may be influenced by hearing the testimony of other witnesses on the same matter, the practice of excluding a witness from the hearing during such testimony has rather limited usefulness. There is little, if any, need to sequester witnesses who are to testify on undisputed matters. Witnesses who are called upon to testify to their understanding of the contract language of their understanding of contract practice wouldn't be sequestered. The only times when sequestration serves a useful role is when two or more witnesses are to testify about the same disputed event and credibility is in issue or when the testimony of prospective witnesses might be affected by overhearing the testimony of the other witnesses. According to the textbook, sequestration should serve these two purposes. Sequestration's role in grievance arbitration should be minimized by the fact that the parties presumably have fully explored the facts during the grievance procedure and have knowledge of what each of the witnesses will testify at an arbitration hearing about any particular disputed event. The need for sequestration is further eroded by the fact that witnesses are likely to have been apprised of the potential conflict of testimony from other witnesses and by the recognition that it doesn't separate witnesses who are excluded from the hearing. Thus, sequestered witnesses are likely to talk about their testimony or the questions that have been asked of them. If asked to stay in the hearing room, their ability to be recalled as rebuttal witnesses may be impeded.

The problem of sequestration is complicated by the right of either party to have an expert advisor present during the proceeding. The expert advisor may be one of the witnesses to testify on the issue of credibility—a witness who would otherwise, but for expert advisor status, be subject to sequestration. The right of union or management to have an expert witness overrides the other side's right to sequester witnesses. The arbitrator may be asked to weigh the expert's testimony in light of the fact that the expert has not been sequestered. The arbitrator then has to weigh that witness's testimony with the knowledge that the expert was the only one in a position to benefit from having heard the testimony of others. The arbitrator will have to determine whether the testimony of that expert witness was fouled by having heard the testimony of the other sequestered witnesses. In such situations, the arbitrator's preference for sticking to the facts of the case rather than getting bogged down by legalistic proprieties may vitiate any benefit sought by the party that originally proposed the sequestration.

Oath

Arbitrators tend to be divided on the issue of whether or not to administer the oath to witnesses at an arbitration hearing. If the parties agree to have an oath, the arbitrator certainly will comply. Likewise, if the parties agree to waive the oath, the arbitrator will comply. The same applies if one of the witnesses opts to affirm for religious reasons rather than "swearing." Dispute arises when one party wishes the oath and the other does not. In those cases, the arbitrator will presumably decide to have witnesses testify under oath. Other arbitrators, of their own volition, request the witnesses to testify under oath without asking the parties' wishes on the issue. When a witness is unwilling to invoke the deity, the arbitrator may ask the witness to affirm rather than swear to tell the truth.

The parties should alert their witnesses to the fact that they may be required to testify under oath. In a surprising number of situations a witness testifying under oath will provide testimony that is contrary to the testimony that the witness had previously promised to give. Thus, when interviewing its witnesses, a party should remind the witnesses that they may be asked to testify under oath and ask them if their answers in that circumstance would be from what they have said in preparation for the hearing. Sometimes, the arbitrator swears in all the witnesses at once. Other arbitrators, who believe the oath or affirmation has an impact on witnesses, asks each witness to take the oath or affirm at the start of his or her testimony.

Partisans on Tripartite Boards

In a situation involving a single arbitrator, there is a procedural decision-making focus. The parties must rely on the neutral's undiluted judgment in making rulings on motions and objections, in allowing or excluding evidence, and in guiding the hearing in the manner best suited to the arbitrator's needs in developing the record for the ultimate decision.

But in the tripartite situation, where each side designates a board member, the neutral arbitrator must expand the foregoing responsibility by becoming a referee for disputes between the partisan members of the tripartite panel.

The tripartite structure creates no problem if the parties don't exploit it. In some relationships, the parties may waive the use of their contractually mandated tripartite panel or may relegate that tripartite panel to a merely signatory role, with the function of voicing either concurrence or dissent after the arbitrator has written the award. In such relationships, the party designees on the tripartite panel may not sit with the arbitrator during the hearing or ask questions of witnesses. In other cases, the parties may ask the arbitrator to proceed with the award and reserve the right to call for a tripartite executive session to discuss the arbitrator's draft opinion. Another format is for the parties on the panel to hold an executive session following the conclusion of the hearing and then, in addition, reserve the right to review the arbitrator's proposed award. None of the foregoing alternatives infringes substantially on the neutral's authority or mandates any different hearing procedure, nor would they have much impact on the arbitrator's role in conducting the hearing. No one would challenge the right of the partisan member to ask questions of the witnesses, as would a neutral arbitrator.

Greater problems arise when the parties have conflicting views over the role of the partisan board members. But the partisan members may go beyond the questioner's role generally ascribed to the neutral arbitrator. They may use their position as arbitrator to serve as adversary. When they assert such dual roles, they disrupt the traditional adjudicatory structure.

The practice may be limited to calling a recess to discuss strategy and questioning with that side's spokesperson or to hand notes to the spokesperson to guide the questioning. It may escalate to partisan questioning of a witness that in effect allows two questioners to that side for examination or cross-examination. That problem is exacerbated when a partisan arbitrator asks leading questions of his or her own side's witness during direct examination. Converting the adjudicatory format to the inquisitorial format, may be a deprivation of due process, unless the neutral chair intervenes to restrict such intimidation.

Even more troublesome is the partisan member who steps down from the board to serve as witness and then returns to the board during the executive session of the board, at which one of the issues may become assessing the credibility of that same person's testimony. If both parties have a tradition of and are comfortable with partisan arbitrators serving as both advocate and witness, the arbitrator usually has little difficulty coping with the bifurcated responsibility. The greater problem arises when one party objects to the other side's partisan asking questions, serving as advocate, or serving as witness. The objecting party may request the neutral to stop the partisan from asking questions or from changing roles, but most arbitrators would take the position that the tripartite structure is the party's own creation.

There should be no illusion that the partisans are neutrals when the tripartite structure places them at the head of the table as representatives for their respective organizations. Some may be more adversarial than others, but the parties' negotiated tripartite structure permits that. The neutral can distinguish and cope with the varying partisan roles while retaining ultimate authority to render the decision as chair of the panel.

Problems created by these conflicting roles of partisans serving as arbitration board members can be readily obviated if the parties agree to restrict their role to a post-hearing meeting at which they get the anticipated "second bite at the apple" through arguments presented there. The neutral is, after all, the primary focus of the facts and arguments presented at the hearing and should be undeterred by partisan activities of the other panel members at the hearing. The responsibility of the neutral to provide a full and fair hearing may lead the neutral to restrict the partisans' questioning if it exceeds the accepted standards for anticipated questioning in direct or cross-examination. It may also require the partisan to take the witness stand when seeking to introduce new evidence for cross-examination by the other side. In addition, the responsibility of the arbitrator would, of course, include controlling the role of the partisans in any executive sessions.

The neutral arbitrator has to protect against such efforts at undermining the decision-making process. It is the parties' machinery and they should be free to utilize it to their respective benefits.

If one believes that arbitration is merely the last step of a grievance procedure in which the parties are duty bound to resolve their grievances, then the tripartite board provides the ultimate forum for the parties themselves to reach agreement. Indeed, it is the format the parties negotiated as their last step in the grievance procedure. They did, after all, decline to follow the general trend of selecting a single arbitrator. Rather, they negotiated a format in which partisans of both parties would have yet another meeting on the grievance. In choosing that tripartite format, the parties could hardly have expected the arbitrator to ignore totally the views of the partisans. On the contrary, the fact that the parties chose to continue the involvement of the partisans almost mandates this neutral entrant into their procedure to facilitate the parties' previously unsuccessful efforts to settle the dispute themselves. The neutral must function as a mediator, helping the parties agree on the issue either in the form of a settlement or by working out agreement on a unanimous award.

Unanimity of award is an obvious goal of the parties because it demonstrates that the parties were, after all, able to resolve their conflict voluntarily, through the assistance of the arbitrator, rather than ceding their rights to an outside third party.

But at the same time, the arbitrator, even as chair of a tripartite board, has the responsibility to issue an opinion and award that are based upon evidence and testimony adduced at a hearing governed by the precepts of due process. That responsibility may be impeded if the partisans go beyond their rightful role as advocates for evidence and positions that were presented at the open hearing.

It is not unusual for a partisan member to offer the "inside story" by presenting evidence that was not produced at the hearing or subject to cross-examination. Nor is it rare for the partisan to take a break from the executive session to report its internal discussions to one or both of the team spokespersons—or to solicit the spokesperson's view of a proposed draft award.

When the contract provides for a majority opinion and award, rather than that of the sole arbitrator, reaching that majority may require the arbitrator to compromise what might be neutral's position in a single arbitrator format in order to secure the necessary majority vote.

Yet that role, too, is considered part of the arbitrator's responsibility for implementing what would be consistent with the parties' intent in opting for the tripartite format.

Exhibits

The presentation of evidence involves not only testimony but documentation or other exhibits to support each side's argument. Sometimes the exhibits are admitted without objection. But at other times there may be varying degrees of opposition to the introduction of exhibits—even to the point of their exclusion. Indeed, some cases may rest on the documentation alone, without the need to question witnesses. In such situations, the parties might forego a formal hearing and instead send the documents and briefs containing their argument to the arbitrator for a more rapid opinion and decision.

Joint Exhibits

If one embraces the view that there should be full disclosure of all evidence at the earliest steps of the grievance procedure to encourage prompt resolution of grievances, then there should be no surprise exhibits introduced at the hearing. Considerable time and, consequently, money can be saved as well if the spokespersons agree in advance on the admission of exhibits. Such agreement should include exhibits that both parties will rely upon in presenting their cases. These joint exhibits usually include, of course, the collective bargaining agreement, universally identified as Joint Exhibit 1, followed by the documents setting forth the trail of the grievance to the arbitration through the several appeal steps of the grievance procedure. The spokespersons might even agree to introduce as joint exhibits any correspondence, photographs, drawings, and so on that they mutually acknowledge to the authoritative and relevant to their respective presentations of the case.

Partisan Exhibits

At times, the spokespersons will agree for convenience to have all exhibits numbered as joint exhibits, even those that one side might view as inimical to its own view of the dispute. But the usual procedure is to have three lists of exhibits: Joint exhibits agreed to as relevant by both parties, and separate sets of employer and union exhibits for items introduced by each team for its own benefit. In most cases, there will be little dispute over the admission of such exhibits if they have been disclosed at the earlier steps of the grievance procedure and have been verified as to authenticity and relevance.

Agreement by one side to the admission of exhibits by the other doesn't acknowledge that these exhibits are controlling, only that they are properly before the arbitrator for assessment of the probative weight to which they are entitled.

As in the case of the joint exhibits, those to be presented by each side should be discussed prior to the hearing, even if over the telephone, to minimize disputes over their admissibility. The exhibits of one side should then be provided at the hearing with sufficient copies for the other side, the arbitrator, the witness being questioned about the exhibit, and the court reporter, if one is at the hearing. If one of the parties objects to the introduction of such documents as immaterial or irrelevant, it is then up to the arbitrator to rule on whether to receive the documents. If the challenge is to relevance, the arbitrator may ask the proferring party how the document is related to the case it is attempting to prove or defend. If the challenge is to materiality, the arbitrator may ask how the document, if admitted, would be of sufficient weight to alter the case.

Once the explanations are given, the arbitrator will rule on whether or not to receive the exhibits. Unfortunately, such exchanges usually occur early in the proceedings, before the arbitrator has fully comprehended the issue being arbitrated and before he or she is able to assess the document's potential impact. Arbitrators generally accept such documents on the assurance that their relevance or materiality will be established later. The final weight, if any, given to the disputed rule or policy is likely to depend on the whole presentation of both parties, but may not be known to the advocates until they read the arbitrator's decision. Arbitrators are reputed to accept documents of uncertain relevance or weight with the rubric: "For what it may be worth." The term may also mask the arbitrator's uncertainty on how to rule on the issue of admissibility. The parties, too, are left in the dark as to what weight, if any, the arbitrator ascribes to the exhibit. It is totally appropriate for a spokesperson to ask the arbitrator to clarify the ruling—at least to the extent of revealing whether some credence is attached to the exhibit—and to ensure that it is not being accepted merely to molify the offering party, particularly if the arbitrator's acceptance of the document shifts the burden of proof.

Voire Dire

Although the exhibits introduced in arbitration are usually known to the parties from their consideration at the earlier steps in the grievance procedure, at times an offered exhibit will be new to the other side. Such a situation may raise questions as to the origins of the exhibit or its authenticity. After the exhibit for identification has been proffered, the other party is entitled to ask questions about the document before agreeing to or objecting to its admission. Such questions are to satisfy the challenging party and the arbitrator that the document or offered exhibit is authentic, that it was properly signed, that it was properly obtained, that it is in the best available form, that it was under proper custody and chain of possession prior to the hearing, or that it can meet any other challenges that might be raised.

The identification and authentification can be achieved by the testimony of the person who prepared the writing, or by identification of the handwriting by one familiar with it, or by comparison to other writing by a qualified expert. Verification may also be established by reliance on the "reply messaged" doctrine, whereby the contents of a writing establish who prepared it. Other writings can be established as authentic by self-authentication, as in the case of public documents, newspapers, official publications, and so on. Authentication may even extend to oral communication, such as a telephone conversation in which the witness may verify the voice by its self-identification, by familiarity with the speaker, and so on.

Once the proffering party has provided answers to the challenges, the exhibit may be still objected to on the grounds that the alleged authenticity or legitimacy has not been established or on the more traditional grounds of relevance and materiality. At that point, the arbitrator will rule on whether or not the document is to be received into evidence; the next step after marking for identification is to mark the accepted exhibits for admission, with the appropriate union or management exhibit number assigned.

Work Rules and Policies

The collective bargaining agreement may not be the only controlling document in determining the outcome of an arbitration case. In discipline cases, in particular, the employer will be eager to enter into the record its disciplinary rules, attendance policy, or other evidence of the work performance standards it has relied on to support the action being grieved.

Even though the work rules or policies may be unilaterally created by the employer, and thus not part of the parties' collective bargaining agreement, their alleged violation might still constitute the basis of the employer's action.

The union's objection that these policies were unilaterally developed by the employer would not bar their introduction. If they were offered by the employer as its rules for governing standards of conduct for employees and for disciplining violations, they would be admissible provided the grievant knew or should have known of their existence.

Thus, if a union objected to the employer's attempt to enter the rules as an exhibit on the grounds that the grievant was unaware of them, the employer's spokesperson might elicit testimony that they were posted, were read to employees, or were sent to employees. Then the union could question the grievant about why he or she had not seen them.

Unless the arbitrator is persuaded that the grievant didn't know or couldn't have known about the rules (that is, if the employer had never posted or sent the rules to the employee, or if it promulgated them after the incident in question), most arbitrators will receive such rules and leave the parties to establish by testimony whether the grievant knew or should have known of them.

In some cases, both parties will want such documents entered into the record so that the arbitrator will have them and so that they may argue from them. In such situations, these policies may be entered and marked as joint exhibits or as exhibits of the party first introducing them.

External Law

The arbitrator's power is drawn from the collective bargaining agreement, and arbitrators are usually asked to interpret and apply that document as the controlling authority on the issue of whether or not an employer or employee's action was justified.

But not everyone in labor–management relations respects the contract as the sole and controlling source for the decision. For many years, there has been debate among arbitrators over whether, on the one hand, the contract should be treated in isolation or, on the other, should be treated as a contract embracing the laws of the jurisdiction in which it was negotiated and signed. This Meltzer-Howlett debate has become more pointed over the years with the expansion of arbitration into the public and federal sectors, in which the governing statutes, municipal bylaws, rules, and regulations so deeply affect the parties' collective bargaining process and the rights of employer and employees to operate as freely as in the private sector, which lacks such legal impediments.[11] The expansion of statutory protection for employees (unionized or not) into Occupational Safety and Health Act (OSHA) and the outlawing of various forms of discrimination have placed even greater pressure on the collective bargaining arena to interpret the contract in the light of the external legal environment.

The problem becomes even more pressing when the parties' agreement refers to such external law in often confusing, and perhaps contradictory, language, such as: "The employer shall not engage in discriminatory conduct which is violative of applicable rulings under federal, state, local and administrative law."

In such situations, arbitrators may be faced with the issue of whether or not to receive in evidence copies of allegedly controlling statues, court decisions, and rulings of administrative agencies that are asserted to be legally dispositive of the issue before the arbitrator. Arbitrators are loathe to exclude such documents, whether or not they are referred to in the parties' agreement, because at the time they are offered into evidence the parties usually have not fully explained the weight to be accorded these external laws—such arguments do not usually come until the parties' closing statements or in post-hearing briefs.

It is incumbent upon the advocates to protect against the arbitrator's being swayed by the other side's exhibits or arguments. Thus, if the document proffered by one side is an old administrative law, ruling, or decision from a court of first impression, the other party should protect itself against a prematurely and unfavorably closed record by seeking an opportunity to examine whether the "law" controls as the other side asserts.

Securing that opportunity may be difficult if the statutes and court decisions have been introduced at earlier steps of the grievance procedure so that the other party has been put on notice that its response should be presented at the hearing. The opportunity to respond may be further clouded by the potential conflicts among federal, state, local, and administrative law. If the evidence is first introduced at the hearing, an opportunity should be provided to test or respond to its validity by calling another hearing to present a response or rebuttal, by reserving the response for submission in a post-hearing brief, or by subsequent exchanges of legal memos. If none of those avenues for response are offered, then the party should urge the arbitrator to ensure personally, by independent legal research, that the "law" matches the claims made about it by the moving party.

Decisions of Ancillary Forums

While arbitrators may feel bound by legislation that confines or usurps the arbitrator's range of discretion, they usually have a different response when presented with the rulings of ancillary forms such as unemployment insurance boards, worker's compensation panels, merit system protection boards, and so on. The rulings of such panels are often introduced to convince the arbitrator to accord full faith and credit to such rulings or, at least, to persuade the arbitrator to rule likewise. Although the issues may appear superficially identical, they arise in a different forum, with different parties and often different standards and burdens of proof. Some arbitrators do accept such rulings "for what they may be worth" and, by so doing, immediately shift the burden to the party found at fault in that ancillary proceeding—making the party which lost in that ancillary proceeding defend or, at least, distinguish the ruling of the outside body with its external standards. The parties are entitled to question the arbitrator about how much weight he or she intends to accord such documents, and when the differences in the forums are explained, most arbitrators are likely to exclude such ancillary decisions.

As noted elsewhere, one of the most common efforts to introduce external legal rulings arises in the case of discipline for actions that may also be subject to criminal charges. Although most arbitrators exclude the findings of unemployment insurance or workers compensation panels as to whether an employee was disciplined or terminated for just cause, they are more troubled by excluding the rulings of full-fledged courts of law. Termination for theft, possession of controlled substances, or driving a company vehicle while under the influence may be routine issues for resolution pursuant to the labor relations' standard of just cause under the parties' agreement. But when the employee has also been the subject of a criminal proceeding, one of the parties is likely to attempt to present the results of that forum to dispose of the issue before the arbitrator or, at the very least, to influence the arbitrator to adopt the same decision on that issue. As in the other ancillary proceedings, the parties, the advocates, and the standards are different, and the arbitrator, recognizing the consequences of the shifting burden, may exclude the findings of the criminal court in such matters.

The exception to that exclusion may be when, in court, the grievant has pled guilty, admitted to the facts, or pled nolo contendere. Such admissions, even though made outside the grievance and arbitration proceeding, and perhaps acknowledging only that the facts are as the prosecutor alleges, are held admissible in arbitration. It doesn't matter what room the employee is in when the guilt or facts are admitted, that admission is properly before the arbitrator. The admission of guilt into evidence still gives the employee the opportunity to explain that admission in an effort to distinguish it for purposes of the just cause issue. Such an explanation may occur, for example, in plea bargaining, where the grievant has pled guilty in the related criminal matter in order to protect against a harsher charge on some other issue unrelated to the disciplinary matter.

Stolen Exhibits

The grievance and arbitration system depends upon good faith between the parties. Unlike some legal court trials, in which the adversaries are strangers except during the case and may never have any further dealings, the collective bargaining relationship is continuing, like a marriage, and can function most effectively for mutual benefit only when there is trust between the parties.

On occasion, however, one of the parties may seek to introduce an exhibit to which the other side objects on grounds that it was stolen or a protected internal work product of its team. This problem may be an outgrowth of more ready access to photocopying facilities and to documents produced in duplicate, which seem to be proliferating in our society. But arbitration is not a court of law. It is a forum in which the relationship between the parties and the party's internal work product must be respected.

Arbitrators are occasionally confronted with requests to accept into evidence internal work products that would be protected and excluded in a court of law or documents that have been stolen. Most arbitrators are reluctant to accept such evidence if they believe the revelation of these documents may have a long-term adverse impact on the relationship, which is, after all, more important than the resolution of any single case. Yet when the document may exculpate the grievant, the urge to protect the parties' relationship may give way to the stronger urge to do justice in the case. It is, in the end, up to the parties to determine whether to introduce such destructive evidence. The same result as admission might be achieved by advising the opposing party of the proposed evidence away from the arbitrator to determine if the objective of its introduction can be achieved by the mere threat of introduction. This tactic could forestall the adverse consequences of following through on that threat. In the long run, the protection of the parties' mutual trust should encourage the parties to work out an alternative to the revelation of stolen documents.

Best Evidence

The prevalence of photographic reproduction facilities may also raise another evidentiary rule in arbitration over what is the "best evidence." The best evidence rule arises from the legal rules of evidence in which it is often crucial to verify whether an offered exhibit is actually the "best evidence" of what occurred. Thus, a photographic reproduction of a signed copy of an agreement is better evidence than a photocopy of an unsigned copy, while the signed original would be the best evidence. An official report of the weather bureau on temperatures or snow fall on the preceding day is better evidence than a newspaper mention of the report, and even better evidence than recitation by a witness of what was read in a newspaper report.

Invocation of the best evidence rule may give the appearance that the challenging party is alert to its legal rules and rights; however, this challenge should not be invoked to impress the arbitrator but to emphasize that a better form of the exhibit would be more accurate and more credible than the form originally proposed.

Withheld Exhibits

Sometimes, evidence that is discovered just prior to the arbitration is properly admitted, after the surprised party is given an opportunity to investigate and respond if it requests to do so. A greater problem arises from exhibits that had been known but not disclosed to the other side prior to the arbitration.

If the parties are to achieve the declared goal of resolving disputes at the lowest steps of the grievance procedure, all the relevant evidence on the dispute should be disclosed to the other side as soon as it is discovered. That standard is frequently codified in the parties' agreement by a prohibition against introducing any new evidence at the arbitration step. Even without such an exclusionary rule, if the frequency and cost of arbitration is to be minimized, it is in the parties' best interest to disclose evidence at the earliest point and to avoid surprises at the arbitration hearing.

Nevertheless, the parties' relationship frequently deteriorates to an adversarial combat in which a "victory" at arbitration become so important that evidence available earlier is garnered and protected to be proclaimed at the hearing to ensnare the other side. While such a tactic may have some limited worth in attempts to impeach a witness, as a general rule it is not to be condoned because it conflicts with the higher purpose of conflict resolution. Once this strategy is employed for victory by one side, it induces comparable behavior by the other side in subsequent appeals and results in abdicating the opportunities to settle earlier and reducing the grievance steps to nothing more than rubber-stamping of the original positions. It also makes increased reliance on the arbitration step inevitable, with its inherent delays, costs, and risks.

When an objection is raised to an effort to introduce "new" evidence at a hearing, the burden is shifted to the arbitrator, who may need the new evidence to reach the proper decision, but who may equally object to failure to produce that evidence at a time when it might have induced settlement. The arbitrator's reluctance to accept such evidence is intensified by the need to provide the surprised party with an opportunity to investigate and respond, which, if requested, may precipitate an additional day of hearing.

Some arbitrators exclude such withheld exhibits on the grounds that if they were known, or could have been known during the earlier steps of the grievance procedure, they should have been introduced in a timely fashion at that point. Such an exclusion would, of course, send a strong message to the parties about their future actions, although it might have a severe impact on the arbitrator's resolution of the pending case.

Most arbitrators, however, would grant priority to rendering a fair decision in the immediate case, accept such evidence, and entertain a request from the other party for an opportunity to rebut the new exhibit—even if this course resulted in an extra day of hearing.

The Grievant's Prior Record

In disciplinary cases, the employer frequently endeavors to introduce the grievant's prior employment record into the evidence, and the union will often object. If the case concerns termination for a "capitol offense"—one for which termination is recognized as justified in first offenses, such as theft or threatening one's foreman—the employee's prior work record would be irrelevant. If, however, progressive discipline would be appropriate for the incident, then the grievant's prior disciplinary record would be relevant. In either case, if the arbitrator imposes a penalty of less than termination, the prior record would be germane to the fashioning of an appropriate remedy in the light of that record. Thus, in most cases of discipline, the employee's prior record is relevant in determining the appropriate penalty if discipline is warranted.

The prior record would *not* be relevant for most arbitrators to prove present wrongdoing by pointing to previous transgressions. Thus, if an employee was caught asleep on the job on three prior occasions, and is accused of it in the present case but denies this wrongdoing, the fact that the grievant was caught asleep previously doesn't prove the employee was sleeping on this occasion. But does a tendency to poor workmanship, as demonstrated by three prior disciplinary penalties, establish a proclivity to poor workmanship in the present case? This record may show a tendency, but such prior infractions do not constitute proof of present poor workmanship. This issue must be proven by the employer irrespective of any similar transgressions in the past.

Testing

One of the parties will occasionally seek to introduce results of a test as proof of whether an employee was under the influence of legal or illegal drugs or whether the employee was telling the truth. If the other party objects to the introduction of the test results, the arbitrator is forced to decide on the admissibility of the exhibit.

The objections may be based on the reliability of the testing, on the chain of custody of the material tested, on the relevance of the test, or on the representations of the test interpreter.

On the issue of reliability of the testing, some tests are objective and clinically conclusive, while others invite more doubt. It is the responsibility of the party offering the exhibit of test results to establish a prima facie case of the accuracy of the results. Thus, the test that measures levels of alcohol in the blood is sufficiently well accepted as proof to overcome any challenge that the test itself is inaccurate. But a test for other drugs may not be so conclusive if the objecting party is able to establish significant challenges to the accuracy of the test results based on its tendency to give false positive and false negative readings.

The uncertainty of such conclusions is nowhere stronger than in the area of polygraph or "lie detector" testing. The test results, which are largely the result of subjective interpretations by readers, are generally held to lack scientific reliability. The 1988 Employee Polygraph Protection Act (PL 100-34) prohibits reliance upon polygraphs for employment purposes except by federal, state, and local governments; it also sanctions use of polygraph testing for employees and consultants to security entities and employees engaged in the manufacture, distribution, and disposal of contraband substances.

Chain of custody issues may also lead an arbitrator to exclude test results, even if the results are scientifically reliable. If the objecting party is able to demonstrate that the urine, blood, or drug sample could have been lost, misplaced, tampered with, or otherwise confused with the sample that was tested, then the exhibit of the test results may be excluded.

The relevance of the test results may also be challenged if they do not constitute proof of wrongdoing—that is, if the sample tested was taken too long before or after the disputed incident, or if the results are otherwise deemed irrelevant to the issue before the arbitrator.

In weighing the admissibility of such an exhibit, an arbitrator looks for the reasonable expectation that the testing was objective and scientific; that the subject matter tested was genuine, without the likelihood of having been tampered with or lost; that the exhibit accurately reflects the test results; and that the arbitrator can weigh the test results themselves rather than a subjective interpretation provided by some outside evaluator.

Medical Certification

Employers have the right to expect employees to attend regularly, but employees also have the right to be absent without penalty at times of legitimate illness or injury. Employees who are rarely absent are seldom challenged to verify the legitimacy of their absences. But in the case of employees who—whether due to poor health or other reasons—tend to be absent with greater frequency or for longer durations, employers frequently require proof of the legitimacy of absences for illness or injury.

That requirement may place a heavy or costly burden on the employee who is asked to provide medical documentation to support the absence, particularly when it is due to the common type of illness for which individuals seldom consult physicians. For employees whose bonafides have been challenged, a requirement to provide certification to avoid discipline mandates visiting a doctor to secure the certification.

Even with the requirement of such documentation, sufficient numbers of falsified, or questionable, certificates have been presented to lead employers to question their veracity occasionally. It is not unknown for individuals to steal pads of medical certification forms. And in the present era of desktop computer printing, individuals have printed such forms so they could write in excuses for their absences.

Employers often counter such frauds by contacting the treating physician or by imposing strict requirements on the content of the certificate. Such requirements for the note might include specifying the dates of absence, a clear statement that the impairment precluded the employee from working on the date or dates in question, and a signature by the physician.

The requirement of such documentation, the empathy of physicians for patients trying to avoid discipline for an absence (even if the patients were not treated for the particular absences), and the pressures of a busy medical practice that leave little time for patients seeking such certificates have occasionally resulted in the issuing of what some call the ten-dollar note, an excuse provided to a loyal patient or for a fee that excuses absences without thorough examination to verify their legitimacy.

Employers may challenge such vague and questionable documents and discipline the employee, thereby setting in motion grievances and appeals to arbitration as to the legitimacy of the doctor's note. If the employer has previously specified the content and form of physicians' notes, the arbitrator will usually expect compliance with that standard. However, the safest way to avoid challenge to the certificate is to ensure that it contains the information that physicians are likely to provide after a legitimate examination of the individual. Those elements are:

1. Diagnosis—a physiological explanation of the ailment. What was wrong with the patient? What organs were affected, and how?
2. How the diagnosis was achieved. Was it through an explanation of the symptoms offered by the patients? Was it through physical examination?
3. Etiology of the condition. What was its cause? Was it an infection?
4. Data, if any, supporting the etiology—that is, probable relevant causes.
5. Impairment rating. Is the employee able to work, or do limited work, and to what extent? Are there restrictions on the employee's walking, lifting, stooping, and so on?
6. Prognosis. What is the patient's prospect for recovery? Is a week's rest needed before returning to full duty? Should the employee remain away from work until another examination or return to work immediately?

Thorough preparation of the requisite documentation can deter cases from coming to the arbitration step.

Conclusion

Ideally, none of the problems discussed in this chapter will arise at the start of the hearing, and the parties will be able to turn directly to presenting the substance of the dispute. But these problems can arise at the start of the hearing and it is wise to be prepared for them, as it is to anticipate and prepare for any challenges to the substantive and procedural arbitrability of the core issue that has finally reached the arbitration forum.

4
Arbitrability

If the parties agree that the issue pursued without resolution up the several steps of the grievance procedure is arbitrable, then the parties should proceed to present the case on that agreed-upon issue. But not all cases have such clear sailing. Frequently, disputes are appended to the processing of the grievance about whether the case should proceed to arbitration and whether the arbitrator has the right to hear and decide it. These are issues of arbitrability.

In some cases, the arbitrability issue is of substance. Did the parties agree that this particular type of issue was to be resolved by arbitration? Is it within the scope of the issues the parties have agreed to resolve by arbitration?

There is also the issue of who is to determine whether or not a dispute is substantively arbitrable. If the parties didn't authorize that type of dispute to be resolved by an arbitrator, should a dispute between the parties over whether an arbitrator has the right to decide the issue be decided by an arbitrator?

Clearly, an arbitrator may decide an issue of substantive arbitrability if the disputants authorize it. But without such agreement, the substantive issue, as well as the arbitrability issue, may be the province of the judiciary for a legal ruling on whether or not arbitration of that issue was comprehended by the parties' collective bargaining agreement. If the parties had not contemplated arbitration of a matter like the one set forth in the grievance, an arbitrator with jurisdiction restricted to the four corners of the agreement would not have authority to decide that issue or even the question of whether he had jurisdiction to decide that issue.

In cases in which there is no question that the substantive issue comes within the four corners of the agreement and is properly subject to arbitration on its merits, there may be procedural challenges to the right of the arbitrator to decide the substantive issue on its merits.

Just as the parties are bound to adhere to the substantive terms of their collective bargaining agreement, they are bound to adhere to the procedural or administrative terms of the contract. Thus, if the contract prescribes certain conditions or requirements for filing or appealing a grievance—such as who should sign the grievance, what it should contain, or the time limits for its initiation or appeal—those requirements are as binding on the parties and the arbitrator as the substantive terms of the agreement. And the party that claims a violation of those procedures or time limits has every right to claim that the other party has infringed any right to have the case resolved

78

on the merits and that the case should not be dealt with on the merits because of that violation.

While arbitrators prefer to have disputes between the parties resolved on their merits, and while they might try to cure procedural defects if feasible, the substantive and procedural challenges to arbitration cannot be ignored or bypassed. Arbitrators may seek to secure voluntary accord on procedural violations to encourage resolution on the merits, but if such efforts are unavailing, they are obligated to interpret all the provisions of the agreement, including those that may preclude their right to decide the case on the merits.

These arbitrability issues are the substance of this chapter.

Substantive Arbitrability

An arbitrator's authority to decide the merits of an issue in dispute presumes that both parties have agreed that the issue is properly before the arbitrator for determination on the merits—whether or not the contract was violated or a disciplinary action was taken for just cause. Sometimes one of the parties objects to the arbitrator deciding the merits issue on the grounds of lack of authority. The objection may be of two types, either substantive or procedural. If a party raises a substantive challenge to the authority of the arbitrator, it challenges the arbitrator's authority to resolve that dispute between the parties by claiming that the parties' contract did not provide for that type of dispute to be submitted to arbitration. Thus, even though the parties may have a collective bargaining agreement containing an arbitration clause, there may still be barriers to taking that case to arbitration.

For example, consider a situation in which a teachers' contract states that "The granting of tenure after three years of teaching is solely within the discretion of the employer pursuant to state law." The union claims that the grievant was automatically granted tenure by the employer's failure to notify him during his third year of teaching that his one-year contract would not be renewed, pursuant to a contract provision that says, "If a teacher is not notified of the nonrenewal of his or her contract by March 15, that person shall continue in the position as teacher." The employer claims that tenure decisions are reserved to management. Whether or not the arbitrator has jurisdiction to hear the issue must be resolved by the arbitrator or a court before the arbitrator can be empowered to rule on whether the grievant is entitled to continue as a teacher with tenure status. If the parties do not agree to have an arbitrator determine the issue of arbitrability, it remains the province of the courts, either through one party moving to compel arbitration or through the other party attempting to enjoin the arbitration proceedings. The *substantive* arbitrability issue is one that the parties may agree to grant to the arbitrator for resolution. If they designate the arbitrator to resolve that substantive issue, they may be deemed to have waived their right to challenge that substantive arbitrability issue later in some other forum. The U.S. Supreme Court in United Steelworkers of America v. American Manufacturing Company (363 US564, 1960) held that the province of the courts is to determine whether a claim is governed by the terms of the parties' agreement, thus the courts would have limited authority to bar arbitration where the parties agreed to submit all questions of contract interpretation to arbitration. Two years later, in Atkinson v. Sinclair Refining Company (370 US238, 1962), the court ruled that issues of substantive arbitrability must be decided by the courts unless the parties' agreement gave the parties' arbitrator that authority.

Substantive challenges to arbitrability may be raised at any time—at the filing of the grievance, during any of the steps of the grievance procedure, at the arbitration hearing, or even after the arbitrator has issued the award. This latitude is based on the theory that because the arbitrator lacked substantive jurisdiction to decide the issue, that decision was null and because the party challenging arbitrability had not agreed in the collective bargaining agreement to the arbitration of that type of dispute, there was no implied waiver by delay in raising such challenge.

Procedural Arbitrability

A different situation pertains in cases of procedural challenges to the arbitrator's authority. While a substantive arbitrability challenge is based upon the absence of any agreement to submit that dispute to an arbitrator, a procedural challenge to arbitrability does not challenge the arbitrability of the substantive dispute. In this case, the parties have agreed that the substantive issue is arbitrable. They have also acknowledged that they are bound by the contract's procedures for bringing that case to arbitration. Challenges to hearing the case on its merits because of alleged violations of the contract's procedural requirements are acknowledged to be properly within the purview of the arbitrator. Thus, because the arbitrator is deemed to have jurisdiction under the collective bargaining agreement to hear the case on its merits, that arbitrator should have the authority to resolve any challenges to his or her right to decide the case on the merits when such challenges arise based on the language of that collective bargaining agreement. According to the U.S. Supreme Court in United Steelworkers of America v. Warrior and Gulf Navigation Company (363 US574, 1960), doubts about arbitrability should be resolved in favor of arbitrability.

When there is a challenge to the procedural arbitrability of a grievance, the parties commonly will list that arbitrability challenge as a part of the issue. Then, while presenting both the arbitrability challenge and the substantive issue at the same hearing, they will give the arbitrator the authority to decide, on the arbitrability issue and then, if the case is found to be arbitrable, on the case on its merits, as well.

Sometimes the parties frame such issues as: "Is the grievance arbitrable? If so, did the company violate the contract when it took the action here in dispute?" An alternative packaging of these issues is to reach agreement on the substantive issue: "Did the company violate the parties agreement as alleged in the grievance?" The statement would then note that the company had challenged the arbitrability of the issue.

In most cases, the facts and timing of the case require a ruling on whether or not earlier conduct was proper or a violation of the procedural requirements of the contract. When the parties are receptive, the arbitrator may seek voluntary rescission of the procedural challenge so that the hearing may proceed on the merits. In other cases in which the procedural defect can be cured without ordering a stay in the proceedings, the arbitrator will undertake to secure the parties' agreement to avoid the extra cost of a stay or the holding of another hearing.

Thus, for instance, if a grievance form on a continuing grievance is unsigned by the grievant, the arbitrator may point out that it is preferable and more economical to permit the signature to be affixed rather than to increase the cost by delaying until there is a signature, a move that would lead to a new demand for arbitration with its additional costs.

Numerous procedural challenges to arbitrability might be raised in processing a grievance and are likely to come before an arbitrator for resolution.

The Probationary Employee

It is generally accepted that the employer has the unilateral right to determine whether or not to retain an employee for permanent employment. Before the employer makes that determination, the probationary employee may be terminated at will. In most collective bargaining agreements, access to contract benefits is triggered by completion of a fixed probationary period from the date of hire. After this period, which may be thirty or sixty days, the employee is granted the protections of seniority and has access to the grievance procedure to guarantee just cause for the imposition of discipline.

Where the collective bargaining agreement has specific language determining the duration of the probationary period, the expectation is that the employer has the right to discipline or discharge a probationary employee and the employee has no right to file a grievance to protest that action. Under these circumstances, questions may arise about the extent to which that probationary clause affects employees who have not completed the specified probationary period.

CASE STUDY: The Case of Underpaid Probationer. Maribeth Haglof was in her third week of employment when she was assigned four hours of overtime. Her paycheck showed that she was paid at straight time for the total hours worked, but was not granted any overtime payment. She filed a grievance. The employer rejected the grievance on the grounds that, as a probationary employee, she was not entitled to file a grievance until she had worked for the company for thirty days. The union objected to the employer's challenge to arbitrability and the case was appealed to arbitration.

The first issue is whether Haglof had the right to file a grievance. At the arbitration hearing, the employer argued that the parties had negotiated a thirty-day probationary period, that employees had no right to file grievances until the expiration of the thirty-day period, and that the employer had the right to terminate an employee at will within that thirty-day period. It asserted that, because the employer had the right to impose discharge without challenge, it should not be penalized for an oversight in payment in this case. The employer concluded that granting permission to grieve would give the employer an incentive to terminate an employee rather than risk having its oversight challenged with a grievance arbitration proceeding.

The union took the position that, although the employer had the right to impose discipline on and discharge probationary employees without union challenge, the grievance in this case did not arise from any disciplinary action. Rather, the union asserted, the matter concerned contract enforcement. The union claimed that it had the right to enforce the contract for the benefit of all employees, probationary or not. By waiving its right to challenge in this case, the union would risk that, in a similar future instance, the employer would claim the union had waived its right to protest the overtime payment issue.

Most arbitrators would take the view that the purpose of a probationary period is to protect the employer's right to terminate an unacceptable employee without going through the grievance and arbitration procedures and without being bound by the standard of just cause. That authority focuses on the right to remove unacceptable probationary employees and should not be used to protect the employer's violation of contract provisions that are applicable to all employees. The union has an obligation to enforce the collective bargaining agreement on behalf of all employees, whether or not they are on probation. The employer has a comparable obligation to conform to the provisions of the collective bargaining in its dealings with all employees, regardless of whether they are probationary. The arbitrator presumably would conclude that the probationary provision did not preclude the grievant's right to protest contract violations that had implications for the entire bargaining unit and would hold the case to be arbitrable.

Discussion Question 1: What would the result have been if the grievance had been filed to protest a five-day suspension imposed upon a probationary employee for insubordination?

In this case, the employer would presumably argue that, because it has the right to terminate a probationary employee without being subject to a grievance by the union, it likewise has the authority to impose a lesser penalty. The company would argue that its effort to impose a corrective discipline on the probationary employee, when it could have terminated the employee without union recourse, demonstrates it willingness to give the employee a second chance to successfully complete the probationary period and should not be subject to challenge by the union.

The union would likely take the position that, although the employer may have the right to terminate a probationary employee without union challenge, when the employer introduces discipline short of discharge, the employee is entitled to protection through a grievance procedure if that discipline is imposed unjustly. The union would argue that failure to file a grievance to challenge that five day suspension would leave it on the employee's record, so that after the completion of the probationary period, any subsequent discipline would be added to the earlier one and could lead to an escalated penalty or perhaps termination for a second offense. In such a situation, the employee and the union would be deprived of any right to protest the earlier penalty on which the termination or heavier penalty would be built.

Most arbitrators would take the position that the grievability of discipline during probation is less clear than a contract enforcement in areas of wages, hours, and working conditions. Indeed, if the employer is willing to refrain from invoking its inherent right to terminate by providing a probationary employee with a lesser disciplinary penalty, the employee would thereby receive a second chance that the employer might not provide if forced to respond to a grievance on discipline involving probationary employees. If the union were permitted to grieve, then in future cases, to avoid such confrontations, the employer could merely terminate probationary employees and deny them the benefit of any progressive discipline.

As to the issue of whether the discipline during the probationary period can be used as a building block toward an escalated penalty after the completion of the probation, most arbitrators would take the position that the probationary period is a distinct time frame during which the employer has unilateral control over the retention or removal of employees. Therefore, by determining that an employee has successfully completed the probationary period, the employer wipes the slate clean of any lesser disciplinary penalties it might have imposed. The union could not have had access to the grievance procedure to challenge any disciplinary penalties during the probationary period and afterward could not reactivate such stale challenges. Nor should an employee who had completed probation be entitled to less corrective discipline because of a minor unchallengeable disciplinary penalty imposed during probation. Once an employee has completed the probationary period, any discipline that might have been imposed will have been wiped off the books, and the employee is viewed as starting with a clear record. Accordingly, the arbitrator in this hypothetical case would presumably deny the union's right to grieve the issue of the five-day suspension during the probationary period.

Discussion Question 2: Would the union have the right to grieve the improper payment even if Haglof, as a probationary employee, could not?

The union clearly has the obligation as well as the right to protect against the violations of the overtime provisions of the parties' agreement by the employer. But the union is bound by the agreement language on probationary periods and union-initiated grievances. Thus, unless the parties' agreement grants the union the right to grieve an alleged overtime violation, or unless it has the right to grieve during an employee's probationary period, its right to enforce the contract in this situation depends upon Haglof's right to grieve. Even if it were held that Haglof had no right to grieve the overtime deprivations, the union's inability to grieve would not necessarily be held against it or constitute an adverse precedent in later cases. The union could simply show that it lacked any standing to grieve the overtime deprivation because that right to grieve did not extend to probationary periods.

Discussion Question 3: What if the case arose in the public sector in which there was no contractual probationary period but there was a three-month civil service probationary period?

If such a case arose over the same issue, proper wage payment, it could be argued that the absence of a probationary provision in the parties' agreement would permit Haglof to file a grievance over the overtime deprivation. The only argument for holding the overtime not arbitrable would be the presence of a contractual probationary period. Without that provision, it would be easier to conclude that Haglof was entitled to grieve the deprivation than in the private sector example.

But if this were a termination case, the absence of a contractual probationary clause would not necessarily grant Haglof the right to arbitrate her removal. The arbitrator might reason that because the contract, rather than the law, controls, the termination case would be arbitrable, thus leaving the employer to go to court to either bar the arbitration or overturn the arbitrator's award.

But the arbitrator might choose to reconcile the statutory probation period with the contractual lack of such a period. That reconciliation could be achieved by reasoning that the civil service probationary period predated the collective bargaining agreement and that the parties negotiated their contact in the context of that statutory three-month probationary period. Because it was so universally accepted that an employer would have the right to terminate without a just cause standard during a probationary period, it should follow that the parties anticipated that the statutory probationary period would control, even without duplicative contract language.

Most arbitrators would probably reason that it would be futile to arbitrate the termination of a three-week employee when the statutory three-month probationary period would prevail.

Although a different decision might result from the absence of a contractual probationary period in the case of wage claim, in the case of termination, the grievance would probably be held to be not arbitrable.

Specificity in the Grievance

When the parties negotiate contract terms, they commit not only to the establishment of substantive terms and conditions of employment but to the procedural language governing the implementation of the agreement in cluding the grievance and appeals provisions. It is assumed that contract language, whether dealing with procedures or dealing with substance, is negotiated with the intent that the parties will comply with it. When the parties negotiate restrictions on the filing or processing of grievances, it is assumed that they intend for both parties to abide by those restrictions and that compliance will be assured by the arbitrator in cases alleging violations of the procedural requirements. Thus, an arbitrable procedural challenge may arise from an alleged failure to abide by any of the negotiated conditions on grievants filing an appeal.

One such requirement that is found in contract definitions of grievances is that the grievance, when filed, should specify the article and section of the contract allegedly being violated by the employer's action.

CASE STUDY: *The Case of the Unspecified Grievance.* Pete Wingate was assigned to work on Veteran's Day, although it should have been his day off. He objected to his foreman when given the assignment, but was told to work the day and then grieve. That is what he did. The grievance said, "The company violated the contract by assigning Wingate to work on Veteran's Day, one of his scheduled days off."

The grievance was then handed in to the foreman who responded, "This grievance is not proper because you failed to specify an article and section of contract, as required by article 3.d of the grievance procedure." Wingate responded, "I think it's specific enough." The case was then appealed to arbitration.

At the arbitration hearing, the employer argued that the contract language specifically required the listing of contract clause and section for any grievance to be appealable and that the grievant should have specified article

5, the provision dealing with compensation, and section 5.c, the provision dealing with holiday work. The employer argued that the language of article 3.d was as specific and as binding on the parties as the substantive language dealing with holiday work and that the arbitrator was bound to enforce the language requiring the grievance's specific contract reference. Under these circumstances, the employer stated, the claim could not be considered on its merits.

The union took the position that the grievance was valid, that the intent of the provision was to provide the employer with clear notice of the facts underlying the grievance, and that the supervisor in this case was aware of the details of Wingate's complaint from the initial discussion held between the grievant and the foreman when the grievance was filed.

The union stressed that the intent of the grievance and arbitration procedure was to resolve cases on their merits and that the employer should not be permitted to benefit from an inartfully worded grievance by a rank-and-file employee. Therefore, it urged that the case be held arbitrable and that the parties proceed to a resolution of the claim on the merits.

Most arbitrators would hold that they are bound as much by the language governing the content of grievances as they are by the language governing substantive matters, such as overtime compensation, and that the parties and grievants are bound by that language. The requirement to cite contract article and section numbers dictates that employees must incorporate such references into the grievance. In the absence of any evidence of a wavier of that requirement, or any evidence of loose or informal application of the contractual grievance procedures in the past, most arbitrators would conclude that they are bound to implement and abide by the requirements of the parties' procedural language, as well as substantive language. Failing to do so would constitute a rewriting of the contract language to exclude from implementation a provision that the parties had clearly entered into jointly with the intent of its enforcement.

Discussion Question 1: Does the supervisor's awareness of the underlying facts overcome the requirement of specificity?

Arbitrators might hold that the intent of the language was to provide the employer with specific knowledge of the nature of the grievance in a timely fashion so that it could prepare an adequate investigation and defense. The arbitrator might rule that this intent was fulfilled when the grievant received his paycheck and asked the foreman about the compensation, thereby making the written grievance a mere formality to initiate a grievance that was already understood clearly by management. Although most arbitrators prefer to resolve disputes between the parties on the merits, they are bound by the contract language; and if the parties have negotiated a specific procedural requirement, it is as binding on the arbitrator as any substantive contract language.

Discussion Question 2: What if the grievance had specified article, but not section?

The parties had negotiated a requirement to cite both article and section. Strict construction of the collective bargaining agreement would require the arbitrator to find that both article and section must be cited in order to meet the specification of the grievance definition. If only the article had been cited, an arbitrator might conclude that there had been substantial, if not complete, compliance with the contract language. If that partial compliance were coupled with evidence that the employer had been aware in advance of the facts relating to the grievance and that the grievant was unskilled in grievance filing, the arbitrator might hold that the failing or violation was deminimis and should not preclude hearing and deciding the case on the merits.

The same result might also be achieved if the correct article, but an incorrect section had been cited. Most arbitrators would probably require accurate citation of both article and section because the parties had agreed to this rule and it presumably reflected intent. If they required the article, they likewise required the section. Some would take the view that there had been substantial compliance and that the error in citing the section should not preclude proceeding with the case on its merits.

Discussion Question 3: Should the arbitrator dismiss the grievance, or should the arbitrator remand the grievance?

The answer to this question would depend upon the relationship of the parties in the processing of the case. Assume the grievance had been filed and that the employer's first- or second-step representative had said that the grievance was not properly filed. If the union then had unsuccessfully sought an opportunity to correct the wording, the union might seek a remand as a way of overcoming the error in the original finding. If, however, the union had such an opportunity but declined it and the case was appealed on the question of whether or not there was a contract violation, then the arbitrator might conclude that his or her jurisdiction was limited to whether or not there had been a contract violation in the filing of the grievance. If the finding was yes, then the grievant presumably would be denied a hearing on the merits. Only if the union brought to the arbitrator's attention that it had sought an opportunity to amend the grievance might the arbitrator, upon finding that the contract language had been violated, accede to the union's request and grant an opportunity to refile the grievance. That decision would not be on the grounds that there had been a contract violation, but that the employer had acted improperly, or arbitrarily or capriciously, in denying the union the opportunity to reform the improperly worded grievance. That decision would probably be the outcome even if the time limits for grievance filing had elapsed before the grievant was advised that the grievance was not in proper form, as long as the employer had been aware of the true issue within the time limits.

Discussion Question 4: Would it make any difference if the union showed that the employer had previously accepted and processed grievances that omitted reference to article and/or section?

If the union could show that the employer had entertained grievances in the past that omitted reference to article and/or section, the arbitrator's decision might take into consideration a past practice by the parties that in effect eroded, if not vitiated, the requirement of citing article and section. If evidence showed only one grievance processed without article and section, the employer might be able to argue that this single instance had been an aberration or error in its procedure, particularly if it was able to show that it had declined to process other grievances omitting reference to article and section.

But if the evidence showed that there had been a pattern or even a mixed practice of accepting grievances without article and section, then the arbitrator might conclude that the parties had, in effect, amended their contract by their practice and that grievances without such specific article and section references would be arbitrable.

If the past practice showed the requirement of reference to article and section had been waived and the employer took the position that the present case constituted a tightening up of a clear contract requirement, most arbitrators would hold that the employer had waived its right to suddenly impose strict compliance. Rather, they would argue, the employer had led the union to assume that the omission would not preclude appeal. Nonetheless, if the contract language required specific wording and the employer announced that in subsequent cases such specificity would be expected, then the arbitrator would uphold that requirement for future cases. This statement would then bring about a return to strict adherence to the requirements of the contract language. But for the case at issue, the past practice would control, so that strict conformity would not be required in that pending case.

Time Limits

As in the preceding section, the negotiated time limits agreed to by the parties for the filing and appealing of grievances are as binding on the arbitrator as the substantive provisions of the parties' agreement on wages, hours, and working conditions.

Negotiated provisions of time limits for the filing of grievances, employer responses, and union appeals to higher levels of the procedure are universally found in collective bargaining agreements. The extent to which arbitrators will rigidly enforce those time limits depends upon how the parties themselves have recognized those limits in their handling of prior grievances. There are a number of standards that the arbitrator relies on in the area of time limits for initial grievances as well as time limits for appeals.

Timeliness in Filing. To hold a grievance to be timely, most collective bargaining agreements prescribe a fixed period after an event for the filing of a grievance. Usually the language prescribes a fixed number of days after the employee knew, or should have known, of the alleged contract violation. Thus, in the case of five-day disciplinary penalty for sleeping on the job, the significant event would not be the date on which the employee was awakened, but rather the date the employee was notified of the imposition of the disciplinary penalty. Although it might have been several days after the offense, the notification of discipline was what informed the employee that there was a basis for grieving to protest the discipline. Unless the employee was alerted to the fact that a contract violation had occurred or that a discipline was being imposed, there could be no basis for grieving. That same standard might be employed in a case in which an employee was denied overtime for holiday work. Thus, the violation occurred on the day of the holiday, when the employee worked the overtime, rather than when the time slip prescribing straight rather than overtime pay was sent in by the supervisor. The working of the overtime may have been the triggering event, but the employee was not aware of being deprived of overtime pay for that holiday and, thus, had no basis for claiming a contract violation or for filing a grievance. The employer could, after all, have corrected the error before the employee was paid. It seems reasonable that the employee's receipt of a paycheck without the extra stipend for the overtime work would be the event informing the employee that there had been a possible violation of the contract's provisions for holiday pay.

Even if the employee didn't notice the improper computation, he still bore the obligation to check for errors. Receipt of the paycheck was the point at which the employee "should have known of the alleged violation." But what if the employee had been on vacation and did not receive the paycheck until two weeks later? Or, what if the employee had had deductions or credit union payments that had terminated on the same paycheck? If the paycheck were larger and carried no notation of overtime pay, so that the employee interpreted the additional amount that week as compensation for the overtime, the employee could argue persuasively that there had been no actual or constructive knowledge of the violation. Perhaps that "knowledge" did not come until a paycheck later, or until a conversation with a supervisor, or until the employee learned from a fellow employee that there was entitlement to the holiday pay. Any of those events could have led the grievant to reexamine his earlier pay stubs.

If possible, it is in the best interest of the parties that the grievances be heard in timely fashion on the merits. It is also in the best interest of the system that an employee wishing to challenge an employer's action not be barred from doing so by a failure to learn of an alleged contract violation within the time set forth in the contract. But time limits for filing are essential to ensure prompt resolution of grievances and to prevent facts and recollections from becoming stable. If the grievant becomes aware of the possible violation within those time limits, they should control and the parties should be bound by them.

The second area of concern in the timing of the initial grievance arises when the employee is aware of an alleged violation but undertakes to resolve the dispute without immediately filing a formal grievance. Thus, in the case of the holiday pay, when learning of the alleged violation, the employee might go to the payroll department or to the supervisor to inquire whether or not there was entitlement to the higher level of pay. The investigation by the company might exceed the time limits for grieving after "knowledge". Some arbitrators assert that a grievant should protect against the expiration of grievance time limit by filing a grievance within the time limits, regardless of whether inquiries or discussions are underway on the resolution of the grievance.

Other arbitrators take the position that as long as the parties are discussing a resolution of a problem, there has not yet been an official violation that could be the subject of a grievance. Under this theory, which is probably embraced by the majority of arbitrators, the time limits are not triggered until the employer has stated that an employee's request for additional compensation for overtime is denied. At that point the employee, according to this theory, has the right to assert that the employer has violated the contract and, thus, the right to file a grievance.

A third area of conflict on the timeliness of a grievance filing occurs in situations in which the employee is not in the active employ of the enterprise—that is, an employee on an unrelated extended leave of absence, or in jail for a nonwork-related criminal violation, or on sick leave. In such cases there is no active employment relationship to trigger the initiation of the time limit. It could be argued that the employee on leave of absence may not come back, or that the employee in jail might not come back. Employees in such unusual situations are not present at the enterprise and do not have access to the employer or to the union for active processing of the grievance. They may not even have received the information that would normally trigger the start of the time limits. Accordingly, arbitrators may hold that the time limits for appeal are not triggered until the employee returns to active employment. That same reasoning would, of course, apply to an employee who is on vacation for a number of weeks, an employee on military service, and so on.

Timeliness in Appeals. The issue of timeliness also has relevance in determining whether the union's appeal from the employer's denial response to grievance had been filed in timely fashion. Here, too, the determination of timeliness depends upon the language of the parties' agreement. If the parties' contract specifies that the supervisor must respond in writing to the appeal of the union within five working days, then the arbitrator must determine whether a second- or third-step answer filed in six or seven days violates the parties' agreement. Most collective bargaining agreements excuse delays on the part of the employer and specify that if the employer does not respond within the number of days specified by the contract, then a denial of that grievance is assumed and union has a right to file an appeal to the next higher step. According to some collective bargaining agreements, the union would be granted the grievance in full if the employer does not respond within the contractual time limits for a grievance answer.

A different situation occurs when considering the timeliness of appeals following the employer's answers. Because the union is the party challenging the status quo by filing the grievance, it has the initiative to pursue that grievance in conformity with the contract provisions. Thus, if the employer denies the claim at step one or two, it is incumbent upon the union to file an appeal within the specified time limits to bring the case to the next higher level. In most collective bargaining agreements, it is the grievant's responsibility to initiate the appeal, although, in some collective bargaining agreements that responsibility is shared by the grievant and the union. Then, either the union or the grievant would have the responsibility to appeal. In most collective bargaining agreements, the union alone has the authority to appeal from the last step of the grievance procedure to arbitration; most collective bargaining agreements do not grant the individual employee the right to appeal to the arbitration step. Therefore, most arbitrators conclude that, at that stage, the union, rather than the grievant, "owns" the grievance and the union alone may determine whether or not to appeal (within the specified time limits) to the arbitration step.

The absence of specific time limits for appeal to the arbitration step probably is because the union rather than any grievant is responsible for the future of the case and because the sequence or even the prospect of appeal may become a political issue in the parties' relationship.

Although most arbitrators would hold that the absence of a negotiated time limit at the arbitration appeal step, in contrast with specific time limits below, relieves the union of any deadline for appeal, the equity concept of laches or undue delay may come into play. It could be argued that failure to complete the requisite procedures for appeal to the arbitration step deprives the arbitrator of jurisdiction over a case in which the prerequisites for hearing the case have not been met. There is a point at which arbitrators may assert that the union has waived its right to appeal to arbitration, particularly where there has been a universal practice of prompt appeal and proof that the employer had been prejudiced by departure from that practice. But the fact that arbitration appeals are often pending for months or years without employer protest makes it difficult for an employer to prevail on the laches theory—that is, the failure to raise the claim within a reasonable time.

More likely, an arbitrator would hold a tardy appeal arbitrable on the grounds that the negotiating table is the more appropriate forum for imposing such a time limit, as the employer had acknowledged in its quest for time limits at the earlier steps of the grievance procedure.

A number of issues arise in determining whether or not to strictly adhere to the time limits set forth in the contract for appeal to the next level of management, even when the contract language may be specific about the number of days for appeal. First, there is the question of whether that time limit has been strictly adhered to in the past. If the union is able to show that those time limits have been waived by the employer's acceptance of grievances that were appealed more than five days after receipt of the employer's action, then the arbitrator may conclude that the parties' past practice has been to overlook or disregard the time limit. If the employer, on the other hand, is able to show that there has been strict adherence to the time limit and that at least one or more grievances have been denied on timeliness grounds and not appealed to arbitration, then the arbitrator would take this history as strong evidence that the union had acquiesced to the company's strict adherence to the time limit.

In some collective bargaining agreements, the parties have negotiated (often following bitter experiences) that exceptions to time limits must be approved in writing. For instance, if the collective bargaining agreement provides that any extension of the contractual time limits must be issued in writing and signed by both parties, then the arbitrator would be bound by that requirement. If the evidence in a certain case showed that no such written extension had been secured, the arbitrator would be required to exclude the grievance on the grounds of time limits. Of course, if the evidence showed that the parties had not adhered to the requirement of a written extension, then the arbitrator would conclude that the past practice has loosened the administration of those time limits, as demonstrated by the loose administration of the requirement of a written extension.

A second area of concern in determining whether or not there has been a timely appeal within the specified days might arise on the issue of how the time period is calculated. Does the five days specified in an agreement refer to five work days or five calendar days? Reference to the past practice of the parties might be instructive, as might a perusal of other provisions of the contract. This evidence might show the arbitrator that the parties' intent throughout the agreement was to consider "days" as work days, and that the same intent applied in the grievance appeal steps, in which the days were counted as work days (or conversely as calendar days). It might behoove the parties in such a dispute to secure some evidence of the negotiating history of the clause to determine whether or not the negotiators had identified the "days" for grievance appeals as work or calendar days.

The third area of concern in appeals is to determine whether the time limits run from the date of the employer's answer or from the time the employee receives that answer. Here, too, the past practice of the parties is instructive, and unless the parties have negotiated specific language to deal with the commencement of the time limit—that is, the sending or the receiving—most arbitrators would follow the same theory appropriate to "knew or should have known" on the grounds that the union did not know of the answer until it was received from the employer. The issue may be complicated by the tardiness of the mail, which may cause the time limit to expire in the delay between the sending of the grievance denial and the grievant's receipt of it. The parties frequently avoid the issue of whether the union is aware of a grievance denial by requiring the union to acknowledge receipt of the denial letter. This procedure triggers the commencement of the appeal time limit and places the burden of notifying the grievant on the union. Even if the grievant or the union is unwilling to sign such a receipt, employers frequently will have a representative of management witness that refusal and annotate the time and date when that grievance denial was given to the union or the grievant.

Sometimes, the grievant or union will claim that the mailed disciplinary notice was not received. It is a presumption in law and arbitration that a letter, if mailed, is received. That presumption may be rebutted by evidence of other "unsent letters" or evidence of other letters being received by the grievant even though sent to the "wrong" address.

CASE STUDY: *The Case of the Continuing Grievance.* On January 2, the grievant, Michael Doika, was assigned to a new position at a higher labor grade. He was unaware of his entitlement to higher pay until February 15, some six weeks later, when a fellow employee looking at his paycheck advised him that he was being underpaid and was entitled to a higher rate. The employee filed a grievance. The employer challenged the timeliness of the appeal by pointing out that the grievant had received five paychecks after assuming his new position, that the position was listed in the contract as paying the higher rate, and that although he may not have had actual notice of the higher labor grade, he was responsible for having learned of it by his presumed knowledge of the collective bargaining agreement. Therefore, since the contract provided a five-day period for filing a grievance, he was responsible for filing that grievance within five days after receipt of his first paycheck on the new job.

The union responded that the grievant was not aware of the new pay rate until mid-February, and that even if responsibility for knowing the rate earlier had foreclosed his entitlement to be paid retroactively back to the day he began the job, he was still entitled to compensation beginning from the five days before he filed the grievance because the violation was a continuing grievance. The employer maintained that the grievance was not arbitrable. The case was then appealed to arbitration on the arbitrability issue.

The employer, at the hearing, contended that the grievant was responsible for knowing the rate of the job, for which he had bid, that the job was listed in the parties' collective bargaining agreement at that the higher rate, and that the higher rate was the grievant's motivation for changing to his new position. Even though he might not have been aware of a contractual violation of January 1, before receiving the first paycheck on the new job, he was clearly on notice of an alleged violation when he received his first paycheck on January 7. The employer argued that the January 7 paycheck constituted the appropriate triggering date for a grievance and that by failing to file a grievance within five days, he had waived his right to protest the improper payment.

At the hearing, the union, on the other hand, argued that the grievant had bid for the job to achieve more favorable hours and a better work location, that the grievant had been unaware of the higher wage rate, that he had not possessed a copy of the collective bargaining agreement, and that he had no cause to look into the agreement to check the appropriate rate for the job to which he had transferred. The union further argued that the grievant had no reason to question the propriety of the pay rate for the new job until some six weeks later, when he was told by other employees that he was being underpaid. At that time, when he first learned of the violation, he filed his grievance. However, the union continued, even if it were held that the grievant should have known of the violation at, or shortly after, January 1, the grievant still had a right to file a grievance in mid-February on the grounds that there had been a continuing violation of the contract and that each day of payment at the wrong rate constituted a new action that could be cause for filing a grievance.

The arbitrator found that the grievant should have known, if he did not actually know, of the appropriate rate for the job on or about January 7, when he received his first paycheck for that job. The arbitrator reasoned that the job was posted, that the job and rate were listed in the collective bargaining agreement, that the grievant was presumed to have access to and have knowledge of that collective bargaining agreement, and that the grievant was required to initiate any protest of his underpayment within five days of receipt of his first paycheck. Although the arbitrator held that, by failing to initiate a grievance in a timely fashion, the grievant had lost his right to reimbursement from the loss effective from January 1, his continued employment in that position at a rate less than that called for by the contract constituted an ongoing violation of the contract that the grievant could challenge through a grievance procedure at any time while that violation continued. Accordingly, the arbitrator found that the grievance filed on

February 15 was timely for challenging the improper payment at that time. The contractual period for filing a grievance—five days after the event—would restrict the grievant's remedy to back pay back to five days prior to February 15, the date on which the grievance was filed.

Discussion Question 1: What evidence could the union have shown to support its claim for retroactivity to January 1?

The union's claim for retroactivity to January 1 would have to depend upon showing that the grievant had been unaware and could not reasonably have learned of the improper wage payment until February 15. To support that contention, the union could have produced evidence that the grievant thought that the job paid the same, or evidence of his preference for different hours or work location as the motivating factor for bidding, or that the grievant was unaware of a contract provision listing the job at a higher rate. If the union was able to show that the position had not been listed by wage rate on the bid sheet or in the contract, or that the grievant had never received a copy of the contract, or that the contract had changes that no one had been given new copies of, the arbitrator might be persuaded that the grievant could not have reasonably known earlier that the job paid a higher rate.

Discussion Question 2: Is an employee responsible for knowing the content of the collective bargaining agreement?

Most arbitrators would take the position that employees are charged with knowing the content of their agreements. Although it may be the responsibility of the union to advise the employees of the content of the agreement and their rights under it, if the employee was given a copy of the agreement, he or she is assumed to have read it and have knowledge of its content. The availability of that agreement would constitute grounds for concluding that there was constructive knowledge of the contract. Actual knowledge of the contract provision, on the other hand, would require showing that the grievant had been specifically shown or advised of that contract provision. If the union sought to show that there had been no constructive knowledge of the contract, it would be incumbent upon the union to show that the copies of the agreement had not been issued to the employees or that the grievant was not present when the contract was distributed to all other employees, or that he was somehow excluded from the opportunity to gain constructive knowledge of the contract's content by language obstacles or other impediments.

A Grievance by a Departed Employee

A collective bargaining agreement is applicable to the employees during the time they are employed by the enterprise. Most collective bargaining agreements will include a provision identifying the means by which employment, seniority, and, therefore, access to the grievance procedure will be terminated. Usually seniority may be severed by the employee's termination for just cause, failure to respond to a recall within a fixed period of time, remaining on lay-off for a certain number of years, resignation, or by any other acts that the parties agree to include in the collective bargaining agreement. Thus, the question arises of the right of an employee to file a grievance when no longer in the employ of the enterprise. If the employee seeks to file a grievance alleging an improper compensation during a holiday, that grievance may be filed as long as the grievant was an employee of the enterprise at the time of the alleged violation. It therefore follows that even if the employee had severed the employment relationship after filing a grievance alleging improper pay, the grievance would still be viable. The employee had the right to be paid the contractual rate for holiday compensation. The union has the obligation to enforce the contract, not only for the departed employee, but for all remaining employees. Thus, the employee who had resigned from the enterprise would have the right to benefit from the union's pursuit of any contract violation allegedly done to the employee during the period of his or her employment. The result would be different, of course, if the employee had, for example, worked on Veteran's Day, discovered an allegedly improper payment on November 25, severed his employment relationship on November 28, and sought to file a grievance on November 30. Most arbitrators would conclude that the grievant could have grieved on November 25–28, and that because the employee had freely chosen to sever the employment relationship with the company, that employee no longer had any access to the grievance procedure.

A corollary right to arbitrate despite the lack of active employee status arises in the case of retired employees seeking to enforce their pension or retirement insurance rights. Usually, the parties' agreement will specify that grievance access is available to such retired employees.

In some cases, however, the contract may be silent on that issue, so it befalls the arbitrator to determine whether, in the absence of specified grievance access by retired employees, that right exists. In making that determination, the arbitrator will be guided by the parties' negotiating history in agreeing to the retirement benefits, by the parties' past practice, and perhaps even by the provisions of statutes on age discrimination and pension rights. Most arbitrators' preference would be to justify the right to grieve and arbitrate so as to assure fair implementation and enforcement of the benefits agreed to in the parties' collective bargaining agreement.

An exception to the right of a grievant to file a grievance after the employment relationship has been severed arises in the case of grievances over employer termination actions. Arbitrators hold that if the employee had been unilaterally terminated by the employer, the new status of "ex-employee" does not deprive the employee of the right to challenge the employer's action in imposing the termination. Otherwise, the employer would be immune from any disciplinary actions undertaken because of its termination of an employee—who couldn't, of course, grieve termination before it happened. Indeed, if employers could avoid grievances over termination, the attractiveness of that action, rather than imposing lesser disciplinary penalties on employees, would be enhanced because it would avoid the risk of grievances over lesser discipline. Arbitrators assume, and the entire grievance arbitration machinery accepts, that discharge effectively terminates an employee's seniority only if the employee fails to grieve that termination within the time limits specified for grievances in the parties' agreement.

In some cases, arbitrators are faced with situations in which the employee submits a resignation and then seeks to file a grievance alleging improper termination. Such a situation may arise when the employer gives the employee the option of resigning or being terminated. If, in such a situation, the employee had agreed to resign and then filed a grievance challenging the employer's action as constructive termination—a resignation obtained under pressure or threat of termination—then the arbitrator must decide whether or not the grievant had standing to file a grievance. If the arbitrator finds that the resignation was not imposed under pressure or threat of termination and that the employee voluntarily resigned without any pressure or desire to continue employment, then the arbitrator would presumably hold such a grievance to be not arbitrable. But if, on the other hand, the arbitrator is convinced that the resignation was a device to deprive the employee of the right of appeal, or to mask a termination, then the arbitrator might conclude that such a grievance is properly arbitrable on the grounds of unjust termination.

Grievance After the Contract Has Expired

A somewhat related issue arises as to the viability of a grievance filed under an expired agreement. In most cases in which the duration date has been reached, but no successor contract agreed to, the parties agree to continue under the prior terms, including the grievants right to enforce that agreement, through the grievance procedure. The Supreme Court in Nolde Bros v. Local 358 Bakery and Confectionery Workers (430 US245, 1977) held that even when the union has terminated an agreement, the obligation of the parties under the arbitration clause of the contract survives unless there has been a specific negation of arbitrability in the contract termination.

Res Judicata/Collateral Estoppel

The legal doctrine of res judicata is intended to prevent repeated litigation of a previously settled issue. It is, on occasion, invoked by one of the parties in arbitration to preclude repeated hearing of a case on the grounds that the issue in dispute has already been resolved by a prior decision, or by an earlier withdrawal of a grievance, that would preclude its reopening as res judicata to that original claim. While that doctrine has its origins and applicability in a court of law with appellate proceedings, where the law is set for disputant parties and those similarly situated, the arbitration forum is different. The parties may agree upon different arbitrators, the collective bargaining agreement may change, and even within the duration of the particular contract the practices of the parties may vary, so there is no guarantee that a second case on the particular issue will emanate from the same facts or result in the same decision as the preceding case.

Thus, in a case in which arbitrator A had decided that grievant Smith was entitled to call-in pay for reporting to work in a snowstorm on January 5, that finding would not be res judicata for arbitrator B, nor would it bar arbitrator B from determining that the grievant Jones is entitled, or not entitled, to call-in pay for reporting during a snowstorm on February 16. The instances are different, the parties are different, and the arbitrator may distinguish between them. Although perhaps relying on the precedent as guidance, the arbitrator would not consider the second case to be a relitigation of the same issue dealt with in the first.

A different result might occur if the second case arose from the same snowstorm. If arbitrator A had decided that the snowstorm on January 5 was an act of God that excused the call-in payment for employee Smith, that ruling could be argued to constitute res judicata for the second arbitrator handling the case of Jones, who also reported for work during the same snowstorm on the same shift. Yet, if Smith and Jones had reported at different times, or on different shifts, then it could be argued that the earlier arbitrator's ruling was not res judicata because the timing and intensity of the storm, the accessibility to the facility, and the availability of notification of a closure were different. Any of these differences could mandate a separate hearing on the second case and permit the second arbitrator to distinguish it from the earlier arbitrator's ruling.

The clearest example in which res judicata would be persuasive would be a case in which a grievant had challenged a disciplinary action by the employer, the case had gone to arbitration, the arbitrator had said that the discipline was for just cause, and the grievant thereafter had filed a new grievance that again challenged that same employer action. Since the second grievance arose from an action that had already been litigated, most arbitrators would conclude that the second case would not be arbitrable and that the first decision constituted res judicata, precluding the second appeal on the same issue.

The legal concept of collateral estoppel has a different impact on the arbitration process. If an employee had been charged with criminal theft for stealing scrap lumber from his employer, and the court had found him guilty and imposed a two-year suspended sentence, the employer, invoking collateral estoppel, would claim that the court determination had established the fact of theft and precluded an arbitrator from independently deciding whether or not there had been a theft. Most arbitrators would take the position that the proceeding before the court of law involved different parties, different quantums of proof, was not based upon an collective bargaining agreement, and therefore should not preclude the union from securing a determination by an arbitrator as to whether or not there was just cause for terminating an employee for theft under the terms of the parties' collective bargaining agreement.

But consider a case in which the office of workers' compensation had found that an employee was permanently disabled by a work-related injury. If that employee were to file a grievance seeking reinstatement to the job, the arbitrator might decline to make an independent determination of whether or not the grievant was permanently disabled and, instead, adopt the workers' compensation finding. The arbitrator might conclude that the parties' agreement, or the union's participation in the workers' compensation case, constituted agreement that the other forum should be the binding decisionmaker on the issue the grievance seeks to reopen. The arbitrator, therefore, might find that the parties are bound by the determination of the office of workers' compensation that the employee was permanently disabled and, thus, bar the employee's effort to return to work under the terms of the collective bargaining agreement.

Most arbitrators view the case before them as justifying a decision based on its own particular merits. At the same time, arbitrators are committed to a system of industrial jurisprudence that precludes excessive litigation and arbitration of shop floor disputes. Thus, if the arbitrators were persuaded that an issue had been litigated, or that the determination of a comparable authority was applicable to the proceeding before them, they would probably heed the theories of res judicata and collateral estoppel—although they might not give them the legal weight that they might be accorded in a court of law. So even if an arbitrator had denied a challenge to arbitrability that raised the doctrines of res judicata or collateral estoppel and proceeded with the hearing of the case on the merits, the arbitrator would still be inclined to endorse the determinations of prior arbitrators that the arbitrator felt would best provide the parties with guidance to prevent repetitive litigation on the same issue in the future.

The same result would occur when the parties had reached a settlement of a grievance—say, on the issue of discipline—by agreeing to reduce a suspension from seven to three days. Once that settlement had been reached, if the grievant sought to pursue that same grievance to arbitration, the employer would properly argue that the third-step settlement was res judicata to the grievant's right to appeal the grievance to arbitration because the matter had already been resolved. If such an argument were raised, then the arbitrator would have to determine whether the settlement was entered into a good faith, whether the employee was bound by it, and whether that precluded continuing the case through appeal to arbitration. Such reasoning and its result might cause the arbitrator to invoke the same concepts that are inherent in res judicata, but he or she would be unlikely to do so using that legal jargon.

Arbitrability of Last-Chance Agreements

In their effort to resolve a termination dispute without going to arbitration, many parties negotiate last-chance agreements to permit the reinstatement of the employee with conditions stringently controlling the grievant's future behavior but providing the opportunity for the employee's rehabilitation. Such last-chance agreements are usually viewed as a negotiated alternative to termination. The union may agree to very restrictive conditions in order to protect the employee's job. The last chance agreement is, in effect, a contract between the union and the employer, presumably with the grievant's acquiescing signature. The arbitrator, who may be called upon to arbitrate a dispute over the last-chance agreement, is as bound by that agreement as by the collective bargaining agreement itself because it is equally an agreement by the parties. Such last chance agreements commonly specify the duration of the probation and grant to the employer the right to determine whether or not the employee has lived up to the conditions of the settlement. Such an arrangement may also contain a provision waiving the right to grieve any subsequent penalties imposed upon the employee.

CASE STUDY: *The Case of the Last-Chance Appeal.* Jonathan Walsh, a four-year employee, had been given two written warnings and two disciplinary suspensions before he was terminated for poor attendance. The union grieved his termination. At step three, the parties agreed to reinstate Walsh on a last-chance basis, with an agreement to which the grievant, the union, and the company were signatories. The agreement acknowledged that there had been grounds for termination and called for a one-year period in which Walsh should reestablish a normal attendance pattern. The settlement agreement also provided that if the grievant were terminated during that period, there would be no right of appeal to the grievance and arbitration procedure.

The evidence showed that Walsh was terminated after three months of the one-year probationary period for four instances of tardiness, ranging in length from ten minutes to four hours. The union grieved. The employer responded that the grievance was not arbitrable and the case came to arbitration on the agreed-upon issue of: "(1) Was the grievance arbitrable?, and (2) if so, was the termination of the grievant for just cause?"

The company argued that the parties had made their last-chance agreement with the acknowledgment that there would otherwise have been grounds for termination. The company also asserted that the one-year probationary period to reestablish a normal attendance pattern was a reasonable standard and time, that the parties had given the employer the right to unilaterally determine whether there had been conformity to the requirements of the last-chance agreement, and that they had voluntarily foreclosed arbitration on the merits of any subsequent termination during that period.

The union took the position that the grievant had the right to file a grievance challenging the final termination under the parties' collective bargaining agreement, that a shop steward signatory to the last-chance agreement had no right to waive the grievant's contractual right to arbitration, that the grievant was entitled to the full range of rights under the parties' collective bargaining agreement, including arbitration of that final removal, and that the arbitrator had the full authority to review the just cause for the removal, including any questions that might arise about the application of the last-chance agreement.

The arbitrator ruled that the steward was a designated representative of the union and that he acted on behalf of the union in agreeing to the last-chance reinstatement. The arbitrator held that the last-chance agreement was as binding on the union as it was on the employer and that the union had agreed to requirements for a normal attendance and employer determination as to whether that attendance had been maintained. The arbitrator reasoned that foreclosure of appeal to the grievance and arbitration system was a valid understanding between the parties and one by which the arbitrator was bound. The arbitrator held that the first question to determine was whether there had been a valid and binding last-chance agreement, and the arbitrator concluded there had. The second question was to determine if the last-chance agreement had been complied with. The arbitrator found that the subsequent infraction was of the type anticipated by the parties and, thus, was covered by the last-chance agreement. Although the arbitrator could have found the company arbitrary and capricious in exercising its authority to determine whether there had been compliance with the agreement, here the arbitrator felt that the company's actions were appropriate under the terms and conditions of the last chance-agreement. The arbitrator noted that there was no dispute over the facts that the grievant had been substantially tardy on four occasions and that those tardinesses fell within the framework of the attendance standards that the parties had empowered the employer to judge. Because the parties had granted to the employer that right to define whether or nor there had been reasonable attendance, the arbitrator held that the parties were bound by that determination. The arbitrator found no grounds for holding that the ruling was arbitrary and capricious, as it might have been after, say, a single two-minute tardiness, and concluded that because the parties had left the definition of reasonable attendance to the employer, the arbitrator lacked the authority to substitute judgment for that of the employer or to rule on the merits of the grievance claim.

Discussion Question 1: What data could the union have presented to support its position?

The union could have produced evidence that the grievant had not been tardy more than most others in the plant, or that the employer tolerated ten-minute tardinesses of other employees, or that one or more of the four instances in the grievant's case were caused by conditions beyond his control, such as child care needs or adverse weather conditions. The union might also have researched the attendance records of other employees during that three-month period to determine if others with more frequent tardinesses had not been disciplined.

Discussion Question 2: Would the result have been different if the last-chance agreement called for "substantial improvement" in Walsh's attendance?

Because the arbitrator limited review in the case to the question of whether or not the player had properly applied the settlement standard of a "normal attendance pattern," the same review would be appropriate if the settlement standard had been "substantial improvement." But using that standard, the comparison would have been the grievant's prior attendance record rather than the abstract norm of the enterprise or area. In such a case, the arbitrator would require evidence of the grievant's prior attendance record to judge whether the employer had conformed to the settlement standard in assessing whether the grievant's attendance had improved and whether that improvement had been substantial.

Discussion Question 3: How could the union have proved substantial improvement?

After assembling the grievant's attendance record for his four-year employment, the union could pick the baseline period for determining improvement—for example, the four-year period, the period since his first attendance warning, or the period between his last suspension and his termination. The tardiness record in any of those periods could then be compared to the tardiness record during the reinstatement period, either as a flat comparison or on a tardiness-per-week or per-month basis to accommodate to the disparate time intervals. The union could also argue substantial improvement if the employee was only tardy now compared to tardiness and absenteeism before.

Waiver of the Objections to Arbitrability

Arbitrators prefer to resolve disputes on the merits of the grievance as filed. Nonetheless, the arbitrators are bound by the contract's procedural language, just as they are bound by the substantive language of the parties' agreement. If there is a procedural challenge, the arbitrators are obliged to resolve the issue of whether or not they have the procedural authority to proceed with the case on the merits.

In their effort to resolve cases on their merits rather than be upheld on procedural grounds, arbitrators will usually be receptive to arguments for waiving the procedural objection, if it can be legitimately shown that the objecting party has failed to assert its protest properly. Thus, arbitrators may conclude that if there is a procedural challenge to arbitrability, the party is obligated to bring it up in timely fashion—that is, at the earliest stage of the grievance procedure, following its awareness of the alleged procedural impropriety. This conclusion is based on several reasons. First, good faith relationships between the parties require that alleged improprieties be notified at the earliest stage to avoid escalation of conflict and to encourage timely resolution of such disputes. Second, one party's timely notification of an alleged violation is crucial to the other's ability to investigate and respond to the allegations. If the violation is brought up months later, the other party might have lost access to information that could have rebutted the challenge to arbitrability. The purpose of the grievance procedure is to resolve disputes at the lowest possible steps. Thus, if one party is aware of a procedural impropriety, it is incumbent on it to alert the other to that alleged violation at the earliest possible step to avoid the escalation to the arbitration procedure, with its attendant cost and use of time. Accordingly, arbitrators invoke the doctrine of wavier if they find that a party has failed to raise in timely fashion information that it earlier had in its possession to support a claim of procedural irregularity. If such wavier is found or invoked by the arbitrator, then the conclusion is reached that the party has sat on its rights, failed to invoke its procedural argument in a timely fashion, and, by its inaction, waived its right to challenge the arbitrability of a dispute. The arbitrator, under such circumstances, will conclude that there is authorization to proceed to hear and decide the case on its merits.

Post-Termination Conduct

On occasion, after the termination penalty has been imposed and while the status of the employment relationship is still not resolved, the discharged employee may engage in conduct that would normally precipitate termination had the employee not already been fired. If the original removal is appealed to arbitration, the post-hearing conduct may give rise to an arbitrability challenge. Unless the parties have agreed to combine the two removal actions into the single grievance that was appealed to arbitration, the arbitrability challenge may arise because either of the parties has attempted to have both cases presented at the same proceeding. If the employer seeks joinder of the two terminations, the union may challenge the arbitrability of the second termination on the grounds that the grievant was never formally notified of the second termination or that the second case had not been properly processed through the grievance appeals steps. If the union seeks joinder of the two terminations, the employer may challenge the arbitrability of the second termination on the grounds that the grievant had already been terminated at the time of the second action and thus had no standing to grieve or that the union had not properly appealed the second case through the grievance procedure. Clearly, it would be most efficient and economical for both cases to be heard at one sitting by the arbitrator. But if the arbitration step is to be useful as the final step of the grievance procedure, the parties must use the preliminary steps as a fact-finding process to settle the dispute. While it might be more efficient if a second termination bypasses the lower levels, and enters the system for the first time at the arbitration step, this process nonetheless contradicts the intent of the procedure. The arbitrator might therefore opt to hear just the first appeal and, if the employee is reinstated, extend to the employer the right to issue a second termination and the union the right to grieve it.

Arbitrators have to weigh expediency against conformity to the parties' appeals procedure. In deciding whether to hear the two cases, the arbitrator might ponder the following:

1. Is the first charge so likely to result in termination that there is scant likelihood of reinstatement and a second appeal?
2. Is the second charge so provable that, even if returned to work after a hearing on the first charge, the second removal is likely to be upheld?
3. Are the facts of the second case undisputed, so that the fact-finding aspects of the grievance appeal have been accomplished?
4. Are the positions on the second case so firmly held that settlement would be unlikely if the case were remanded?
5. Does contract language affect the issue, such as a requirement of, or a bar against, one grievance being arbitrated at a time?
6. Has there been any waiver by either party that would undercut their contentions on the cases being joint or severable?
7. Would economic hardship befall the employer or the grievant by separating the case and handling the second removal as a separate case?
8. Are there any precedents in the parties' relationship in which a similar situation arose?

The answers to these and other questions along the same lines probably cannot be secured through the formal presentations of the parties. But it would not be improper for the arbitrator to meet jointly outside the hearing room with the team spokespersons to attempt a resolution of the problem. This meeting might lead to an agreement on proceeding without prejudice; it might lead to an adjournment to process the second appeal; it might lead to submitting the issues of both terminations to the arbitrator for a resolution; or it might result in proceeding with the first termination and leaving to the parties, and perhaps to a new grievance, a resolution of the standing of the second removal and grievance.

Union-Initiated Grievances

Most collective bargaining agreements assume that a grievance will be filed by an employee affected by the employer's action. This expectation is usually reflected in the language, which refers to the "employee grieving" or the "employee submitting the grievance." The grievance form will contain a space for the grievant's signature, and some collective bargaining agreements specify that the grievance be signed by the employee. Occasionally, the grievant does not sign the grievance or it is signed by a union official. This irregularity may precipitate an arbitrability question over the right of the union to grieve. In some contracts, there is a joint right to grieve, and the language empowers "the grievant or the union" to initiate the grievance. In other contracts, individual grievances are to be submitted by the affected employee, while certain other grievances, such as those related to the contractual rights of the union (dues check-off, or posting on the union bulletin board) are to be filed by the union and resumably signed by the pertinent union officer. Union-sponsored grievances are often introduced into the grievance procedure at the second step.

Arbitrability questions usually arise when a union official seeks to grieve on behalf of an individual employee.

CASE STUDY: *The Case of the Recalcitrant Grievant.* Andrea Gager had sixteen years of seniority, had always worked available overtime, and was being considered for promotion to a managerial position. She was at work on the Wednesday before the holiday, when the foreman solicited volunteers for holiday work. But Gager was not informed of the overtime work until she learned the following week that everyone else in her shop had worked the overtime, including employees junior to her.

She told the stop steward, Cathy Groves, what had happened, and Cathy urged her to file a grievance. Andrea declined on the grounds that the complaint might jeopardize her chance for the promotion.

The next day, unbeknownst to Andrea, Cathy filed a grievance on Andrea's behalf and signed it "Cathy Groves, shop steward."

The foreman rejected the grievance as improper, citing article 3, section 2 of the parties' agreement, which read:

Step one
The aggrieved employee has five days from knowledge of an alleged violation to file a grievance with the foreman.

Step two
The union my file grievances affecting bargaining unit rights at step two.

The case was appealed to arbitration.

At the hearing, the employer argued that the grievance was not arbitrable, that the right to grieve was personal to Andrea, that she had exercised her option not to grieve the oversight, that the shop steward had no right to grieve on behalf of an individual in this case because bargaining unit rights were not at issue and that, in any event, union-initiated grievances had to be filed at step two, not step one.

The union argued that Andrea had been intimidated from filing the grievance because of her pending promotion, that the union had the obligation and right to police the contract for its membership and its individual members, that the employer's failure to solicit an eligible employee for overtime work had an impact on all employees, and that it was within its purview to police the agreement for the benefit of the bargaining unit.

The arbitrator held that the case was not arbitrable. Article 3, section 2, specified that the right to file resided in the "aggrieved employee," that the union's right to file was restricted to issues of bargaining unit rights, that this case involved an individual's right to be solicited and not the rights of the bargaining unit as a whole, and that the filing at step one rather than step two showed that the shop steward was exercising an individual right on behalf of Andrea rather than a union right.

Discussion Question 1: What if Andrea had been a probationary employee?

The right to grieve is personal to the grievant regardless of whether that employee is a probationary or a regular employee. The question of whether or not a probationary employee would have had the right to grieve in this case is one that only the employee could assert. As noted earlier, the union would not be disadvantaged in its protection of bargaining unit rights if a probationary employee declined or was refused the opportunity to grieve a bypass in overtime solicitation.

Discussion Question 2: Doesn't the union have the right to protect against the adverse precedent that might be set by the failure to challenge a contract violation?

Adverse precedent might be established by a failure of an individual to grieve an alleged violation, but if there were an adverse precedent it would be set against Andrea and not the union. Individual employees have the option of grieving. They are not required to grieve, nor is the union required or authorized to grieve on their behalf.

The union might be bound by that precedent in cases where the union had the right to grieve and failed or declined to do so. In this case, however, there was no union right to be policed so the union would not be bound by any precedent in situations it lacked the right to grieve.

Discussion Question 3: What if there had been no separate union right to grieve at step two?

If the contract had contained no special grieving right for the union, the arbitrator might have held that it had the right to grieve on Andrea's behalf. But the phrase "The aggrieved employee has five days" suggests that this right is unique to the employee.

A different result might have ensued if Andrea had asked Cathy to file the grievance on her behalf. That request might have been viewed as a ministerial delegation of the writing and filing of the grievance, which Cathy exercised as an agent of, and at the direction of, Andrea. In that situation, the arbitrator would probably have held the grievance arbitrable, unless the contract specified that the grievance had to be signed by the grievant or that only the grievant could submit a grievance.

Separate Ruling on Arbitrability

Efficiency and economy may require the parties to fully present their views on procedural issues as well as on the merits of a particular case at the same sitting. The arbitrator may also prefer to have the parties present their arguments on both procedure and the merits in order to gain all the information necessary to proceed to a determination on the merits if the case is found to be arbitrable. But occasionally the party challenging arbitrability will insist on a ruling on arbitrability before agreeing to proceed to a resolution on the merits. In some cases, that position is based upon an unwillingness to proceed to consideration of the merits by the same arbitrator if the case is held arbitrable. If the party challenging arbitrability loses, it would have the option of having the merits determined by a different arbitrator.

A request for a decision on the arbitrability issue alone may be based upon an unwillingness or inability to fully prepare what might be a very protracted case on the merits. The party challenging arbitrability may seek a preliminary ruling on that issue to avoid the necessity of preparation of what might be a very long and complicated case on the merits. A third reason for a ruling on arbitrability alone may be the challenging party's fear that, if given the authority to proceed on both issues, the arbitrator's self-interest would lead to holding the case arbitrable to secure further hearings and writing time on the merits.

This latter fear may be particularly apparent in cases in which the employer challenges the right of an arbitrator to hear more than one case, even though the grievance or demand for arbitration encompasses multiple grievances. If the arbitrator retains jurisdiction over both the procedural issue and the merits, a ruling that multiple cases be processed from one grievance or demand for arbitration would lead to substantial work and economic benefit for that arbitrator who maintains jurisdiction over all the cases. Arbitrators who are sensitive to such charges, but who are equally concerned about a possible effort to run up the cost of arbitration by requiring individual processing of each of the multiple cases before separate arbitrators, might decide the arbitrability issue and just one of the several cases of the merits. Then, if the arbitrability issue is decided in favor of having multiple grievances heard by the single arbitrator, the arbitrator could leave to the parties the choice of coming back to that same arbitrator for the hearing of the remaining issues or of choosing a second arbitrator to hear the remaining issues.

Thus, when dealing with the question of the separability of the arbitrability challenge from the merits, arbitrators must not only effect the goals of speed and efficiency in processing cases on arbitrability and on the merits, but they must also respect the right of the parties to a separate ruling on arbitrability without imposing themselves on the parties by asserting jurisdiction over the substantive issue. It should remain the choice of both parties whether to grant such jurisdiction to the arbitrator.

When there is an objection to proceeding to the merits until there has been a ruling on arbitrability, the arbitrator may face a demand from the party against whom the arbitrability challenge is raised to proceed to hear the case on the merits. Obviously, there is no problem if the parties agree to have a written decision rendered on arbitrability before proceeding to a second hearing on the merits. Nor would there be a problem if the parties agreed to go forward on the merits with the understanding that the arbitrator would only rule on the merits if the case proved arbitrable. The problem for the arbitrator and the parties arises when the party challenging the arbitrability refuses to participate in a hearing on the merits, while the other party insists on the arbitrator going forward, even if the other party leaves the proceedings. Although the threat of an ex parte hearing might induce the threatening party to remain under protest, most arbitrators, given the prospect of conducting an ex parte hearing under these circumstances, would grant the request for a ruling solely on the arbitrability issue and arrange for a second hearing on the merits if the case is to be held arbitrable.

Combining Procedural and Substantive Issues
before a Single Arbitrator

In some cases, the arbitrability challenge is quite distinct from the issue sought to be arbitrated on the merits. Such a challenge might be whether three separate grievances slated for arbitration should be heard by a single arbitrator or three different arbitrators. But in most cases, the facts that give rise to the merits are interrelated to the facts that give rise to the challenge to arbitrability. For example, in the case in which a probationary employee grieved a denial of overtime pay, the issue of the right of a probationary employee to file a grievance on such a claim necessitated testimony on both the procedural issue of her entitlement to file a grievance and the merits of whether she was entitled to the overtime. A case in which the union claimed that the settlement of the grievance barred the disputed termination that followed would present a similar combination of issues.

Because of the overlapping testimony on procedural and substantive issues, most parties prefer to present both issues at the same hearing and to authorize the arbitrator to deal first with the procedural issue and, if the case is found to be arbitrable, to proceed to the merits. Such combining of procedural and substantive presentations is a practical way of gaining information on both issues and is economical in avoiding the need for second day of hearing if the arbitrator finds that the case is arbitrable. When the parties are unwilling to combine the two processes, it may be necessary for the arbitrator to hear the case and render a decision on arbitrability before the parties proceed to a second day of hearing. In other situations, one of the parties may be reluctant to commit to having the arbitrator hear both issues and would permit the arbitrator to hear only the threshold procedural question. After learning of the arbitrator's decision, the parties can then decide whether to proceed with this or some other arbitrator on the merits. Such bifurcation of procedural and substantive issues may result not only in repetitive presentation of evidence but in additional costs for the extra day of hearing. In addition, there will be further delay if the parties do not plan their second day of hearing until after their receipt of the arbitrator's award on the issue of arbitrability.

Arbitrators are sometimes faced with an insistence by one party that issues concerning both procedure and merits be heard at the same hearing, even if presented sequentially. Although that format may be acceptable to both parties, the desire of one party to bifurcate the proceedings may elicit a formal request to the arbitrator for a ruling. Arbitrators have been known to order the parties to be prepared to proceed to the merits after arguing the arbitrability issue. Indeed, in some cases arbitrators have even insisted on proceeding ex parte against the wishes of the party that left the hearing room after requesting the bifurcated proceedings. But most arbitrators will respect the wishes of the party requesting bifurcation and, despite the extra cost and time entailed, will undertake to hear and rule on the arbitrability issue before hearing the merits of the dispute, or perhaps even before scheduling the second hearing. One would expect the parties to turn to arbitration to resolve the basic substantive issue that is disrupting their otherwise smooth relationship. But just as they and the arbitrator are bound by the substantive terms of their collective bargaining agreement, they are also bound to adhere to the procedural rules set forth as the precondition for any ruling on the merits. Only when such procedural issues are fully and fairly aired and decided can credibility be attached to the substantive rulings of the arbitrator.

Conclusion

Arbitration is proclaimed as the fastest, cheapest, and fairest method of resolving disputes between the parties. It could be argued that protests over arbitrability mock that standard by imposing legalistic objections to hearing cases on their merits. But for arbitration to fulfill its goal of bringing finality to a dispute, the legal authority of the arbitrator to issue a binding award should be clear. Challenges to substantive arbitrability are therefore crucial to ensure the competence of the process.

The same legal authority could be analogized for procedural challenges to arbitrability. The parties' collective bargaining agreement is the legal document that creates the arbitrators' authority. The arbitrator is as much bound by the substantive provisions as by the procedural requirements for bringing the case to arbitration. If arbitration is to maintain credibility as the means for assuring contract compliance, it is important that procedural issues over access to the process be resolved in a manner that gives full support to the parties' agreement and practices. Once the arbitrability issues are heard, it is time to proceed to the hearing on the case itself.

5
The Hearing

The format of the hearing is designed to provide the arbitrator with the most accurate recitation of the facts of the case and with the arguments of the spokespersons as to why their side, rather than the opposition, should prevail.

The hearing commences with each party giving an overview of its side of the case in the opening statement. Following this step, the issue should be "joined." The spokesperson for each side will give its view of the facts together with an assurance that its recitation will be more persuasive than that proffered by spokespersons for the other side. The opening statement is not proof; rather it is an assertion of what that side claims will be proven.

Once the hearing proceeds to the evidentiary phase, the filtering process commences. Each side's witnesses testify in response to direct questions, which are calculated to elicit the facts in a manner that buttresses that side's view of the dispute and its interpretation of the contract. But a single witness's recital of alleged events in response to a sympathetic questioner does not constitute proof. Rather, testimony that remains unshaken, despite cross-examination and efforts at contradiction by other witnesses, comes the closest to truth according to our adversarial legal system. Truth, as noted below, is often difficult to establish, in part because of spokespersons' skill in sowing doubt about the veracity of a witness's recital. Thus, although it may be impossible to determine what is true in a particular recitation of facts, the adversarial procedure requires only that the neutral be more persuaded by one side's version of the facts than the other side's or, at least, that the neutral be convinced that there was greater probability that one side's version of events occurred than the other side's.

The strategy for meeting that requirement to persuade guides the choice of witnesses, the order of their selection, their questioning, and the evidence that is introduced to bolster their claim. It also guides any objections to permitting those witnesses to testify, to the introduction of certain evidence, and to the questions that are asked (or omitted) during cross-examination or rebuttal.

Once the spokespersons have had full opportunity to question and cross-examine witnesses and to introduce exhibits they deem relevant, the next step is for the spokespersons to summarize their positions in the closing statements. In these statements, they point out how their original positions, as articulated in the opening statement, have withstood the efforts of the other side to undercut them and why, having survived the evidentiary onslaught, their view of the contract should prevail.

This chapter explores many of the tactics that are utilized by the parties to make their case during the hearing.

Opening Statement

By the time the case has reached the arbitration hearing, the parties should be aware of their respective positions on the dispute. Their mutual inability to convince the other side to alter its position has brought the case to this stage. But the arbitrator hasn't shared that history and—except for some information that may have been gained while jousting over the framing of the issue—probably doesn't know why the parties need an arbitrator.

The opening statement is designed to give each spokesperson the opportunity to present a concise forecast of the evidence that side intends to produce, together with an explanation of the controlling contract provisions which it expects will lead the arbitrator to issue a ruling in its favor. The opening statement is a roadmap of what each party intends to prove.

But beyond that theoretical framework, the opening statement alerts the other side about what is to be emphasized and what must be responded to. If the first opening statement is responded to at the start of the hearing by a comparable statement by the other side, the two statements should reveal where the parties agree and narrow the area of focus and testimony to those aspects of the case in which they conflict. If the parties have used the grievance procedure efficiently, the lines should have been well drawn before the arbitration step, but the opening statements may disclose emphasis on additional or different contract provisions, reliance on different or even surprise evidence, or the development of a totally new theory of the case. A party's desire to draw the arbitrator to its view of the dispute may be offset by a reluctance to reveal its case to the other side. As a result, opening statements by the moving party may be very short.

It is not uncommon for the responding party to defer its opening statement until after the moving party has called all its witnesses and completed its presentation of its case (except for possible rebuttal). This failure to provide an opening statement containing some forecast of the forthcoming testimony and documentation deprives the arbitrator of an overview of the case and of an opportunity to focus on the areas of conflict that will ultimately need resolution. That problem is even greater when the responding party makes no opening statement, but it is not common in contract interpretation cases, in which the employer, as the responding party, is usually eager to get its position on the table. This strategy is more common in discipline cases, in which the union, as responding party, will wait to determine whether the employer is able to present a prima facie case. The arbitrator is then unable to determine what is agreed, what is merely accepted or acquiesced, and what is objected to in the other side's presentation.

Moreover, the absence of a responding opening statement makes it impossible for the arbitrator to rule intelligently on objections over relevancy if kept in the dark about the claims and theories of both parties' cases.

On the other hand, an excessively detailed opening statement may reveal facts that could be more dramatically or effectively handled by direct testimony—or even more so by cross-examination. Sometimes spokespersons who deliver a detailed opening statement forget that the recitation does not constitute proof: it is merely an assertion of what that party proposes to prove. To the extent that the other side's statement repeats or agrees with the assertions, the need for proof is alleviated. But the other side will also point out the areas in which it disagrees with the opposition's opening statement, thereby focusing the hearing on those disputed matters, for which each party will undertake to prove its contentions. It is a cardinal rule that the opening statement must not be interrupted by the other side. If there is any objection to the content, the other side may respond by noting such objections and their basis in its own opening statement.

It is not common to have rebuttals following the opening statements, but if one of the spokespersons were to begin with an offer to the arbitrator to further narrow the issue by agreeing with some of the assertions made by its adversary, this move might elicit a comparable response on some other aspects of the case from the other side and, thus, narrow the conflict.

If the parties have properly utilized the grievance procedure to fully explore all facets of the case, the opening statements are unlikely to provide any surprises. But if the grievance has been prematurely pushed to arbitration, or if the spokespersons are new to the case and hadn't jointly discussed it, the opening statements' full revelations of each parties' assertions might encourage the spokespersons to step outside the hearing to discuss either a stipulation or agreement about the undisputed facts of the case or, even better, to the entire dispute.

Who Goes First?

The opening statement is to introduce the case to the arbitrator. It matters little to the arbitrator which party makes the initial opening statement and proceeds first with its witnesses because the objective is merely for each party to introduce its position. After the opening statement there should be ample opportunity for response and for the examination and cross-examination of witnesses. If the parties dispute which party should go first, the arbitrator will usually fall back on the theory that the burden of going forward falls on the party that instituted a change in the parties' standing relationship. Therefore, in contract interpretation cases the union usually goes first; in disciplinary cases, it is usually the employer. Occasionally, as in the case of a demotion, it is difficult to determine whether or not a grievance involves discipline. The union might assert that the demotion was disciplinary and that the employer must therefore establish just cause. The employer, on the other hand, may argue that the demotion was taken for normal business reasons and had no disciplinary overtones to it. The arbitrator would then have to determine, on the basis of introductory arguments by the spokespersons, which side should go first. In the event of a stalemate or prolonged silence, the arbitrator may ask the employer to go first because it has greater command of the facts of the case.

When one side makes the first opening statement, it may gain a momentary advantage by having an opportunity for an uninterrupted recitation of its assertions and argument. But that advantage is immediately dissipated by the other side's comparable effort. At the end of that exchange, the arbitrator should be able to focus on the specific areas of conflict. When one side goes forward with direct testimony of its witnesses, the same momentary advantage again arises and, again, is defused by the other side's opportunity for cross-examination.

The burden of going forward should not be confused with the burden of proof. The burden of proof concerns not the order of the proceedings, but rather the ultimate disposition of the case: Did the party prove its case? Who won and who lost? That burden, generally ascribed to the employer in cases of discipline and discharge and to the union in cases of contract interpretation, may shift far more often. As one side makes an assertion, claim, or statement, it becomes incumbent on the other side to rebut or refute that statement. Failure to do so may lead the arbitrator to conclude that the assertion is proven or, at least, agreed to. And the arbitrator relies upon such conclusions in determining the outcome of the case. Thus, it is important for the spokesperson who disagrees with the content of the other side's opening statement to respond by stating that an opposite position will be proven or, at least, by reminding the arbitrator (and giving notice to the other spokesperson) that an assertion in an opening statement is merely that. Such assertions are not accepted as evidence or as proof and must be proven through witnesses and by documentation.

Admitting Weaknesses

Honesty is important in opening statements. The other party may challenge an assertion by stating its intent to prove the opposite or by reminding the other party and arbitrator that an assertion is not proof. Even if the second party in its opening, fails to challenge a statement in the first opening statement, the arbitrator will not necessarily accept that statement alone as a fact or as proven. The arbitrator may be skeptical of the assertion or may ultimately conclude that it is inconsistent with testimony and proven facts. Thus, it is risky to include matters that can't be proven in opening statements.

An opening statement that recognizes that unsupported assertions can be contradicted by testimony from the other side is far more effective. The other side may be disarmed by an opening statement that admits weaknesses that the other side intended to emphasize. The arbitrator, too, may be more sympathetic to an opening statement that admits such weaknesses and focuses on what the admitting party believes most important.

Suppose a spokesperson for a grievant accused of punching his supervisor stonewalls in the opening statement, in which the grievant is portrayed as a nonviolent, saintly victim of an angry and hostile supervisor. Such an image can be readily eradicated by the testimony of that supervisor and others describing the grievant's frequent threats, shovings of supervisors, and challenges to settle disputes in the parking lot. This rebuttal testimony could be effectively deflated by an opening statement in which the provocative behavior is admitted, but characterized as playfulness, as tolerated behavior, or even as the basis for the supervisor's vengeful behavior in the case in arbitration. In this area of human endeavor (as in others) it is important not to promise more than can be delivered.

If this latter approach is taken, when the employer seeks to introduce evidence of the grievant's provocative actions, the union spokesperson would be in a position to agree that the incidents did occur and then to propose that the arbitration focus on the particular incident. This strategy deflects the impact that testimony of previous wrongdoings might have had on the arbitrator.

The Role of Argument

The opening statement should focus on the facts that the party intends to prove, including the forecast that they will lead to a favorable conclusion under the terms of the parties' agreement. While it is, of course, acceptable to spell out in its presentation of the facts, the detailed contractual argument that the party expects the arbitrator to adopt, such a recitation as part of the opening statement is premature. It may flood the arbitrator with too much material too early, without the filter of either direct testimony or cross-examination. It may also raise false expectations that may be deflated by unanticipated contradictory testimony or documentation presented by the other side.

Thus, a detailed, complex examination of the facts and parties' argument is better deferred to the closing statements, when the arbitrator has heard the conflicting testimony and has drawn tentative conclusions from the evidence that had been presented. At that point, the spokesperson can more effectively focus the arbitrator's attention on the testimony and proven facts and can present arguments as to why a certain conclusion must be reached based upon the evidence.

Evidence on the Requested Remedy

The union, in its opening statement in a disciplinary or discharge case, will usually conclude with a request that the grievant be reinstated with full backpay or be made whole for lost earnings and benefits. It is not unusual for the union spokesperson to detail what it seeks as restitution for the alleged wrong, whether in discipline or contract interpretation cases. But it is unusual for the employer to respond with any discussion of possible remedy because it fears that its statement would be interpreted by the arbitrator as a sign of weakness in its position or as a signal that it might entertain some alternative to the action that precipitated the pending grievance.

By the recitation of its proposed remedy, the union, at the least, places that issue on the table and alerts the employer to its obligation to present alternative testimony or else risk the arbitrator's acceptance, in the absence of any response to the issue, of the union's claim for remedy.

If the union does not volunteer its position on remedy during the opening statement, the arbitrator may ask the union what remedy it seeks. That request is usually enough to put the issue of remedy on the table and to alert the employer to the need to respond if it wishes to prevent the arbitrator from embracing the union's assertions on remedy. However, employers are generally loath to discuss any remedy. They posture that their position will prevail and that, therefore, no remedy will be needed, because there was no wrong. Employers tend to feel that, if they discuss the issue of remedy, they are suggesting that they are less than completely positive that their case will prevail. But unless the employer has presented some evidence of its view of an appropriate remedy, if any, if the union prevails in whole or in part the arbitrator has no guide except for the union's position to what recompense is fair or reasonable. However, arbitrators are unlikely to ask the employer for its position on remedy because the question would suggest that the arbitrator intends to grant the union's claim in whole or part. The arbitrator may merely desire the employer's view on remedy in case the union prevails in whole or part, so that such a request of the employer does not mean the arbitrator has prejudged the issue or reached a conclusion on the basis of opening statements. Such a question is usually the arbitrator's way of alerting the parties to the fact that they may need to present evidence on the issue of what the grievant has done during the period since termination or on how a contractual violation by an employer should be remedied. But, in general, because employers read such questions as evidence that the arbitrators have prejudged the issue in favor of the union, arbitrators are usually reluctant to ask the employer of its position on the remedy issue.

Witnesses

Perhaps the most important part of the adversarial process, and the one that distinguishes arbitration from mediation, is the testing of the statements of individuals who allegedly witnessed events about their participation in the events in dispute.

Those statements may not always be accurate recitations of what transpired. There may be failures of observation or perception. The witness may be sure that she observed the incident, but contradictory evidence may show that from her workstation, where she testified she was standing, her observation could have been obstructed by a building column, a pile of cartons, or a burned-out light bulb. Similarly, she may have thought she heard what was said, although machine noise might convince the arbitrator that she couldn't have heard it with the clarity she alleged. Such errors or failures of observation or hearings are not infrequent and are not deliberate falsifications of testimony. The witness may really believe that she observed the action, but her conviction may have been based on oral input from others, on having heard the relevant sounds, and on subconsciously filling in details she had missed between the events she had unquestionably seen or heard before and after.

The testimony of witnesses may also be affected by weaknesses in their memory of what they heard, saw, or felt. They may not accurately recall the event. We all suffer from weaknesses of memory. We can recall distinctly what we had for breakfast today and what we wore yesterday. But what about breakfast yesterday, or the day before? Can one really expect to totally recall events that occurred some six months ago, especially when it seemed that no one else expected an account of these events. Some people do have the exceptional ability to recall details over long periods of time. Others may recall incidents that were out of the ordinary, that were called to their attention as important, or that they felt were important to remember at the time. But most people forget lots of things. Details may only be recalled when one is reminded or when they are triggered by the memory of some other detail. For this reason it is important in case presentation to secure written statements of their observations from witnesses as soon as possible after the incident. Then, months later, when the witness is trying to reconstruct the sequence of the event, a rereading of the earlier notes will likely stimulate recollection of what transpired, including peripheral matters that might not have been part of that written recitation.

Testing the recollection of witnesses through cross-examination is crucial to verifying that they actually experienced or perceived the events they recall. It is not unusual for a witness to testify with real conviction to remembering a certain sequence of events. But on cross-examination it may be revealed, at times to the genuine embarrassment of honest witnesses, that what they believed they saw, heard, or felt was told to them later, or was the result of imagining that, because they saw A and C, they therefore "logically" had to have seen B. Their sincere motive of trying to relate the whole truth may have led them to believe B when, as demonstrated in cross-examination, they hadn't seen B.

The third failing of testimony may occur in the recitation. Even when the witness's observation is unquestionable and the recollection unchallengable, there may not be a perfect recitation at the hearing. Different witnesses react differently when called to the witness stand. Those with experience in the process and an overview of where their testimony fits in the presentation are more likely to serve as good or credible witnesses. On the other hand, those who are new to the process, unfamiliar with the role of their testimony, or nervous at being the focus of everyone's attention may bungle their testimony. Anyone might be so affected. Speaking hesitantly, misunderstanding the questions, missing cues, or misspeaking are often signs of pressure or discomfort. These behaviors should not be misinterpreted as signs of lying or of lack of credibility. Demeanor evidence can be most misleading.[12]

It is important for the spokesperson to put the witness at ease, particularly if the person is inexperienced or nervous, so that he or she can provide the most persuasive testimony. Preparation for that testimony, including some of the questions to be asked and those that might be asked in cross-examination, helps the witness gain a level of comfort concerning the role. If the spokesperson has had prior experience with the arbitrator hearing the case, it is helpful to alert the witness to the role the arbitrator will play, particularly if the designated arbitrator is activist or interventionist. A role play of the whole proceeding, if there is an opportunity, is even more helpful. But, practice in the company of friends and supporters can't be preparation for the sheer terror that some people feel when called to the stand, administered the oath, and suddenly aware that all eyes—particularly those of the opposing counsel and the arbitrator—are focused on them. To reduce the panic, it is common to begin by asking the witness simple and unthreatening questions: name, length of service, current work, positions previously held, and history of involvement with the present dispute. The arbitrator may help set the witness at ease by a word of thanks for the testimony, but out of concern that there may be a perception of treating witnesses differently, the arbitrator usually leaves it to the spokesperson to set the witness at ease. Once the witness gains some self-confidence through questions with easy answers, it is time to plunge into the more controversial subjects of the grievance. Questions to the witness should be brief, simply stated, and clear. They should be asked one at a time and should not be negatively worded or argumentative.

Direct Examination

The questions asked of witnesses indirect examination are intended to elicit the statements about what they observed, saw, or felt. In some cases, particularly when the witness is articulate, strongly conversant with the case, and comfortable in the role, the spokesperson might simply initiate the recitation by a question such as "tell us about your involvement in this case." It is prudent to make sure, before inviting such a free description, that the witness is not too garrulous, too prone to dwell on trivia, or too likely to meander into areas not germane to the grievance. Such wanderings may be curtailed by interrupting the witness's recitation, but to do so may negatively suggest that the witness has been stopped before entering into less secure or more troublesome areas. Such a witness is generally an asset rather than a liability, however, if only because the ability to relate a story in a clear, flowing manner tends to heighten its credibility.

At the other extreme is the introduction of a witness's testimony by a series of questions eliciting short but, ideally, accurate responses. It is proper to ask what the witness saw, felt, and heard. Beyond those limits, the questions may prompt objections if the witness is asked for opinions that are properly the domain of expert witnesses who are qualified and recognized by the parties as such or is asked to draw conclusions from the evidence that are more properly the domain of the arbitrator. The questions may assume and include factual matters that are not in dispute, but about the disputed matter it is crucial that the witness express his or her own observations and not merely confirm or deny the facts contained in the questions asked. Such a usurpation of the answer by a question that assumes an answer and relegates the witnesses' testimony to yes or no, constitutes a leading question. While such a question is permissible on cross-examination to cause the witness to give a false or contradictory statement, it is improper in direct testimony, where the testimony of the witness, not that of the questioner, is sought.

Thus, if the testimony is undisputed that the witness punched in at 8:00 A.M., and the issue is whether or not the witness observed the grievant's time card being punched at 8:08 A.M., the following questions would be permissible:

Q. After you punched in at 8:00 A.M., did you see the grievant?
A. Yes.
Q. Tell us what you saw.

If the time of the incident was in question, or if there was a question of whether the grievant was in the area, then the following questions would be appropriate:

Q. What time did you punch in?
A. 8:00 A.M.

Q. Did you see anyone in the area?
A. Yes.
Q. Whom did you see?
A. A, B, C, and the grievant

The questioner must be careful not to assume a fact that is not in evidence. Thus, in the foregoing exchange, if the questioner went from the first question, "What time did you punch in?" directly to "Whom did you see?", that second question would assume a fact not in evidence: that there was someone else in the area.

Constructing the foregoing exchange into a leading question, might yield something like: "At 8:08 A.M., after you had punched in at 8:00 A.M., did you see the grievant standing next to the time clock?" Obviously, the leading question doesn't elicit much, if any, independent testimony from the witness; it is merely a confirmation of the assertion by the spokesperson. Since it is inappropriate to place the spokesperson on the witness stand for cross-examination—particularly since the spokesperson didn't observe the incident—it is important that questions be framed so that the witness provides the testimony during cross-examination, rather than the spokesperson.

In those rare instances in which the spokesperson was a witness to the events, it would be proper to let the spokesperson testify in narrative form or, if the other side objects to this course, to have a team member serve as substitute counsel.

The First Witness. After having made its opening statement, it is important for the moving party to determine who can explain the relevant background and provide the most credible and comprehensible chronology of the events leading to the arbitration and to then call that person as the moving party's first witness. As the first witness it is preferable to have someone who is able to bring the case into focus on the matters in dispute. A chronological approach is most important to help the arbitrator understand the matters in contention.

In disciplinary cases, in which the employer calls the first witness, the testimony may begin with a recitation of how the alleged wrongdoing came to the employer's attention. For example, if the case involves employee theft that was reported by an undercover investigator, the personnel director may seek to introduce that investigative report into the evidence. Although such evidence is clearly admissible as the document that triggered the employer's disciplinary action, the report itself does not constitute proof of the theft.

The union, in such a situation, might properly object to the introduction of the exhibit as hearsay, because the person to whom the report was submitted and who testified about receiving it cannot be cross-examined as to the truth of its content. The union might stipulate that a report was prepared and submitted to the personnel director and used as the basis for the disciplinary action. This step would eliminate the need to introduce the report as the triggering incident that led to the grievant's termination. Such a stipulation should also resolve any questions that the employer arbitrarily singled out the grievant for its disciplinary action and may help the union avoid having the document admitted into evidence, at least by a witness other than the person who wrote the report.

And even the writer could only testify to what he personally saw, heard, or felt. If the writer of the report had not directly observed the incidents, he could only be questioned on what the spotters had reported to him. The writer could not establish whether the spotter reported the truth. Only cross-examination of the spotter as a witness could achieve that goal.

If the employer presses to admit the report at that stage, despite the objection concerning hearsay and the offer to stipulate that the discipline was not precipitated by animus or arbitrariness, the arbitrator may accept it into evidence in order to temporarily avoid the issue of how much weight, if any, should be given to the hearsay in the report. This acceptance may be under the rubric "for what it may be worth." When that statement is used, either party is fully within its rights, although perhaps somewhat at its jeopardy, to ask the arbitrator to estimate the worth of the report, if any. This right is granted because admission of the report may shift the burden to the union, which must endeavor to rebut a written accusatory document whose author may not be called to testify or be subject to cross-examination.

The Grievant as the First Witness. Each party should be free to select as its witnesses those individuals whose testimony would be most likely to help prove its case. There is also a value to having as initial witnesses those who can shed the greatest light on the facts that have led to the dispute. Thus, in a contract interpretation case, it is not unusual for a union to call a representative of management as its initial witness to provide an overall view of the operation in dispute, to describe the equipment that gave rise to the controversy, or to set up the sequence of events that led to the grievance.

Similarly, for cases of discipline or discharge, where the employer has the burden of going forward, the employer should call as its initial witness the individual with the greatest knowledge of the facts that gave rise to the imposition of the discipline. In most cases, the employer will seek to make its prima facie case on the basis of testimony from supervisors who were familiar with the dispute that resulted in the discipline. Usually, employers decline to call employees as witnesses to protect them from the rancor of other employees who might resent their action on behalf of the employer. In some cases, however, the employer seeks to call the grievant as its initial witness by claiming that it has the burden of proof and that it should have the right to call any witness it believes will help it meet that burden. If the union has no objection to the grievant being called as first employer witness, no problem arises. The difficulty comes when the union objects to that call. The arguments against the calling of the grievant as the first witness usually include five lines of reasoning.

First, the employer has the burden of making a prima facie case against the grievant based upon evidence to which supervisory personnel could testify. The union would argue that the employer's burden of proof requires it to make an independent showing that it had grounds for imposing the discipline—the employer should not need the testimony of the victim of its action to establish its case.

The second argument often raised by unions is that the employer has that burden of proving its case, regardless of whether the grievant opts to attend the hearing. Thus, if the grievant were absent, the employer would still have to show that its disciplinary action was taken for just cause. That burden, unions argue, should not in any way be altered by the presence or absence of the employee.

The third argument often raised is that calling the grievant as the employer's witness would violate the employer's longstanding practice of not calling bargaining unit members as employer witnesses because of the adverse effect it would have on the employer–employee relationships on the shop floor.

The fourth argument is that the union reserves the option of determining whether or not the grievant will testify, as it reserves the option of determining whether any grievant would testify at a contract interpretation case. The union might feel the grievant would make a poor witness, would not appear credible, or would be easily confused. Accordingly, the employer should not have the right to force the union to have the grievant testify if the union prefers not to have such testimony.

And finally, the union would argue that if the employer calls the grievant as its witness, the employer would be bound to the answers that the employee provides, which might be contrary to the employer's best interest in seeking to prove the grievant culpable of some impropriety. If the employer's inclination is to declare the grievant as a hostile witness, the union would respond that the grievant is entitled to an initial inquiry by more supportive direct testimony. The employer will still have the full opportunity to question the grievant afterward, through the normal channels of cross-examination.

The employer's response to the union's argument would focus first on the right of either party to call as witness any participant that it deems appropriate to proving its case.

Second, the employer might maintain that the grievant is the person with the greatest familiarity with the incident and should, therefore, be the individual to initiate the testimony that provides the background from which other testimony would evolve.

Third, the employer could argue that the presence of the grievant at the hearing makes it reasonable for the employer to call the grievant as its first witness in case the grievant at some point might depart from the hearing and deprive the employer of that opportunity.

And fourth, the employer would argue that it has the right to call bargaining unit members as witnesses if it chooses to do so, but that it has refrained from doing so in prior cases because of the subsequent impact on the bargaining unit. In this case, however, the merit of the employer's argument ensures that the employee will be found unfit to return to duty and, thus, the testimony would not have any adverse impact on the future relationship of the parties.

In the event of such a dispute, the arbitrator must often determine whether the grievant is to testify as the first witness. Some arbitrators see no basis for such denial and will order the grievant to testify. Other arbitrators will deny the request and sustain the objection for any one or more of the reasons listed by the union.

The union can often defuse the problem by assuring the employer that the union will be calling the grievant as its witness, so that the employer will have the benefit of cross-examining the witness at the conclusion of the union's direct testimony. Arbitrators will frequently make that suggestion as a means to avoid having to rule on such an objection and will assure the employer that it will have the right to examine the grievant, even if it calls the grievant as a rebuttal witness. The employer is frequently assuaged by that assertion. If the union indicates that it has no intention of calling the grievant as a witness, then the arbitrator who would bar the initial call will usually grant the employer the right to call the grievant after the other witnesses have testified if it still needs that grievant's testimony.

Hearsay. Hearsay is second-hand evidence. Testimony like "I heard him say————" doesn't provide any chance to question him. It is important to recognize why the issue of hearsay is so critical in arbitration. Although arbitration is less legalistically encumbered than a court proceeding, it nonetheless incorporates the adversarial format of the right to examine witnesses for their testimony about a disputed event, and the even more crucial right to test that testimony on the crucible of cross-examination. That procedure is easy when the person called to the stand was an eyewitness to the event. Witness Rachel can be questioned about observations, sounds, light, distance, and so on. And on cross examination, she can be questioned on whether her early testimony was correct. How many people were present? Who was closest to the time clock? Had any threat or promise been tied to the testimony? Hadn't the witness told the grievant they'd find a way to fire her that very week?

If Rachel, however, testifies that she was told by Jon that he had seen the grievant punch someone else's time card, the questioning and cross-examination of Rachel could only cover the conversation between Jon and

Rachel; it could not test whether Jon was telling Rachel the truth about his observation. Thus, the introduction of the content of Jon's statement into the record, through the witness's recitation of what she had been told by Jon, places that report in the record for "the truth of the matter asserted" without any opportunity to challenge it through Rachel. And if Jon doesn't testify, that report might not be subject to any challenge at all.

If, however, Jon had been called to testify, his recitation of the same story would be admissible because he, the original storyteller, would be subject to not only direct examination but, more importantly, to cross-examination. Permitting Rachel to testify about the story she had heard from Jon would introduce that story into evidence and, if not challenged, would obviate any need for that party to call Jon or risk subjecting him to cross-examination that might have altered or discredited that otherwise unchallenged story. That result occurs if the other side fails to challenge the introduction of the hearsay testimony or if there is a challenge to its admission that the arbitrator improperly overrules, even if only "to take it for what it's worth." In either case, the hearsay testimony is in the record as evidence of the facts asserted. Its admission may shift the burden to the side denied the right of cross-examination, which must now prove that Jon's statement was inaccurate. What would have been a burden to prove positive in the first situation is now converted to a burden to prove negative.

The same problem would have existed if Jon had handed Rachel a written report. Rachel could testify and be cross-examined on the conversation with Jon, but the report would be hearsay if she sought to introduce it. If, however, Jon were called to the stand, as its author he could testify and be cross-examined about the report and its content.

In determining whether a statement or document made outside of the arbitration hearing is admissible, it must be determined if the statement or document is relevant for a use that does not depend upon its truth. If so—for example, as a spotter's report that there had been theft as the triggering event of an investigation—it would be admissible, but not for the truth of the spotter's assertions. If the statement or document is being used to prove its truth, is it exempted or an exclusion from the hearsay rule? If it is, then it would be admissible; if it is not, then it is hearsay and its admission is at the discretion of the arbitrator.

In some situations, documents are admissible when testified to by other than their author. For example, a time card, if authenticated, would be admissible as proof of the times listed without the testimony of the person who punched it. A routine personnel card listing date of hire, pay raises, job held, discipline imposed, home address, and so on would be admissible as an ordinary business record without need of the testimony of the people who made the various entries. So, too, for other records taken or kept in the ordinary course of business: attendance forms, absentee call-in sheets, logs of shipping orders, and so on. These routine business records are generally considered an exception to the hearsay rule provided they (1) are in writing, (2) are recorded or entered contemporaneously to the event cited, (3) are authenticated as genuine, and (4) are taken in the regular course of business.

Other exceptions to the hearsay rule will permit the introduction of material that, on its face, would constitute hearsay. Whether or not such hearsay will be admitted at a hearing is, of course, at the discretion of the arbitrator, because the formal rules of evidence do not apply in arbitration hearings. Among these exceptions are records of admissions made by the witness, records of the witness's present or former mental or physical state, official written statements of public officials, witnesses' prior testimony in a former hearing or deposition, and prior statements that are inconsistent with the witnesses' current testimony. Prior consistent statements may even be admissible to rebut a charge of recent fabrication of testimony.

Failure to object to hearsay may fatally affect either side's efforts to win its case. But that risk is inherent in the adversarial relationship. It is crucial to the preservation of that system to ensure that only credible evidence that has withstood the test of cross-examination is admitted. That standard may mean an occasional miscarriage of justice if the party is unable to establish that kind of evidence by other witnesses. But that price is minimal compared to the injustice that could result if the parties were able to convict an innocent employee by flooding a record with unsubstantiated, unchallengeable, or, perhaps, totally fraudulent statements or documents that overturn the traditional safeguards and shift the burden of proof from the parties to the victims of such hearsay admissions.

Grievant's Prior Record. In discipline cases, direct examination of the personnel director, the foreman, or even the grievant may be used to seek to introduce the grievant's prior employment record into evidence. If that record is quite favorable, the union would probably seek its introduction; if less than favorable, the employer would probably attempt its introduction. The introduction of such a record might be objected to on several grounds.

First, although the formal record is, strictly speaking, hearsay, that objection would be overcome by the fact that the employer's personnel record for the employee would be a record kept in the normal course of business and, thus, constitute an exception to the hearsay rule. Second, the introduction of the record might be objected to on grounds of relevance.

CASE STUDY: The Case of the Capital Offense. The grievant, Jonathan Walsh, was terminated pursuant to the following notice:

Mr. Walsh:

Effective immediately, your employment is terminated because of your theft of company property.

At the arbitration hearing, the company sought to introduce the grievant's personnel record. The union objected on the grounds that the employment record was irrelevant.

The union argued that the basis for termination was a single offense of theft. It acknowledged that proof of theft constituted grounds for termination on first offense, but maintained that the employer could not, after the fact, add to the grounds for removal or tilt the record against the grievant by an ex post facto reliance on a record that was not invoked at the time of termination. At that time, the union continued, only one reason was cited for termination: that particular theft. Thus, the union argued, the employer's case must rise or fall on proving that theft. It urged the arbitrator exclude the personnel record.

The employer argued that it was standard procedure to introduce the grievant's prior record at arbitration hearings, that the union's objection to its introduction arose from its fear that the grievant's unsavory record would undermine its position, and that admission of the record was essential to show that the employee's performance was marginal, thus making it reasonable for the employer to terminate him for theft. Additionally, the employer argued that the introduction of the record would be important in determining the remedy if the arbitrator should order the grievant's return to work.

The arbitrator reasoned that the personnel record, while hearsay, was a document prepared in the normal course of business and, thus, could be admissible as an exception to the hearsay rule. However, the arbitrator excluded the offered exhibit on the grounds that the employer had imposed one charge: theft. If that charge were proven, then, pursuant to the union's acknowledgment that proof of theft justified termination on first offense, the grievance would be denied and the termination penalty endorsed. If, on the other hand, the employer did not meet its burden of proving there had been theft in the incident, there would be no grounds for any discipline, let alone termination, because no other charge had been filed against the grievant. Accordingly, the arbitrator continued, there was no justification of a discipline of less than termination and, accordingly, the prior record would have no relevance.

Discussion Question 1: What if the termination letter had been worded differently?

Assume the letter had read:

Mr. Walsh:

After the evidence of your theft, the employer finds that in the light of your prior record, a termination penalty is ordered.

By wording the termination record to embrace the employee's prior record, the employer still might not have been able to enter the prior record into evidence. The record would not be admissible to prove the theft or to show any propensity to theft based on prior discipline for wrongdoing. Proof of that theft would depend on the employer's ability to convince the arbitrator that it had occurred as charged. Even if Walsh had been previously charged with theft, that record would not be admissible to prove theft in this case. Furthermore, if the parties had stipulated, as in this case, that theft was grounds for termination on first offense, the employer's case would rise or fall only on the basis of proving that theft. If Walsh were found to have stolen, he would be removed; if the theft were not proven, he would be reinstated with full black pay, because the precipitating incident that triggered the discipline could not be proved. Therefore, the prior record that might have been used to alter that discipline would not come into play.

The prior record might be introduced and admitted into evidence early in the hearing as an essential element of the charges against Walsh. However, in a theft case, unlike others, in which termination is not imposed on first offense, the record might not be relied upon by the arbitrator.

Discussion Question 2: What if the union had not stipulated that proof of theft justified termination on first offense?

If the union had not agreed that the termination penalty was appropriate for theft, the prior record might have had considerable bearing, whether or not the personnel record had been cited in the letter of termination.

One could readily assume that theft, as that term is commonly understood, justifies termination on first offense. The employer need not tolerate thieves in the workplace. New hires should properly assume that proof of theft is grounds for termination, if not criminal proceedings, whether or not termination is prescribed in the company rules. In addition, no union wants to devote its resources to defending thieves, whose actions undermine the profitability of the enterprise on which the employees depend for survival. Arbitrators, too, do not condone theft and would not want to unleash the flood of grievances that would result from the reinstatement of a proven thief. Doing so would create a precedent of allowing one proven theft per employee before imposition of the termination penalty.

But occasionally the employer may have, in some measure, condoned a type of theft and reduced its penalty from automatic termination to penalties subject to progressive discipline. In those situations, the prior employment record, whether or not cited in the termination letter, would be admissible. Such reasoning might apply in cases in which the grievant took home a peanut butter sandwich from a peanut butter factory where employees were allowed to consume the product without discipline within the plant; or in which the grievant took home scrap moulding from a carpenter shop where the employer had acquiesced to employees taking home unwanted scrap materials. A lesser penalty might even be imposed if the grievant's locker was found to contain a jar of unopened peanut butter in a peanut butter factory, if the employer had only terminated employees who took the product off the premises.

Discussion Question 3: Would the prior record be admissible to establish the grievant's date of employment?

Information on date of employment, which is routinely introduced into evidence in most disciplinary cases, might be relevant in the theft case if there were a question of the grievant's entitlement to retire, for example. But if either side intends that simple datum to introduce the prior record for other less relevant purposes, the introduction can be avoided by offering to stipulate on the date of employment as set forth in that employment record, without putting the entire record into evidence.

But it must be borne in mind, notwithstanding the foregoing examples, that in cases in which termination has been imposed for an infraction that is not stipulated as justifying termination on first offense, the employment record displays the grievant's prior work and discipline history. This record would probably be admissible for the purposes of assessing, on the one hand, the appropriate penalty in the light of the collective bargaining agreement's goals of constructive progressive rehabilitation or, on the other hand, whether the grievant's offense is but another example of incorrigibility that has, perhaps, escalated to justification for termination.

Parol Evidence Rule. When a document is introduced into evidence, it is not unusual for the sponsoring party to consider its language as dispositive of the issue in dispute. That stance is as true of language from the collective bargaining agreement as it is of the language of ancillary letters of understanding or even of an unchallenged note or notice. If the opposing spokesperson accepts that document as clear on its face, there is no need to go behind those words to ascertain the intent of the draftsman. In such cases, the legal standard of res ipsa loquitor—the thing speaks for itself—is accepted as controlling.

Under the traditional standards of contract interpretation, no evidence may be admitted to vary or contradict the terms that the parties memorialized in writing as their agreement. Through the negotiating process, the parties are assumed to have wrestled with different words and concepts before writing the terms that they intend to be bound by. Those words are thus to be respected as the embodiment of their intent, and they should prevail over any alleged oral agreement that seeks to vary or alter that written agreement.

But many disputes are entirely based upon differing interpretations of the same words. In such situations, the witness may be questioned about the circumstances in which the document was drafted. Among the questions asked might be: Who participated? What changes were proposed? Were there were earlier drafts? What did participants say about the intent or meaning of the proposed words? The sponsoring spokesperson would most likely invoke the theory of res ipsa loquitor and argue that the language is clear in its wording and that it reflects the parties' agreement. The spokesperson may acknowledge that negotiations over the language took place but note that when the parties considered other proposals or alternative language and reflected on it, those ancillary concerns were all taken into account and the parties then agreed upon the written terms and signed them. The time for adjusting those agreed-upon words, the theory goes, was during negotiations. If one of the parties' intent differed from the clear statement in the words, it was incumbent on that party to press for the adjustment prior to the conclusion of the negotiations; having failed to assert itself, that party must be viewed as bound by the language that evolved from that negotiation. In theory, one cannot use oral testimony to vary from the written agreement.

But if the party challenging the clarity of the language can show that the written terms could be subject to more than one interpretation, then the arbitrator would be likely to permit testimony that might alter or refine the arbitrator's conclusions about the meaning of the document language.

One common example of such parol, or oral, evidence used to interpret or amplify the written language is in the use of the term *day* in calculating a five-day period for filing a grievance. Does day mean calendar days? If so, wouldn't that interpretation discriminate against an employee on vacation at the time or having scheduled holidays during that appeal period? Or does day refer to work days? If so, wouldn't it discriminate against employees whose triggering event occurred on a Monday, thereby depriving them of the weekend to think about it, compared to an employee who learned of a disciplinary penalty on a Tuesday? What about those whose triggering event occurred the day before their vacation? Or, when if days means work days, should it be interpreted as the enterprise's work days, normal work days, the employee's personal schedule of working days? And what if some employees, or the grievant, are scheduled for overtime work on their regular days off or on a holiday? Are those work days?

If the contract language can be shown to be subject to more than one interpretation, it becomes important to determine the parties' intent in agreeing to that language. The procedure for that determination is through testimony and documentation about what the drafters of the disputed language had in mind when agreeing simply to the word "days."

An inquiry into what transpired in negotiations may bring some witnesses to testify that they assumed, meant, preferred, or demanded work days, while others may testify equally strongly that they fought for calendar days. After weighing the testimony, the arbitrator may conclude that those intending work days had not articulated their position or that they had demurred when the other side clearly stated "we all know we mean calendar days, so just inserting the word *days* will suffice."

In that case, the arbitrator would probably conclude that there had been an agreement on calendar days. But, alternatively, the parties might have been in such a heated deadlock that they were unable to agree on either, so that they put down the single term "days" as a midnight compromise to end the negotiations. If that were the case, it would be incumbent upon the arbitrator to resolve that deliberate ambiguity based upon the evidence of what transpired at the negotiations, what had been the parties' prior experience in accommodating to the word day, and what had been the understanding using the term days elsewhere in the parties' agreement.

Direct Versus Circumstantial Evidence. One would assume from the preceding consideration of hearsay that the only evidence acceptable to the arbitrator would be the direct testimony of witnesses who participated in the events.

Such direct evidence may be the most persuasive in establishing facts, but facts may also be proven by circumstantial evidence—that is, facts that can be inferred from other facts. To be admissible, these other facts have to have bearing on the core facts to be proven.

Some examples might be a medical record of a bruise, although no one saw the fight; a telephone record of a call to the grievant's home when the grievant denied having made any calls from work that day; or a time card showing the grievant had arrived late, despite testimony of prompt reporting.

CASE STUDY: *The Case of the Personal Phone Call.* Glendon Roy, a telephone reservations clerk, was given a letter of warning for making personal long-distance telephone calls on company time. Janice Summ, the supervisor, testified that she saw Roy dialing an outside call and heard him begin the conversation with, "Hi, Mom, this is Glendon."

On cross-examination, the union established that Summ was two desks away and asked the arbitrator to visit the telephone room. The visit disclosed that the room was quite noisy and crowded, with twelve operators answering and occasionally making phone calls.

After resuming the hearing, the company called the office manager, who submitted company telephone records for the day in question. These records showed that a telephone call had been made to a number in area code 203, that the phone number was listed in the name of Glendon's father, and that Glendon had been assigned to work that day at the desk from which the call was made. The union objected to the offer of the records as irrelevant and hearsay, but was overruled by the arbitrator, who accepted the record.

On cross-examination by the union, it was shown that the call was made at 12:35 P.M., that employees were at lunch from 12:00 P.M. to 1:00 P.M., that there was no personal code for accessing outside lines, and that any number of people who knew Glendon's mother could have made that call. Union witnesses were called to establish that Ms. Roy was a frequent visitor to the area and that a number of operators knew her although, on cross-examination, none of the union witnesses admitted to calling her that day.

The company argued that Summ's direct testimony was credible and constituted proof of the calls, but that, in any event, the circumstantial evidence of company records established that Glendon had made the call.

The union asserted that Summ could not have overheard the call because of her distance and the noise in the area, that the records were hearsay, that anyone could have made the call, and that the company had failed to meet its burden of proof.

The arbitrator held that Summ's testimony was not persuasive because of her distance from Roy and the surrounding noise, but that the telephone records—which were admissible as a record kept in the normal course of business and were therefore an exception to the hearsay rule—did establish that a call was made to Glendon's mother. From that circumstantial evidence, the arbitrator held that there were grounds for a reasonable inference that Glendon had made the call. He concluded that the evidence that it had been lunch time and that other operators knew his mother, did not overcome that inference and the arbitrator therefore sustained the imposition of the letter of warning.

Discussion Question 1: If the employer had sought to introduce evidence of three earlier calls that Roy had admitted making to his mother, would that evidence strengthen the employer's claim that he had made this one?

The fact that Roy made calls to his mother in the past does not prove that he made this one. Prior similar incidents may prove that the employee knew the number or person called, but the employer still has the burden of proving that Roy made this call. For example, if the grievant had claimed that an accident was caused by a faulty ladder, evidence of previous accidents on the ladder might be circumstantial evidence that the ladder was faulty, but an accident on that ladder by the grievant must still be proven.

Cross-Examination

Once the witness has been asked all questions that his or her own sides' advocate deems desirable, the opposing spokesperson is given the opportunity to question the same witness on the subject matter covered in the direct testimony examination. Cross-examination is intended to discredit or contradict the witness or the testimony in an attempt to aid one's own case. Unlike the questioning during direct examination, which should not lead the witness, questioning in cross-examination may be more pointed, and the opposition spokesperson may lead the witness by asking the type of question that is prohibited on direct examination, such as: "Isn't it true that you couldn't see the time card area from where you were working?"

If one accepts the rationale that cross-examination should test the veracity of the testimony presented during direct examination, it follows that questions directed to trip up or contradict the witness would be admissible. In a sense, such questions lead the witness to a particular answer, and it becomes incumbent on the witness to answer them in a manner that reinforces the direct testimony and to avoid falling into the contradiction trap that comes from a pliable answer to the leading question.

But it also follows that this tactic must be limited in subject matter to those areas that were covered by the witness during direct testimony. The scope of cross-examination is therefore limited to the areas covered in direct examination. If the opposing counsel seeks to question a witness on matters that are not within the scope of the direct examination, it should be done without benefit of leading questions. In this case, the arbitrator might propose that the cross-examiner recall the person to the stand as that side's own witness, thereby permitting direct examination by that opposing advocate and cross-examination on the new matters by the spokesperson who originally called the witness for the original direct testimony.

Cross-examination of witnesses can be dangerous and should be carefully thought out. Nothing requires the cross-examination of every witness. Indeed, prudence may dictate waiving the opportunity to cross-examine, particularly when the witness in direct testimony has been assertive, clear, and at ease.

If the witness seemed uncertain in an area of testimony and the opposing counsel has reasonable cause to believe that the witness's testimony could be discredited by cross examination, it should be undertaken, but only in that narrow area. It is far better to suppress the natural fighter's instinct to attack the smooth and persuasive witness of the other side, than it is to attempt to undercut that testimony while at the same time providing a forum for the repetition and reconfirmation of everything that witness had said in answer to the direct questioning.

The old saw that is uniquely suited to cross-examination on questionable matters is, of course, "Don't ask the question if you don't know the answer, or unless you are prepared to prove a contrary answer is false." If the witness has not hurt your case, don't cross-examine.

The enthusiastic cross-examiner may also unintentionally bolster a witness's direct testimony by arguing with the witness. Cross-examination, despite its inherently adversarial nature, is not negotiations or a grievance appeal step, and it is not a forum for changing the other side's mind. It is particularly difficult to those who have repeatedly engaged in confrontations across the table from each other to adapt to the fact that arbitration is quasijudicial forum, in which the goal is not confrontation or argument, but rather the presentation of acknowledged divergent views, testimony, and evidence for the dispassionate decision of the arbitrator. Perhaps the most likely argumentative trigger of a repeat recitation of what was already testified to on direct examination, is the question "Why didn't you?" One should keep away from this question unless there is a masochistic desire to hear a replay of the direct testimony. When they call for arbitration and then use it only for hostile exchanges, the parties' reversion to across-the-table arguing, bullying, and finger-pointing can only erode the arbitrator's confidence in the parties' sophistication and maturity. Indeed, such a display might tilt the arbitrator from skepticism over the witness's testimony toward questioning the position of the cross-examiner who is so dogged and abrasive.

Other questions should be avoided on cross-examination. For example, the loaded questions like "When did you stop beating your wife?" are objectionable on both direct and cross-examination because they assume a fact not in evidence—that the witness had beaten his wife. As noted earlier, such questions properly invite an objection, which the arbitrator will unquestionably sustain.

Another form of counterproductive questioning on cross-examination arises from the tendency of opposing counsel, when surprised or resentful about an answer, to repeatedly ask the same question and, thus, elicit the same unacceptable answer. One of the dangers of questions about the unknown, when asked of the opposition, is that the questioner becomes bound by the answer.

Impeachment of the Witness

There is, however, an exception to the rule against going beyond the scope of the direct testimony during cross-examination. Such questioning is permitted in an effort to impeach a witness. This move allows questions that are not only beyond the scope of the direct testimony, but even questions that may be beyond the scope of the arbitration.

Undertaking to impeach a witness is to try to demonstrate that the witness is not truthful and that, if the witness lied on one matter, he or she cannot be relied upon to tell the truth on the subject matter of the arbitration. The impeaching evidence must show bias, defects in perception or memory, untrustworthiness, or a material inconsistent statement.

Usually, the effort to impeach a witness requires advance knowledge of some fact that the witness is likely to deny; the more embarrassing or more secret the fact, the greater the prospect of the witness denying it. Thus, in cross-examination of a witness on an attendance matter, if the questioner asks "Have you ever been convicted of perjury?," this question will undoubtedly be objected to as irrelevant and extraneous, but it would be permissible as an attempt to impeach the witness. If the witness answered no and court records are produced to contradict that response, the inference is that, if the witness lied on one answer, he or she might have lied on other matters.

Of course, a truthful response to a question asked in an effort to impeach will tend to reinforce the credibility of the witness's testimony on other aspects of the case.

The common law rules of evidence do not permit the impeachment of one's own witness.

Admissions/Confessions

Cross-examination of the grievant by the employer may be the context in which the employer seeks to introduce into evidence an earlier confession or admission as to the event in question. Generally written, confessions are admissible into evidence and may be dispositive of the dispute. Where or under what circumstances the admission was made is not very important. Whether that admission was made at the time of the incident or as part of a tangential criminal proceeding also doesn't matter. A confession is admissible and subject to inquiry about the circumstances of its making. Unquestionably, such an admission does not constitute proof, but it does shift the burden from the employer seeking to prove guilt to the union seeking to discredit what, on its face, appears to be an admission of guilt. Such an effort may not be futile. Suppose that the grievant's spokesperson is able to show that the grievant was terminated was for admitting to possession of cocaine. If the grievant persuasively testified that he did not possess of cocaine, but merely falsely admitted so as part of a plea bargain to avoid a trial and potential conviction on a much harsher—though equally unfounded—charge, the arbitrator may be convinced that the confession should not be accepted as proof of guilt.

The only area in which a confession might be barred from admission is if made as part of an effort at grievance settlement. That situation might arise if the employer were to introduce into evidence testimony of a third-step grievance settlement in which the grievant had offered to acknowledge guilt in exchange for a penalty less than discharge but the settlement subsequently fell apart. Such an offer of compromise in lieu of proceeding with the discharge action should be excluded from the record because of the chilling effect it would have in future efforts to settle grievances if those exploratory efforts were to be introduced later into evidence. Such a confession does not constitute proof of guilt but, more likely, an effort to avoid the arbitration and resolve the dispute. Thus, if the settlement effort had failed and the employer opted to pursue the grievance to arbitration, an admission, whether or not true, made as a component of a failed settlement package would be excluded. That exclusion would be consistent with the preferred policy of encouraging settlements and protecting the sanctity of such discussions, even if the settlements failed.

Cross-examination is undoubtedly an art. When used with care and discretion, it may expose the weakness of the testimony of the other side and bolster the cross-examiner's case. But this procedure has risks for the fierce partisan and the unwary questioner. It can have the unintended consequence of securing victory of the other side—even when that side might otherwise have been defeated.

Rebuttal Testimony

After the moving party has presented its witnesses for direct testimony and cross-examination, and after the responding party has done the same with its witnesses, the hearing may be over unless the party that went first opts to call a witness for testimony in response to what had been placed into the record by the other side. The rebuttal testimony may come from one of the witnesses who had testified earlier in the moving party's direct presentation or it may come from a witness who had not testified earlier. The purpose would be to contradict the testimony offered by an earlier witness from the other side.

In either case, rebuttal testimony, as in the case of cross-examination, must be confined to the scope of the evidence already adduced. It is not an opportunity to introduce new testimony that was earlier forgotten or newly discovered. This testimony is no more than a response or rebuttal to opposition evidence that the original moving party believes it can contradict, discredit, or dilute. In that respect, a rebuttal can also be used to reinforce testimony offered earlier for that side by the same or other witnesses.

Expert Witnesses

In a sense, every witness is an expert on what he or she saw, heard, or felt—as long as that person had sufficient opportunity to perceive. This expertise makes the testimony of observers to an event so important to establish a believable recitation of what transpired. But two witnesses to the same scene may offer differing testimony about what happened. As noted earlier, an acknowledged observer's testimony about what was seen may be compromised by failures in observation, retention, and/or recitation. That fallibility may make the arbitrator responsible for determining which of those two observers provided the more credible recitation of what transpired. Certainly, cross-examination helps in that regard.

But some witnesses are classified as "expert witnesses" because they possess a knowledge that transcends individual observation of an event. Their expertise comes from extensive experience or professional training in the subject matter of their testimony. Their testimony about a particular observation may be no more credible than that of any other observer, but their statements do have greater credibility when they concern matters beyond common understanding within the witness's field of expertise. Their expertise is established by their ability to testify from the vantage point of accumulated observation, experience, and study. Unlike the individual untutored observer of a single event—who is presumed able to testify only about what was heard, seen, or felt—the expert witness is able to draw on accumulated observations and study to testify about conclusions that might be drawn from that observation. Such testimony may be claimed to be objective, but these witnesses may be paid by, or at least partial to, the side that sponsors them. And they may be contradicted by equally "objective" experts from the other side. But to have a witness's testimony classified as expert, it is first necessary to establish the witness's qualifications as an expert by evidence of education, training, and experience in the matter in dispute. If the individual's qualifications as an expert are established, that person's contribution may expand beyond the observation of a single incident to an opinion or to conclusions to be drawn from the incident.

To take a simple example, suppose that any number of fellow employees testify to the fact that the grievant was coughing, wheezing, and sneezing. But only an individual who has experience with coughs, wheezes, and sneezes and who has studied those symptoms and their cause can credibly testify whether that individual had a virus, asthma, or some other respiratory malady. If such a witness has trained as a physician, that background is deemed sufficient qualification to provide expert testimony on the individual's medical condition.

But not all experts are equally credible. Their relative persuasiveness may stem from their academic training in their field of specialization or the extent of their experience with the matter in dispute. The expert testimony of the company nurse on the grievant's condition may be more persuasive than the testimony of fellow employees, but it may be outweighed by the expertise of the company physician, even though the physician had trained in occupational health rather than chest diseases. These battles of the experts may pit nurse, physician, chiropractor, social worker, and so on against one another. In this example, the arbitrator might rely most comfortably on the testimony of a physician with board certification in thorasic medicine or infectious diseases. But if the issue concerned the amount of lifting or distances of walking in the plant, the nurse who had worked there for years might be more credible than a physician who had never set foot in the plant.

But what if one party relied on the one expert, while opposing conclusions were put forward by the other? Obviously, expert qualification does not guarantee that the arbitrator will accept the expert's opinion or conclusion as dispositive of the issue, particularly if there are competing views between or among experts.

Nor do experts qualify as such merely because of professional study or accumulated graduate degrees. Their qualification to testify depends on the nature of the dispute. If the contract or rules authorize absence in the event of verified illness, then medical expertise may be controlling; but, if the issue concerns machine malfunction, the mechanic from the machine maintenance company may equally qualify as an expert, with the right to give as testimony opinions on the reason for the malfunction or conclusions about what went wrong.

The parties should be prepared to demonstrate the qualifications of the witness they wish to offer as an expert, either by an oral recitation of background in the area of expertise or by provision of a written curriculum vitae. And opposing counsel must have the opportunity to question the witness about the expertise. Acknowledgment by the opposition that the individual is qualified as an expert witness does not bind that party to the expert's testimony any more than it binds the arbitrator to accept the expert's opinions or conclusions.

Once the qualifications have been offered and opposing counsel has had an opportunity to challenge those qualifications, the arbitrator is able to determine whether or not to accept that witness's testimony as expert. When that designation is granted, the expert witness may testify about conclusions drawn from the presented evidence. In addition, hypothetical situations, perhaps matching the facts of the case in dispute, may be placed before the expert witness for an opinion.

The authorization to provide an opinion or conclusion and for answering hypothetical questions is unique to those who have qualified to testify as experts. This edge is not provided to the average witness.

Advocate Witnesses

A unique role is sometimes played by the team spokesperson who seeks to testify as a witness. It could be argued that such testimony should be barred and that the party whose spokesperson was close enough to the case to become a potential witness should be required to secure alternative counsel. However, the informality of the arbitration process, together with the prior practice of the parties, will usually lead the arbitrator to allow the spokesperson to testify as a witness.

The spokesperson may have negotiated the contract or taken certain actions in processing the case to arbitration and may therefore be in the position to testify on the facts that are in dispute and shed light on them.

In an arbitration hearing, there is no jury to be led astray by dual role playing and the arbitrator and the parties are able to discern which hat the advocate is wearing. It makes little practical or economic sense to require that another advocate be summoned.

In most cases, the spokesperson merely offers a recital of what transpired, but occasionally the other side will object to such a recital on the grounds it has no way of objecting to the testimony because there are no questions to preview the issues raised by that testimony. As a consequence, in some situations the spokesperson first asks the question and then answers it.

The superfluousness of this procedure can readily be established by the spokesperson, in the role of witness, asking him- or herself, in the role of advocate, to repeat the last question.

Missing Witnesses

Arbitration hearings are scheduled weeks and months in advance and all the participants are notified of the time and place of the hearing. They rightfully anticipate that those whose testimony is pertinent to the prosecution or defense of the grievance will appear to testify and be subject to cross-examination. Despite this clear notice, and despite the crucial nature of their testimony, some witnesses do not appear. In some cases, the absence is beyond the witnesses' as well as the parties' control. Witnesses who observed the disputed event may die, move away, or become lost to contact by the parties. Others, although accessible, are unwilling to take part in the proceedings. Still others simply get confused: they mix up or forget the day of hearing, report to the wrong place, or find more pressing engagements for the day of the hearing. The burden of producing the witness is on the party planning to call that witness as part of its case.

What to do in the absence of an important witness must be confronted by the parties or if, they dispute the issue, by the arbitrator.

The Missing Grievant. One would expect the individual who precipitated the dispute, the grievant, to be present at the hearing. If the facts of the grievance are undisputed and the focus is on the contract or contractual rights, the testimony of the grievant may be unnecessary and the union that opted to proceed to arbitration may well decide to present its case without the grievant, or through another witness. The presence of the grievant may not be necessary unless there is a need to question him or her about some disputed aspect of the case. In cases involving contract interpretation, it may be possible to stipulate the facts or agree, through an offer of proof, about what the grievant would have testified if present.

But in cases involving disputed facts or disciplinary matters, the testimony of the grievant may be crucial to the union's presentation of its case. If the grievant's absence is due to injury, illness, or even a jail sentence, the parties may agree to postpone the hearing until the grievant can be available. Such postponements are usually agreed to, sometimes with the understanding that, in the event of a sustained grievance, the employer will be protected from any cost associated with the additional delay, such as compensation for the period between the scheduled day of hearing and the postponed hearing date. The parties may make arrangements to secure a deposition from the grievant at a time and place mutually convenient to all. Under that arrangement, the spokespersons would be able to question and cross-examine the witness, with a written or videotaped record being preserved for presentation to the arbitrator. That deposition is, in effect, a substitute for the testimony at the arbitration hearing. Although the arbitrator would not be present, this type of deposition preserves the adversarial elements of the process. Alternatives such as a written statement from the grievant are admissible only if acceptable to both parties. If the opposing party objects to the written statement as biased, or depriving it of the opportunity for cross-examination, the statement would presumably be excluded by the arbitrator. Otherwise, admission of such written documents would deprive the employer of its crucial right of cross-examination and provide the arbitrator with a one-sided, unchallenged view of the dispute.

In the event that the parties are unwilling to agree to a postponement or alternative, such as a deposition, that the employer insists the grievance be dismissed for lack of a grievant, and that the union insists on proceeding, it becomes incumbent on the arbitrator to decide the status of the case. Several options are open to the arbitrator. If convinced that the grievant had notice of the hearing and merely opted not to attend, the arbitrator might request the union to withdraw the grievance, might dismiss the case, or might request the parties to proceed and put in their evidence in the absence of the grievant, thus providing a basis for a decision despite the grievant's failure to attend. In disciplinary cases, that prima facie presentation by the employer in the absence of a response by the grievant will usually result in a denial of the grievance on its merits.

In cases where the grievant fails to appear, despite having been notified by the union of the time and place of the hearing, and the union is willing to proceed, the arbitrator might specify in the opinion the efforts by the union to notify the grievant in order to protect the union against any possible suit for a breach of the Duty of Fair Representation.

When the union makes a persuasive claim for an extension on the grounds that it expected the grievant to be present or that the absence was beyond the grievant's control, the arbitrator might agree to postpone the start of the hearing until later that day to provide time for the grievant to appear or be found. Alternatively, the arbitrator may agree to a postponement to a time in the near future, with the understanding that the union would withdraw the grievance if the grievant could not be found or that the hearing would proceed to finality on the rescheduled date, regardless of the grievant's absence.

Employer Calling a Missing Union Witness. Many employers abide by the precept that it is too disruptive to the labor–management relationship to call a union member to testify as a company witness. To be identified as a company pawn would place the employee in an uncomfortable, if not risky, position among fellow employees. Yet, at times, employees make statements to company officials that support the company position on what occurred at a disputed event.

Often the company is relieved of the need to call the union member when the union calls that person as its witness; the company is then in a position to cross-examine that witness about what was said to the supervisor. But if the union does not call the employee and the employer is anxious to have the employee's statement placed into evidence, there is a temptation for the company to call that witness.

Clearly, testimony of the supervisor about what a bargaining unit member told him would risk being excluded as hearsay. But many arbitrators, sensitive to the jeopardy in which an employee would be placed if called as a company witness, have made a unique exception to the hearsay rule by admitting such reporting of what the employee said to the supervisor. They allow such hearsay testimony into evidence as the preferable alternative to having the company call the employee and leave it to the union to call the employee as its witness to rebut that hearsay testimony. Then, if the union does not call the employee to testify, the hearsay report of what was told to the supervisor stands as proven.

The Missing Accuser and Other Missing Witnesses. Because arbitration hearings often involve many witnesses, it is not unusual for one or more of the anticipated witnesses to be absent from a hearing. Producing witnesses at the designated time and place is the responsibility of the side that intends to call them. Failure to produce witnesses may be fatal.

CASE STUDY: The Case of the Missing Accuser. The grievant, Michael Dojka, is a bus driver who was disciplined for unsafe driving after a passenger car driver, Anthony Bedwell, wrote to the company that Dojka had swerved in front of him. Bedwell, the protesting passenger car driver, resides in Marshall, Michigan. The hearing was scheduled for a date in February in Philadelphia after Bedwell agreed to attend at the bus company's expense. A snowstorm prevented Bedwell, the accusing driver, from getting to the hearing, although everyone else was present.

The employer proposed that the hearing proceed and that the arbitrator accept into evidence the original letter of protest to the bus company and the transcript of an interview of the passenger car driver and wife, which was conducted in Marshall, Michigan, by the company's attorney. The counsel argued that the absence of the witnesses was due to an act of God, and that it would be excessively expensive to reschedule the hearing.

The union spokesperson asserted that the disciplinary penalty must be set aside, that the employer had failed in its burden to prove the grievant at fault by its inability to produce the accusing party, that the admission of the letter and the transcript of the interview with the auto driver and his wife deprived the grievant of the opportunity to confront his accusers and the benefit of a cross-examination, and that the grievance should be sustained.

The arbitrator admitted into evidence the original letter of protest as evidence of the complaint that led to the employer's action, but with the caveat that the letter did not constitute proof of what it asserted. The interview transcript was excluded on the grounds that it lacked any cross-examination and was, thus, self-serving for the employer.

The arbitrator held that the written assertion provided by Bedwell did not constitute proof of the alleged reckless driving and decided that, because the absence of the accusing driver was beyond the control of Bedwell and the employer, the hearing should be rescheduled at a time and place acceptable to the parties.

Discussion Question 1: What if the union had refused to agree to a postponement unless the company bore the full cost of the arbitrator's second day of hearing?

Any dispute over who is to pay for the additional cost resulting from a postponement constitutes a separate issue over which the arbitrator has jurisdiction only if both parties agree. Without such an agreement, the arbitrator has no authority to rule on the assignment of costs. And even if the parties agree to permit the arbitrator to rule on that issue, most contracts provide for the sharing of the arbitrator's fee and the arbitrator would be bound by such language.

The union's effort to have the employer assume the cost of the second day of hearing might be a matter that the arbitrator could discuss informally with the parties. If the employer fears that the arbitrator might not postpone the hearing because of the added financial burden on the union, it might volunteer to absorb the extra cost as a means of mollifying the union. That offer might induce the arbitrator to view the request for postponement more favorably.

Discussion Question 2: What if the accusing party had written to the employer to say that he did not have the time or inclination to come to Philadelphia for a hearing and that he felt his letter and the transcript of his interview ought to suffice?

The employer in a disciplinary hearing has the burden of proof, and the grievant has the right to a fair hearing and to confront his accusers. The employer's burden is not met by providing recitals of one side's view of the facts unless there is an opportunity to cross-examine the authors of such recitals.

Even though an instance of reckless driving might go unpunished by sustaining the grievance, in the absence of direct testimony, subject to cross-examination, such reckless driving is not proven. Among the options that arise from the company's failure to produce the accusing witness, it is preferable to allow the alleged reckless driving to go unpunished than to discipline an innocent driver of an offense he did not commit.

Discussion Question 3: What if the accusing driver's wife, rather than her husband, had come to the hearing?

Two people were apparently in the car, although the husband, the driver, wrote the protest letter. Unquestionably, as driver he would be the preferred witness. But the wife, too, was in the car and had standing to testify about what she observed, felt, or heard. If she were present, the case would go forward as scheduled, with the wife available for examination and cross-examination. The absence of the husband, while not fatal to the company's case, would be a proper subject of questioning by the union spokesperson. Regardless of whether the husband or the wife is selected by the employer as its accusing witness, it is bound by the testimony resulting from that choice.

Discussion Question 4: What if the wife testifies and the company, thereafter, seeks another day of hearing for her husband, the driver, to testify?

If, at the conclusion of the wife's testimony, the company requests another day of hearing so that it can bring the husband as a rebuttal witness to bolster his wife's testimony, the arbitrator would question why the husband was not present at the scheduled hearing. If the answer is that he is ill and unable to attend, the arbitrator might take the position that the employer should have postponed the proceeding and that by proceeding with the wife the employer had made a commitment to rely solely on that proof. The arbitrator might reason that the company should have foreseen the nature of the wife's testimony and that it should have had Bedwell available for rebuttal or enforcement, if that were to be his role. To permit the company an extension to salvage what it now perceives as a possibly weak case would be unfair to the grievant and to the union. They have the right to expect and rely upon a speedy hearing of the case and a resolution of the dispute on the date scheduled.

Discussion Question 5: What if the case involved a reported threat against the life of a witness, who refused to testify out of fear?

It is universally accepted that the employer, in a case involving a terminated employee, has the responsibility to present a prima facie case before the accused employee is expected to testify to rebut those charges. But should that standard apply when the threatened victim has a legitimate fear of reprisal for testifying? Clearly an oral or written report of the threat is hearsay and would not constitute a prime facie case to shift the burden of response to the alleged accuser, but it would also enable the grievant to avoid any responsibility for testifying or answering the charges. Strict adherence to the rules of evidence would endorse such silence. But in at least one case in South Africa, OK Bazaars and Commercial, Catering and Allied Workers Union, the arbitrator, Edwin Cameron, ruled that the written statement of a store customer alleging a death threat by a striking employee was admissible in order to elicit a response from the accused, with the expectation that the statement would not support any penalty if a reasonable explanation were forthcoming from the grievant.

The Arbitrator Calling a Missing Witness. The recognition of arbitration as an adversarial process in which the parties are responsible for selecting their spokepersons and for presenting their respective cases assumes that they bear the burden for what they put into evidence as well as for what they omit. That view of the process dictates that the parties select their own witnesses and bear the consequences of omitting witnesses. However, recognizing such responsibility means that arbitrators may not secure the benefit of testimony from witnesses whom the arbitrators deem should be called. This restraint places arbitrators in a dilemma.

Most resolve the problem by accepting that it is the parties' responsibility to mount their own cases and select their own witnesses, even if the failure of a party to call a particular witness may jeopardize its chance of victory. This school holds that if the arbitrator calls a witness who was not called by either party, the arbitrator serves as an advocate for one of the parties by calling a witness that the party declined (or forgot) to call.

But rather than accepting an incomplete record, some arbitrators will enter the breach by calling witnesses on their own. In this case, the arbitrator asks questions of the witness and both parties may cross-examine. While there is no question of the right of an arbitrator to call witnesses, arbitrators are split on the question of whether or not such an action constitutes a role that more properly belongs to the parties. Filling that vacuum to "complete the record" risks that the arbitrator may open a can of worms, which the parties, in their judgment and experience, would prefer to avoid.

Privileged Communication

Over the generations, society has developed traditions that protect free and unfettered communications between certain individuals and that have become enshrined in law. Among these is the protection of verbal communication between attorney and client to ensure the sanctity of confidences, to encourage socially important relationships that require mutual trust and confidence, and to safeguard such confidentiality. The same protection is afforded to verbal communication between physician and patient to assure the patient that anything revealed to the physician as an essential component in an appropriate medical treatment is not subsequently revealed when the physician is called to court to testify. Society has placed a high value on free and confidential communication between husband and wife, attorney and client and physician and patient and seeks to protect this privilege. Under common law, only the holder of the privilege—the client or the patient—can waive the privilege. The lawyer and the doctor are bound by the holder's decision. The same principle governs the relationship between patient and psychotherapist and clergyman and confessor.

Similarly, in communication between husband and wife, the courts have deemed it socially beneficial to protect familial confidences as a facet of the sanctity of the home. Society has also banned revealing classified information, grand jury testimony, and communication with mediators.

But arbitration is not a court of law. Should the traditional privileges be protected, or should they be extended to cover communications between grievant and union representative?

In the case of attorney–client and physician–patient communication, the privilege encompasses a legal obligation that the attorney or the physician not testify against client or patient, as the case may be. If the privilege is invoked by a lawyer or physician, the arbitrator will generally respect it, particularly because the arbitrator lacks the judge's authority to hold them in contempt. The response would hold for the husband–wife privilege.

But arbitration proceedings differ from court proceedings. The penalties for wrongdoing may result in the loss of job or earnings, but they do not embrace incarceration or loss of liberty.

Arbitrators are responsible for determining facts. Invocation of any of the legal privileges by the grievant might be viewed by the arbitrator as an infringent on that responsibility, particularly if the privilege is invoked by a grievant unwilling to permit testimony concerning communication with a physician or attorney. Arbitrators will often threaten to draw an adverse inference about the party declining to provide the necessary testimony—that is, the arbitrator would threaten to credit the allegations of the other side if the witness is silent on the matters being questioned. This prospect induces the desired testimony or encourages the client or patient to release the evidence or documentation sought in the matter.

The arbitrator may make such a threat when the employer refuses to release its medical evidence concerning an employee. Although many employee medical examination forms authorize the employer to release their content for internal management use, the employer may invoke the privilege to keep those records from the arbitrator. Agreement to their release by the employee—as is his or her right—or the suggestion by the arbitrator of an adverse inference would usually secure the desired information. When the grievant refuses to release the medical records held by an outside physician to the arbitrator or the employer, the same threat of an adverse inference usually triggers a waiver of the privilege and the release of the requested evidence.

Offers of Compromise and Settlement

The underlying precept of arbitration is that it should be avoided by the parties' resolution of their disputes at the lower steps of the grievance procedure. In the overwhelming majority of grievances, that is exactly what happens. The union withdraws the grievance, or the employer grants the grievance, or the parties reach some sort of settlement that resolves the dispute without the need for appeal to arbitration.

During the settlement talks, offers of compromise, admissions against interest, and case weaknesses may be discussed and mutually exchanged in the effort to reach agreement. But sometimes those settlement efforts do not result in agreement, the settlement talks come to an end, and the case is put back on the track to arbitration.

It is only natural in such circumstances, when the parties have returned to the barricades, that the other side's admissions, statements of weaknesses, and sharing of confidences during the settlement talks should become savory items to place before the arbitrator. The introduction of evidence that a case is insecure might inspire the arbitrator to rule for the party that knows it is right and against the party that, in settlement discussions, acknowledged the weakness in its case.

But even though the admission of such evidence would make the arbitrator's job easier and would help the arbitrator issue a decision more closely resembling the parties' settlement discussions, such testimony is universally excluded by arbitrators. Indeed, if there is so much as a hint that a party is endeavoring to introduce evidence of what transpired in settlement discussions, arbitrators on their own initiative are likely to take the rare step of intervening without waiting for a formal objection.

The reason for this sensitivity is obvious. The parties must be free to discuss settlement without concern that any statements they make in such efforts might come back to haunt them in the arbitration proceedings. Furthermore, it is not clear that statements made in an effort to settle a grievance, including offers of compromise, are admissions of weakness or guilt. They may merely reflect an effort to reach a compromise to avoid the cost, consequences, delay, and perhaps even the risk of an adverse decision in arbitration. Thus, even if evidence of the settlement discussions were to be admitted, that evidence can never clearly demonstrate whether it was genuinely an acknowledgement of a weak case.

To bolster the parties' efforts to resolve their conflict as early as possible and to encourage their freedom to do so in future cases, arbitrators invariably exclude evidence of offers of settlement or compromise.

Plant Visits

Many cases involve testimony about the details of equipment, or the flow of an operation, or the layout of the site where the dispute arose. The parties endeavor to provide the arbitrator with as much testimony—documented photos, plant layouts, floor plans—as they can to enable the arbitrator to fully grasp the environment of the area.

But usually no oral or documentary evidence can substitute for a visit to the machine, operation, or site in question. Such visits present little problem if the hearing is being held at the work facility. The parties may agree to have the arbitrator visit the site prior to, during, or at the end of the hearing.

Such a visit may be more of a problem if the hearing is held away from the site or if one of the parties objects to the plant visit. Even if the provision causes inconvenience to one or both of the parties, the guidance of the code is clear:

> Part 5, Sec D—Plant Visits
>
> 1. An arbitrator should comply with a request of any party that he or she visit a work area pertinent to the dispute prior to, during, or after the hearing. An arbitrator may also initiate such a request.
> a. Procedures for such visits should be agreed to by the parties in consultation with the arbitrator.

Thus, under the code, the right of either party, or the arbitrator, is clear; only the procedures for the visit are unresolved. The language suggests that the arbitrator should try to work out an accommodation with the parties about the procedures for the visit.

Closings

After the spokespersons have called to the stand and examined all the witnesses, after they have been cross-examined, after all the relevant documentary evidence has been received into evidence and there is no request for further input from either party, and after the submission evidence comes to an end, it is time for the spokepersons to draw upon the factual record and the received documentation to fashion a summary of what has transpired and to argue why, on the basis of the evidence and the parties' collective bargaining agreement, the arbitrator should rule in its favor.

Oral or Written Summations

The summation may be given orally at the end of the hearing or in writing for submission after the hearing by a mutually agreed deadline. The arbitrator usually leaves the choice to the parties. Obviously, the costs are greater if the parties reject the oral closing statements in favor of a summary written later. Occasionally, the parties choose to do both, arguing orally and later filing written post-hearing briefs. If one side seeks to argue orally while the other party requests an opportunity to file a written brief, the arbitrator will usually grant the request for written closings.

Part 6A of the code requires the arbitrator to comply with mutual agreements of the parties on the filing or nonfiling or post-hearing briefs or submission, although the arbitrator may request that briefs be submitted or that none be filed. In the even of conflict, part 6.A1b is relevant:

> b. When the parties disagree to the need for briefs, an arbitrator may permit filing, but may determine a reasonable time limitation.

If there is objection to that ruling by the party seeking an oral argument, the arbitrator may offer to hear that side's oral argument at the point. The arbitrator will exclude the other party and its witnesses from the oral summation so that they do not secure any advantage in rebutting the other side's oral arguments when writing their brief.

Occasionally when the parties opt for written post-hearing briefs, there may be a request for reply briefs to be filed in response to the arguments raised in the initial briefs. If both parties agree, the arbitrator merely sets the date for such submissions. But if there is disagreement over whether or not there should be reply briefs, many arbitrators will rule against reply briefs. There are several reasons for such a ruling: First, arbitration is presumed to be expeditious. The preparation of transcripts and written briefs adds an additional month or two before the arbitrator is able to write and render the decision to the grievant. Second, arbitration is presumed to be an inexpensive, informal process. Opening the door to written briefs and then to reply briefs epitomizes the growing legalistic trend that forces the parties to pay ever-rising costs in their efforts to resolve their disputes. Third, arbitration is supposed to be a process in which the parties have already raised all the relevant arguments in their across-the-table efforts to resolve their dispute prior to arbitration. By the time the arbitration is held, there should be no mysteries or surprises, but merely a presentation of the divergent arguments so that the arbitrator can choose the most persuasive and end that particular dispute. If the goal of the entire grievance and arbitration process is to encourage the parties to resolve their disputes mutually at the earliest-possible stage, there should be no surprises at the arbitration stage, let alone afterward in post-hearing briefs. Permitting post-hearing briefs tacitly acknowledges the propriety of introducing surprise arguments, which call for response in the briefs; discouraging post-hearing briefs encourages the parties to bare their arguments earlier. Most of the arguments are already familiar to the other side, and there is little benefit to the arbitrator or the parties to justify the delay and additional cost of reply briefs.

Both oral and written summations follow the same format, beginning with a chronological recitation of the facts that bolster the side's position and seeking to discredit or discount the facts that tend to bolster the other side's position. There then follows a recitation of the contractual provisions that are expected to induce the arbitrator to conclude in that party's favor.

An oral closing better meets the objectives of speed and economy than a written brief, particularly when the parties request more time than was agreed to at the hearing to submit their briefs. An oral closing enables the spokesperson to capitalize on the freshness of the presentation, which the arbitrator has just heard, and on the arbitrator's greater sensitivity to the immediacy of an oral rendition of the facts so fresh in the arbitrator's mind. It is certainly appropriate to request a few minutes of privacy at the conclusion of the evidence in order to gather one's thoughts for the oral argument. Being tied to a previously drafted closing argument is risky and often self-defeating, because the writer becomes wedded to the words and may include facts that were not proven at the hearing or omit facts that unexpectedly surfaced for the first time at the hearing. Following a previously prepared script may result in missing the benefits and the persuasive impact of spontaneity that one expects in oral closings. A previously prepared checklist of the facts and arguments to be covered may provide greater opportunity to work into the closing any surprise facts or arguments heard at the hearing for the first time.

Perhaps even more valuable to the parties is the chance to listen and respond to the oral argument of the other side. There is no limit to the duration of the closing or to the opportunity to respond to the other's side's closing. Hearing the other side's argument also provides an opportunity to object to any effort to introduce new evidence. Any effort to keep new evidence out of post-hearing briefs is dissipated by the fact that the arbitrator may have read and absorbed the objectional material before the objection can be lodged.

Arbitrators have no preference about which party makes the first closing statement because there is full opportunity for rejoinder by the other. Some arbitrators have the party that made the first opening also make the first closing. Others believe the party that goes first should close last. Generally, it is preferable to abide by the practice the parties have followed in the past, with which they are comfortable.

But written briefs do have advantages. Provision of written briefs may be a practice of the parties or may be requested by the arbitrator. Aside from demonstrating to the client that the advocate has done the most thorough job possible by taking the time and care to write formal briefs, they also provide a less harried context for setting out the party's position. Formal briefs sidestep the pressure of the hearing and protect against the omission of crucial facts and arguments that might result from a hastily assembled oral closing argument. Written post-hearing briefs provide an opportunity for reflection, for careful scrutiny of the notes or transcript of the hearing and full scope to structure a detailed recitation of the favorable facts while criticizing facts that might be disadvantageous. Written post-hearing briefs also foster a more orderly presentation, one that may be so appealing to the arbitrator that it provides a readily adoptable model for the arbitrator's own reasoning and conclusions. Such briefs may be of particular interest to arbitrators in more complex cases or to arbitrators who long ago, put aside their notes of the hearing and await the briefs to bring them up to speed again, despite the skewed recitations of carefully selected facts that such briefs usually contain.

Arbitrators who undertake more prompt writing of awards may already have written their own recitation of the facts, unsullied by the partisan histories that tend to characterize post-hearing briefs. Such arbitrators may prefer oral rather than written summations so that the argument has been set forth when they write the facts and they can write of their conclusions at the same sitting, thus closing out the case. However, if the parties feel the arbitrator is inexperienced or has not fully understood the case, the briefs may provide an additional opportunity to get the message across when the arbitrator rereads and examines the positions of the parties.

Once the hearing is declared closed, the record is closed as well, and both parties undertake that the closing presentations, oral and/or written, will not include evidence that was not presented at the hearing. Prior arbitration awards between these and other parties are exempt from that commitment, because each arbitration decision stands on its own, with adherence to prior decisions between the same parties being a matter of arbitrator's discretion.

Prior arbitration awards are usually introduced as part of the closing argument. If they were between the same parties, it is presumed that both sides are aware of them, have access to them, and are alert to which are relevant to the present dispute and subject to introduction by either party. It is up to the spokespersons which, if any, are to be introduced, and they need not be introduced as part of the evidentary presentation.

Arbitration decisions between different parties, lack any evidentary value, except for the reasoning of the arbitrators in those cases, which are asserted by the spokespersons to be analogous. Either party may introduce such awards at any time, including in the post-hearing brief, as long as copies (or, if published, citations) are provided to the other side as well as the arbitrator.

Delay in Submitting Post-Hearing Briefs

The goal of expeditiousness in arbitration is often derailed by extensive delay in the provision of post-hearing briefs. Usually the parties agree to a deadline for the submission of post-hearing briefs based upon their schedules and the pressure of their other work. If an unexpected problem precludes submitting the brief by the date previously agreed upon, there is usually mutual accommodation to a delayed deadline. But at times one of the parties fails to meet the specified deadline and does not provide the agreed-upon brief.

This failure places the arbitrator in the awkward position of having one brief submitted as agreed and no access to the brief of the other party. Part 6.A2 of the code specifies that "An arbitrator must not consider a post-hearing brief or submission that has not been provided to the other party."

If the parties had agreed that the arbitrator should not consider any brief filed after the deadline, part 6.A1 would permit the arbitrator to decide the case without tardy brief: "An arbitrator must comply with mutual agreements in respect to the filing of post-hearing briefs or submissions."

How an arbitrator should proceed if no authorization has been granted to decide the case when one brief overdue was decided by the Committee on Professional Responsibility and Grievances in Opinion 8 on May 16, 1981:

> An arbitrator does have Code responsibilities when a post-hearing brief is not filed by an agreed upon date, even where the parties have made no agreement as to the effect of a late filing. These responsibilities arise primarily from the arbitrator's Part 2-J.2-Duty to cooperate with the parties in avoiding delays. After a reasonable period (allowing for possibilities such as a delayed mail delivery or an unannounced agreement by the parties to an extension), the arbitrator should make appropriate inquiry and take appropriate action. At some point, it may become incumbent upon the arbitrator to give notice that the decision may be issued after a certain date, whether or not the tardy brief has been received by that date.[13]

Clearly, the arbitrator is at a disadvantage when only one brief has been provided and the argument of the other side must be extracted from its opening statement or, perhaps, its oral closing. But that disadvantage is the responsibility of the delinquent party. The arbitrator's greater responsibility is to the primary goal of the process—to issue the award in a manner that will resolve the dispute with minimal delay.

Post-Hearing Evidence

Once the hearing is closed, neither party has any right to provide the arbitrator with evidence, other than prior arbitration decisions, that could have been presented in the hearing and subjected to objection, voire dire, and/or cross examination.

Yet evidence is sometimes offered for admission after the hearing by a party that believes it should be considered by the arbitrator. Sometimes, the party has belatedly thought of evidence that would effectively rebut the other side's presentation. At other times, the evidence is newly uncovered and was not known or available at the time of the hearing. To be considered for receipt by the arbitrator, such post-hearing evidence should be new or newly discovered and should not have been available or accessible at the time of the hearing. Additionally, the timing of offering that evidence is crucial. There are three time windows for considering the admissibility of such evidence. First, it may be offered after the hearing, but before the arbitrator's decision is rendered. In this window, it may be weighed by the arbitrator for the limited purposes of discovering (1) whether it is truly newly discovered evidence, (2) whether its material weight might be enough to alter the outcome of the case, and (3) whether it is acknowledged as admissible by the parties or must precipitate a reopening of the hearing to resolve any challenges to its admission, with the time and costs that such a reopening would entail.

The second window would be if the new evidence were submitted with the post-hearing brief. If the evidence is cleared with the other side and submitted with the brief without objection, the arbitrator would receive and consider it. If it accompanies the brief without such clearance and is objected to by the other side, the arbitrator would refuse to receive or consider it. That decision would be made on the grounds that the evidence should have been presented at the hearing or, if newly discovered after the hearing, that it should have been presented by petition to the arbitrator to introduce it in a reopened hearing, at which it could be introduced and submitted to cross-examination. Such an exclusion is usually ordered for several reasons. First, allowing such evidence would deny the other side access to the procedural safeguards provided by the hearing for testing the authenticity and admissibility of evidence. Second, its admission would place a premium on withholding evidence until the filing of post-hearing briefs, thus subverting the goal of resolving disputes well prior to arbitration. Third, acceptance of this evidence would place the other side at a serious disadvantage because it would not have advance knowledge of the evidence, would not be able to consider it in its closing argument, and would not have any opportunity to rebut it.

Nonetheless, if the new evidence were offered prior to issuing the arbitrator's opinion and award and had not been available by the close of the hearing despite due diligence by the party seeking to introduce it, and if the offered evidence were pertinent and likely to affect the outcome of the hearing, the arbitrator would probably entertain a motion to order a reopening of the hearing so that the newly discovered evidence could be considered for admission and, if received, be subject to cross-examination and possible rebuttal. That result, of course, would open the door to new closing arguments and, if that were the parties' choice, to submission of new briefs and perhaps reply briefs as well.

The third window for post-hearing evidence would be after the arbitrator has issued the decision. By that time, the arbitrator has ceased to have authority over the case and is *funtis officio*. The case was heard, the decision rendered, and any authority the arbitrator had has ended. The parties may, on their own, consider the impact of the new evidence on the arbitrator's decision or on their relationship. But that choice is up to them and beyond any role of the arbitrator. If the evidence is to be brought before the arbitrator or is recognized as having a material effect on the case, both parties would have to agree to reopen the case for the submission of the new evidence to the arbitrator and to give the arbitrator an opportunity to amend, revise, reaffirm, or reverse the previously issued opinion and award. The arbitrator has no right to reopen the case on the petition of one party once the decision has been rendered. Arbitration is, after all, to be binding on the parties.

Evidence on Remedy

As noted earlier, even if the union presents evidence during the hearing on the subject of remedy, on what a terminated employee lost during the period prior to reinstatement, or on how a contractually deprived employee should be made whole for that violation, the employer usually demurs. Other than perhaps some questions raised on cross-examination, the employer is unlikely to present contrasting evidence or otherwise to call to the arbitrator's attention the fact that it is even thinking of a penalty less than the one imposed or that its action was other than totally justified.

That strategy is usually maintained in the oral closing or written post-hearing briefs. The union is likely to reemphasize any questions asked about remedy during the hearing, and the employer is likely to adhere to its position that any other action it might have taken would have been unjustified or impermissible.

Occasionally the employer will argue that if its primary position is not fully sustained, the position of the union should not be fully sustained either. In this context, the employer may suggest to the arbitrator some remedy less than that sought by the union.

Even if the employer does not consider the remedy question during its closing, at the end of the closing the employer will sometimes ask the arbitrator to retain jurisdiction in the decision. Then, if the employer fails to secure a total victory from the arbitrator and it deems some other remedy appropriate, it can present its position on the remedy. This step may require a new hearing at which evidence would be presented to show that a remedy less than that requested by the union should be accepted by the arbitrator.

Conclusion

The foregoing recitation of what transpires at a hearing and of the problems that may arise should not give the impression that all of the cited problems occur in every hearing. On the contrary, most hearings flow smoothly, with the parties harmoniously presenting the evidence they think the arbitrator needs for a fair decision. However, problems of the sort covered here arise from time to time and it is important, particularly in the murky area of the rules of evidence, to know what is necessary to ensure that the arbitrator receives all the evidence necessary for a fair consideration of the issue and to protect against either side securing an unfair advantage that might lead to an unfair opinion and decision.

The preceding exposition of the sequence of a hearing incorporates several evidentiary matters as well. Rulings on admissibility of evidence is essential for the arbitrator to properly assess the materials and testimony presented at the hearing. Weighing that procedural and substantive evidence and argument is the next task of the arbitrator.

6
Decision-Making Procedures

A book devoted to the procedural issues facing the parties in the arbitration process cannot avoid addressing the consequence of their presentations, the greatest procedural issue of all: the procedure used by the arbitrator in deciding and writing the opinion and decision that seal the parties' fate.

Obviously, the process of making and writing the decision is unique to each arbitrator. While parties may try to ascertain how an arbitrator will decide a particular issue by examining that arbitrator's previous awards, there is no real window into how the arbitrator reasons through to this decision, except in what the arbitrator writes to educate the parties. That formal decision may try to bolster any uncertainty during the decision-making process and try to persuade the losing party that all of its arguments were carefully weighed but found lacking when compared to the overwhelmingly persuasive reasoning of the winning party. Some arbitrators reveal their indecisiveness about difficult cases in their opinions; others, reluctant to intensify the losing party's handwringing, set forth their reasoning very assertively so that the losing party is more likely to conclude that the case was open and shut and that they had never really had a chance.

Yet all arbitrators go through a set of similar procedures in reaching the conclusions they set forth in their opinions. That process may commence as early as the first announcement of the issue, with a visceral tilt to one side or the other. The arbitrator's opinion will then shift from one side to the other throughout the hearing and will probably solidify by the end of the hearing. By then, all arbitrators will have a "gut" reaction to the presentation about which side has won or about how the case should be resolved. That tentative initial conclusion is usually reached without a thorough reading of all the exhibits and contract citations and may be arrived at even before reading the closing arguments of the parties in their briefs.

That initial impression may, of course, be reversed by subsequent reflection and examination of the documentation. Sometimes, the case presentation of the parties may not be evenly matched. One side's spokesperson may be more experienced or may be an attorney, while the other's is not. (But this comment should not suggest that an attorney would be the preferred presenter.) Although arbitrators do not often rescue the party with the weaker presenter, they probably leave the hearing with awareness of the disparity and perhaps with an increased sensitivity to the problems faced by the less experienced advocate. That sensitivity, however, does not necessarily translate into a bias toward the underprivileged if the presentation didn't provide the necessary evidence. But, in most cases, the arbitrator's initial visceral feeling controls or is bolstered by the evidence. In other cases, a minority, the arbitrator exits the hearing undecided and hopes that study of the exhibits and opposing arguments will shed sufficient light to guide an intelligent and persuasive opinion.

I don't mean to suggest that arbitrators make up their minds only on the basis of what is stated at a hearing, but rather that, like anyone, they form certain impressions that, using their experience as decision makers, they test against the evidence. If the evidence suggests an alternative reasoning or even a different decision, they will readily adjust their initial impression to conform to the weight of that evidence.

It is the role and impact of that evidence that creates the procedural issues in the decision-making process. That fact is the thrust of this chapter. The evidence presented by the parties controls, rather than any subsequent independent research. Arbitrators refrain from independent research unless it is authorized by the parties so that the parties' presentation of evidence constitutes the environment from which the arbitrator draws conclusions based on fact and reasoning .

The data before the arbitrator, in the form of exhibits, direct examination and cross-examination, objections, and opening and closing argument, provides a diverse menu from which the arbitrator often could readily extract a reasonable decision supporting either the union or management position. Indeed, cynics could contend that arbitrators' agility in developing rationales for their decisions is governed by pragmatic self-interest, so that decisions are driven primarily by the selfish goal of client acceptability and the potential for reemployment that flows from it.

That suspicious view suggests that once one side has won a case before an arbitrator, it should avoid any further encounter with that same arbitrator, who would manipulate the decision in the next case to give a victory to the loser in the previous encounter. Yet parties with a marketplace containing five thousand arbitrators to choose from usually return to the neutrals they have dealt with before, even though one of the parties must have lost numerous cases before that arbitrator.

Those who reselect the same arbitrator appear to believe that arbitrators decide cases on their merit rather than on the basis of any scorecard. It seems likely that the parties can evaluate the strengths of their cases fairly well and know whether they have a reasonable prospect of winning or losing. When reusing an arbitrator, that expectation may even be fine tuned, so that a surprise decision from the arbitrator will be unsettling. An unanticipated victory where the evidence pointed to a loss would probably discredit the arbitrator and make the parties hesitant to use that arbitrator in the future out of fear that a strong case the next time could equally irrationally go to the other side, despite its weaker case. Assuming that the parties generally know when their case is strong or weak, the arbitrator's professional survival is best assured by deciding each case on its merit or weakness, without any calculation of whether the decision will protect the arbitrator's caseload.

Thus, if the arbitrator's decision is based on the evidence rather than its results for the arbitrator, the process of deciding the case requires a careful weighing of the evidence. That process involves numerous versions of evidence or testimony from which the arbitrator must choose and on which the decision may rest.

Is the grievant's recitation persuasive enough to control over the contradictory testimony of several management witnesses? Is the testimony of a negotiating team member so persuasive that the arbitrator believes the parties intended the contract language to mean something other than what appears on its face? Should the clear contract language control over or fall to an unchallenged practice that the parties acknowledge has continued for years without challenge? Should new contract language control over language that was repeated without protest through several contracts? What if the new language is more general than the earlier language?

While it is probably true that arbitrators have an intuitive sense at the end of the hearing about which party is likely to prevail, and while that intuitive sense can develop into a firm opinion and decision by careful culling of the evidence, arbitrators usually place that intuitive hunch into a mental recess while objectively assessing the evidence and repeatedly bouncing that hunch off of it to determine whether the hunch is supported by that evidence. If not, the hunch will fall in favor of the evidence, for the evidence controls. Once the decision has been made, it is the arbitrator's responsibility to corral that evidence and to put it on paper in a formal and, ideally, persuasive exposition of reasons for the decision.

This chapter focuses on decision making as well as decision writing and concludes with an examination of the finality of the award, despite the onslaught of efforts to introduce new evidence and to get the arbitrator to change the opinion and decision that so much effort has gone into reaching.

Credibility of Witnesses

Often the contradictory stories told by observers to the same event catapults a case to arbitration. Indeed, if there were no conflict over fact and the case depended solely upon the arbitrator's choosing one of two theories or contract provisions, there would be no need for a hearing and arbitrations could more speedily, efficiently, and economically be resolved by mailed stipulations of facts and submissions of briefs.

Whether the case involves conflict over what transpired before the imposition of discipline or over what was said during negotiations of a disputed contract provision five or ten years ago, most arbitration cases involve some disputes over fact that justify a hearing so that the arbitrator can observe the witnesses and hear the direct and cross-examining testimony that is the prerequisite to any meaningful findings of fact.

It must be borne in mind that, like all of us, witnesses are subject to lapses of memory. Even if the witness clearly observed the incident in dispute and clearly grasps all the details and peripheral events of that observation, the power of that testimony may still be affected by a failure to retain all those details in memory, the input of supplementary information by others in the period since the observation, and the witness's ability to fully recall or persuasively recite all that was observed and retained. Numerous psychological studies show that individuals may believe they observed things that were only suggested to them after the observation or that were suggested by the manner in which questions about those observations were asked.

How the arbitrator makes findings of fact from such contradictory evidence is difficult to determine. Some arbitrators claim they are able to judge whether or not a witness is telling the truth from the witness's demeanor. Some state that a witness who is explicit in recalling detail in testimony is more credible than one who is vague or uncertain. But such detailed recollection may, instead, be a consequence of good preparation for the hearing, or of a detailed writing of the event at the time or even of mere bluffing. Most arbitrators, however, realize that demeanor is not an infallible indicator of truth and that there are too many cultural differences in appearance, language, and gestures in our increasingly multicultural work force to support a judgment that a certain movement, look, or attitude is proof of truth or falsehood. Too many persuasive witnesses are just good liars. The stakes in an arbitration case, whether a potential loss of employment or a costly interpretation of the collective bargaining agreement are too great to hinge on some undocumented old wives tale that a lying witness won't look you in the eye, or that glancing upward to right or left before answering a question indicates that a false or true answer is forthcoming.

Some arbitrators claim that the testimony of witnesses must be weighed in the light of their motivation for telling the truth or lying. An employee whose job is at stake, for example, has the motivation to do whatever is possible—including lying—to protect that job. Thus, this reasoning continues, the supervisor is more credible because he or she has no motivation for lying. This rather simplistic view of witness credibility shifts the burden of proof in discipline cases from the employer to the grievant, and ignores the fact that a supervisor, who may have wrongly imposed the discipline, has a great deal of motivation to protect his or her credibility with the employer and with subordinates in future encounters, and even to ensure continued employment. Thus, the fact that the grievant's job survival may coincide with proclamations of innocence does not necessarily mean that the grievant is guilty and lying.

Arbitrators are more likely to rely on whether a proclaimed sequence of events is plausible in the light of the admitted evidence, the cross-examination and contradictions, and the available circumstantial evidence.

The ever-shifting burden of proof is very valuable in such an endeavor. Thus, when the employer's witnesses can testify that an employee was seen with a company volt meter in an inspected lunchbox while leaving the plant, that conduct would constitute a prima facie case of attempted theft and the burden of proving that there had been no theft would shift to the grievant. If the grievant then testifies to purchasing the volt meter at the company's surplus warehouse, that statement would appear to constitute an adequate rebuttal to the evidence of theft. If the employer failed to rebut that evidence, the arbitrator might reasonably conclude that the volt meter had been the grievant's property, so that there was no theft. But if the employer countered with testimony that volt meters were not sold in the surplus warehouse, that might switch the arbitrator's leaning from innocence to guilt. Then, too, there might be a rebuttal by producing the receipt from the warehouse for the sale of the volt meter. This shifting of burden can make the arbitration like a ping pong match, with the ball bouncing from team to team until it is not returned or falls at the feet of one of the teams.

The arbitrator's most trustworthy tool is seeking to resolve contradictions or differences in testimony is the burden of proof, which falls upon the employer in cases of discipline and discharge and upon the union in cases of contract interpretation or application. Under that theory, a tie is decided against the party having that burden of proof.

In the classic example of the supervisor who calls an employee into the office for a discussion and then emerges to report to the personnel director that employee had hit him so the employee was fired, the burden of proving that the attack took place is on the employer. The arbitrator may believe the supervisor if the grievant does not deny the assault, if there is corroborating evidence from the nurse that the supervisor's chin was cut, if there was evidence of a contusion, or perhaps even if the supervisor testified bargaining unit witnesses were present but were not called to testify and be subjected to cross-examination. Conversely, the arbitrator may believe the grievant if union witnesses testify that the supervisor had taunted the employee, that the supervisor had falsely accused this or other employees of assault in the past, or perhaps even that an assault by a 98-pound grievant on a 240-pound supervisor is not likely.

In a true test of credibility, where there is no evidence except the supervisor's claim of being hit and the grievant's denial or any physical contact, where there is no corroborative or circumstantial evidence, and where there were no witnesses, the traditional burden of proof standard would dictate that the grievant wins because the employer in such a discipline case had the burden but couldn't prove just cause for its disciplinary action.

The old saw that arbitrators do not know who is telling the truth, only whom they believe, is ultimately the standard the parties must accept when submitting issues of credibility to arbitration. The burden on the parties is to corral and organize the testimony and evidence so that when they are presented to the arbitrator in closing statements or briefs, they provide a reasonable explanation of what that side asserts transpired. When coupled with challenges to the rationality or believability of the other side's recitation, such proof is intended to provide the more—or the only—rational explanation of what actually took place. If the arbitrator goes along with that chronology, the case may be won.

Procedures in Deciding Contract Interpretation Cases

In nondisciplinary cases in which the arbitrator is required to resolve disputes over the ambiguous interpretation or application of the contract in which issues of credibility do not arise or have been resolved, the arbitrator may rely upon certain accepted standards of contract interpretation as guideposts for resolving claimed conflicts in contract language. Those guideposts are as appropriate to questions of arbitrability as they are to the merits of the case.

Compatibility with the Rest of the Contract

One of the basic standards of contract interpretation is that the interpretation of any single contract provision must be compatible with the collective bargaining agreement as a whole. For example, a new article 14 of the parties' agreement, "Labor–Management Cooperation," states:

> The parties will endeavor to resolve any disputes informally through joint labor–management meetings, which will be held monthly and at which any issues may be raised by employees who are present.

If the grievant seeks to utilize that forum to raise a complaint concerning a failure to promote him to a higher position, the employer would argue—and the arbitrator would probably agree—that the parties negotiated a grievance and arbitration system to handle allegations of contract violation, that the collective bargaining agreement sets forth the standards of behavior expected of both parties, that the Labor–Management Cooperation provision was not intended by the parties to supplant the grievance appeal procedures, and that consistency in applying the contract as the procedure for enforcing any alleged rights would dictate appeal to that grievance procedure. The Labor–Management Cooperation provision would simply be an informal, but nonadjudicatory, addition to any individual rights enforced by the contract.

It is not unusual for parties swept up in negotiations to introduce new language that seems to create new rights independent of the contract. Arbitrators, with their backgrounds in collective bargaining, are alert to these variations, but are also sensitive to the need to protect the contract and the rights enumerated therein as the most important document protecting the overall relationship of the parties.

Presumption Against the Drafter of Language

If, in the foregoing example, the evidence shows that the employer drafted the provision stating that the joint meetings "will be held monthly" and that it failed to call meetings for two months and then claimed that the holding of such meetings was at its discretion, a claim by the union that the monthly meetings were mandatory would probably be upheld by the arbitrator. In relying on the principle of presumption against the drafter of language, the arbitrator might hold that the employer, as drafter, had the option of inserting the word "may" instead of "will" before "be held," that it could have inserted language calling for bimonthly or regular meetings or meetings at its discretion, and that, when it used the term "will be held monthly," it committed itself by its own language to do just that. Thus, the union would be within contractual authority to expect the employer to live up to the commitment it had made to have required monthly meetings.

Earlier Versus Later

The parties' collective bargaining agreement is a continuing document. Some agreements have histories that can be traced over decades; many predate the 1935 National Labor Relations Act. Certainly, each individual contract is finite—often one to three years—but each time it is renegotiated, most of the former language is continued without change. Only those provisions that caused the parties difficulty during the prior contract term or that are anticipated to cause difficulty in the forthcoming contract term are placed on the bargaining table. All unoffending provisions are left unchanged, perhaps for decades.

At times, the parties may renegotiate or add new language but neglect to search through the remaining provisions of the agreement to ensure that all the related preexisting provisions have been amended to conform to the changes resulting from that negotiation. Arbitrators tend to follow the legal standard that later language on a subject controls over earlier agreed-upon language. Their reasoning is that when they changed the prior language, the parties had that prior language before them. The changes they agreed to reflected their perception of a need that had to be addressed and that they believed they had addressed by adopting the new language. But with that contract revision came the obligation to review the entire document to bring over preexisting provisions into conformity with the new language. The parties viewed the new language as revising the contract in the light of their more recent experience and needs—that is, as replacement of any prior language on the subject. Arbitrators tend to embrace this interpretation as the more accurate view on the issue in dispute.

CASE STUDY: *The Case of the Newer Standards.* In their first agreement in 1972, the parties negotiated a just cause provision which read:

> The school district agrees to adhere to the principles of just cause in any action it takes in imposing discipline, nonrenewal of teaching contracts, or discharge.

That provision was never cited in any grievance or arbitration appeals following its 1972 adoption and was retained in all intervening negotiations. However, in negotiating the 1990 agreement, the district proposed a new provision dealing with nonrenewal of nontenured teachers:

> In handling the nonrenewal of teaching contracts of nontenured teachers, the parties agree to follow the procedures of State Statute 189:72.

That state statute provided for appeal to the state Board of Education of any disputes over the nonrenewal of teaching contracts of nontenured teachers.

The union objected to the proposal, but when its adoption remained the final obstacle to a much-wanted salary increase, the union acceded to its introduction.

Doug Kaden, the grievant, had completed one year of teaching when advised that his contract would not be renewed. An effort to arbitrate the nonrenewal as not being for just cause was rebuffed by the district, which held the Kaden's only route of appeal was through the statute to the state Board of Education. The union protested, and the issue was referred to arbitration on the sole issue of arbitrability.

The union argued that nonrenewal of teachers' contracts was tantamount to dismissal and that the parties had recognized this fact when they included nonrenewal along with discipline and discharges as matters that would be subject to the just cause standards of review. The union argued that the 1990 amendment constituted a restriction imposed on the union under pressure, that the union's had not acquiesced to the surrender of its preexisting rights, and that at the very least, the language must be interpreted to permit appeals through both forums.

The district took the position that even if the parties had inserted the language of just cause for nonrenewals in 1972, there had never been any test of whether it applied to nontenured teachers, and that the 1990 contract amendment was mutually intended to clarify that issue of applicability. The district asserted that the new language was clearly aimed at precluding the invocation of the just cause standard for nonrenewal of nontenured teachers, that the union had agreed to it as the sole route of appeal, and that the grievance should be found not arbitrable.

The arbitrator held that the 1990 contract provision controlled over the earlier language because it had been adopted later, that the later language was the more contemporary expression of the parties' view on how to challenge nonrenewal of contracts of nontenured teachers, that the parties to the 1990 negotiations had been notified of the restrictions contained in the district's proposal, and that they had also been alerted to the need to determine the impact of the new language on the parties' pre-existing language. It was, according to the arbitrator, the responsibility of the union to protect against any excision of any earlier rights by restricting the district's new proposal or by introducing language that ensured the continuation of any related nonrenewal rights in the just cause language.

The arbitrator found the new language applied to all nonrenewals of contracts of nontenured teachers and that the language of the parties agreeing to the statutory appeal made that route the exclusive avenue for appeal and precluded any secondary appeal through arbitration under the just cause standard.

Discussion Question 1: What if the union had argued that the 1990 negotiations focused only on future teachers or that the agreement was never intended to foreclose access to arbitration?

This question illustrates the type of case in which the intent of the parties in agreeing to the new language would help in ruling whether the restriction was applicable in the manner the district asserted. In the absence of such parol evidence, an arbitrator could readily conclude that the 1990 agreement to go to the State Department of Education contained no language making it prospective in application or exclusive in route of appeal. It would, of course, be incumbent on the union to prove that the intent of the agreed-upon revision differed from what was written. To prove this intention, the union would have to provide supportive testimony of the negotiators' evidence that the district had accepted, though not codified, its interpretation. But if the district's witnesses testified differently from the union witnesses, then the arbitrator presumably would find that the union had not met its burden of proving the parties' intent differed from the clear words of the provision.

The burden was not on the employer to solidify its achievement beyond the language. The written language would control unless the union could prove a different intent or even prove there had been no meeting of the minds on the restriction the arbitrator held the district had achieved. The union might have succeeded if it could have persuaded the arbitrator, not that the new language did not say what the District avers, but that the union agreed to the language thinking it meant something different.

Discussion Question 2: What if the district had argued that the 1972 just cause provision applied to nonrenewal of only tenured teachers?

Arbitrators follow the precepts that all contract words are to be given their common meaning, that parties occasionally draft new language without resolving ambiguities it creates in preexisting retained language, but that if the parties have left that preexisting reference to nonrenewal, it should retain some meaning and relevance, despite the new addition.

The district's effort to distinguish the new from the preexisting language is in line with the goal of giving all provisions full meaning while reconciling any differences between provisions. Also, the offer of an explanation to support a consistent meaning between two apparently inconsistent provisions enables the arbitrator to avoid ruling on what might otherwise appear to be a deliberate contradiction between contract terms.

In this case, the district's distinction—particularly because of the evidence that no prior grievances had been filed by nontenured teachers— would support the assertion that the original language was intended to be limited to tenured teachers but had never been tested. This distinction would also overcome the alleged contradiction between the just cause provision and new language by noting that the latter was confined to nontenured teachers and that the original language applied only to tenured teachers.

Discussion Question 3: If the parties had been silent on whether or not any earlier grievances had been filed on nonrenewal of contracts, should the arbitrator have asked?

Arbitrators are loathe to ask questions that one would expect the parties to have asked in their questioning of witnesses. The silence of both parties on the issue of whether any grievances had been filed on nonrenewals might signal to the arbitrator that both parties want to leave this area unexplored. Arbitrators usually sense and conform to such unexpressed preferences.

But an arbitrator does have the obligation to reconcile two apparently contradictory provisions. Inasmuch as the arbitrator bears the responsibility for a rational, well-founded decision, the experience of the parties before the new language was adopted would appear to be vital to understanding how the parties viewed the old language and whether that practice had caused any need to change the language.

If the parties were silent because there had been no prior experience, the arbitrator's question would raise no problems. If, on the other hand, both parties were seeking to suppress some prior experience, one or both parties could explain by mutual agreement these prior cases were to be without precedent.

General Versus Special Language

A related situation involving the weighing of two potentially contradictory contract provisions occurs when the language of one provision is more detailed than that of another. When the parties have general language covering their relationship and also have negotiated more detailed language, it is assumed that the more specific provisions for handling a problem control over the more general language.

Suppose that the parties have negotiated a Management Rights Clause that includes the phrase "and management has the right to maintain discipline within the enterprise including the right to hire, discipline, and discharge employees." In their grievance article, the parties have also negotiated a provision that reads "The employer must adhere to progressive standards in imposing discipline."

Even if both provisions were adopted in the same negotiations, there is room for arguing that they contain a contradiction. In the Management Rights Clause the parties have enumerated a number of rights that management retains, so it could be argued that the parties ceded to management the right to discipline as well as discharge without any requirement of progressive discipline. It could also be argued that, if the employer retains the right to discharge employees, it should not be restrained by any requirement to discipline employees by imposing lesser escalating penalties.

But the parties that recognize the employer's managerial right to discipline and discharge also have negotiated a provision requiring progressive penalties. Inasmuch as the Management Rights Clause does not specifically preclude adherence to progressive discipline, there is no direct contradiction between the clauses. The fact that the grievance article does require progressive discipline means that it would control.

It must be assumed that the parties were alert to the language of the general Management Rights Clause when they negotiated the grievance article, whether or not it was negotiated at the same time or in a later negotiation. In the grievance article they imposed a restriction on what would appear to be a broad right to hire and fire, and that specific provision is superior to the more general language. Even if the parties had negotiated the Management Rights Clause after they had negotiated the grievance article, they would be held bound by the specific language if they had not somehow cited it, overruled it, or distinguished it when agreeing to their general language.

Ordinary Meaning

If the language of the Labor–Management Cooperation agreement discussed earlier in this chapter had called for regular meetings, and the employer had held them three times in January, once in May, and twice in September, the arbitrator might well sustain a grievance in which the union protested that the meetings were not being held regularly. In deciding whether the meetings were regular, the arbitrator could turn to the dictionary meaning of regular as "reoccurring at fixed intervals" and require the meetings to be held monthly, or every six weeks, or at some other periodic interval, instead of sporadically, as seems to have been the employer's practice.

If the contract language involved words with specialized or technical meaning, the arbitrator would interpret such language in terms of the meaning usually given to such technical terms. But for nontechnical wording that is based on normal human intercourse, the arbitrator will often turn to the dictionary definition of words as the parties' presumed intent in drafting contract language.

Residual Rights

For many years, there has been a debate between those who contend that all rights not negotiated by the union into the contract reside with management and those who contend that the collective bargaining agreement is a treaty between two parties with equal rights. Under the latter theory, the union has the right to provide or withhold services, while the employer has the right to provide the compensation and exercise such rights as it enumerates in the management rights clause.

Most observers and arbitrators have embraced the former alternative by reasoning that, before collective bargaining, the employer possessed all the authority in the workplace and that the union achieved recognition and restrictions on those all-powerful rights only insofar as it was able to extract concessions through collective bargaining.

This debate bears on the standards of contract interpretation because when the parties have failed to negotiate a particular benefit or protection, most arbitrators embrace the residual rights theory. Arbitrators reason that the employer retains any rights that are unrestricted or unmentioned by the contract and that in contract negotiation the burden was on the union to achieve any additional rights from management. Failing that effort, management retains any unspecified residual rights.

Past Practice

In many cases, one party will rely on what appears to be the clear language of the contract, while the other party will assert that, despite what that language says or omits, the parties have consistently adhered to a practice that might appear to violate that contract language, but that would control.

Inasmuch as the parties cannot negotiate every eventuality that might arise in the employment relationship, it is not unreasonable to conclude that, if the parties have followed a clear, consistent practice that is not restricted by the contract language, that practice should be permitted to continue. In effect, the parties, upon entering a collective bargaining agreement, have frozen the status quo on extracontractual conditions that have been previously in effect; the party seeking to alter that status quo would have to do so by seeking agreement on new contract language.

A different situation occurs when the contract language varies from preexisting practice. Some arbitrators take the strict view that explicit contract language controls. That view may be particularly prevalent when the arbitrator is ruling on contracts containing a zipper clause, which specifies that only the written contract is relevant and that any oral understandings must be excluded because they violate the parties' expressed commitment to the written word. In such cases, evidence of contradictory practice may be excluded. But most arbitrators hold that the controlling standard is how the parties apply the agreement. Following that model, if the employer declines to impose the strict requirement of the parties' written agreement in favor of continuing a practice that is acceptable to both, it could be reasoned that the parties have in effect recast the contract to embrace the mutually accepted practice.

For example, suppose the contract specifies that "Employees shall remain at their work stations until the end of their respective shifts" but, in contradiction to that language, the foreman had allowed employees to wash up in the locker rooms five minutes before the end of their shifts. Or suppose that the contract requires submission of a written request for a personal day five work days in advance, but the practice has been for the employer to accept and process oral requests in less than five days before the day of leave.

In both cases, the contract language is explicit, while the existing practice violates that language. Most arbitrators are willing to admit evidence of practice that contradicts specific contract language. In some cases, the parol evidence rule might be relied upon to explain that the intent of the parties, as manifest by their practice, is at variance with or contradicts the agreement language. In other cases, the arbitrator will admit evidence of the contrary practice as evidence that the employer has waived implementation of the agreement.

As in the case of a company rule that has been consistently violated, arbitrators are unlikely to find a contract violation if there has been a consistent history of the employer abandoning its right to expect adherence to the contract. That conclusion is usually founded on the precept that the employer cannot suddenly revise a practice to which it has acquiesced. If it wished to do so, the employer could readily reestablish the supremacy of the contract and terminate the violative practice by simply issuing notice that, thereafter, the practice must be terminated and the contract or rule requirement must be adhered to.

The following questions comprise a convenient checklist for determining whether or not a past practice has the standing to be accepted as on a par with or more persuasive than contrary contract language:

1. Did the practice concern a major condition of employment? Is it something that concerned few employees, or isolated plant locations? Was it widespread?

2. Was the practice established unilaterally? Did the employee know of it? Was it something that the employees did on their own, or was anyone in management involved in its evolution?

3. Was it administered unilaterally? Was it something that existed within the ranks of the employees? Did the employer permit it to continue or acquiesce or approve of the practice?

4. Did either side ever undertake to insert the practice or its prohibition into the contract? Was it ever the subject of negotiations between the parties?

5. Was the practice repeated frequently? Was it routine?

6. Was the practice longstanding? Had it existed under prior agreements?

7. Did the employees rely upon it? Was there a social, or economic benefit from the practice?

8. Was it specifically detailed, open, and known? Was it known to any or all levels of management? Was it kept from top managers by participating subordinates?

Negotiations History

In many cases, the parties merely ask the arbitrator to interpret the wording of their agreement on its face. Sometimes this request may occur in connection with a dispute about other contract terms, perhaps involving the earlier versus later or general versus specific standards. But the parties seldom base their positions on the words themselves. It is much more likely that each side will seek to persuade the arbitrator that its interpretation is more valid because it reflects the culmination of what that side was striving for during the negotiations that led to that language.

The generally flexible attitude of arbitrators toward the parol evidence rule reflects their view of the labor–management relationship as a continuing partnership that is periodically reduced to writing in collective bargaining agreements and ratified by the parties. The agreement is not a one-shot contract negotiated like a purchase between parties that must detail their mutual understanding of their "deal" in jointly acceptable written language. Because of the continuing labor–management relationship, the parties' most recent contract is only a reflection of the parties latest thinking; it was not developed like a purchase and sales agreement for a house or a load of steel. Rather, the most recent contract has a negotiating history built into it that is based on prior written agreements and the negotiating histories that went into them.

Thus, when an arbitrator is confronted with a dispute between the parties over the meaning of the contract's written language—even language that superficially might appear to be clear—that dispute shows that the parties do not agree on the meaning of the terms and, almost by definition, that there is ambiguity in the jointly agreed language. In such situations, arbitrators feel compelled to listen to evidence about what preceded the agreement on that disputed language so that they can more accurately assess each party's individual intent and their mutual intent when agreeing to it. Comprehending the confusing and often protracted presentations of the negotiating history may be crucial to the arbitrator's rendition of a fair award. In this type of dispute, the arbitrator's experience in and familiarity with negotiation procedures will ensure the parties of a more informed arbitral result.

Arbitrators may rely upon several aspects of negotiations history in seeking to satisfy themselves about the meaning of the disputed contract language.

The Negotiations for the Most Recent Contract Change

Of most immediate relevance to the arbitrator is what the parties intended when they agreed to the present language. To help determine that intent, the arbitrator would benefit from presentations about what transpired before that new language was agreed. The record, at best, will be fuzzy. Obviously, witnesses who were present at the negotiations will provide testimony of their recollections of what they and others said at the hearing. If unrebutted, such testimony is usually persuasive to the arbitrator. But if rebutted or contradicted, the testimony's value is harder for the arbitrator to ascertain because acceptance of challenged testimony depends upon resolving threshold credibility, which usually is not as apparent as arbitrators would like. Of greater help to the arbitrator is written documentation, which may be individual notes taken by participants in the negotiations or a sanitized set of mutually agreed-upon minutes. But the latter, if edited, while perhaps clear, may be more diluted than the handwritten contemporaneous notes of the participants, with their occasional quotations of what the spokespersons said.

Perhaps the most informative report of what transpired on the way to the agreed-upon language is any record of the proposed language and the responses that were exchanged between the parties during the negotiations. When timed and dated and marked as employer or union offerings, such records provide a more accurate insight into the parties' intentions on each proposal. These records, coupled with the notes of the participants and the oral testimony of witnesses, give the arbitrator the tools for a reasonable assessment of the parties' intent in agreeing to the disputed provision.

Prior Contract Negotiation

As indicated in the discussion of earlier versus later language, it is often necessary to go behind the contract words to secure evidence of the intent of the parties during negotiations of more than the most recent agreement. Since each contract is only a temporal codification of the parties' relationship on the date of signing, the effort to prove intent may lead the parties to present evidence of negotiations for a number of contracts dating from the time the disputed issue was first before the parties.

Tracing that history may be very time-consuming and may absorb much arbitration hearing time, but it is important for the parties to provide those data to the arbitrator. And, for the arbitrator, tracing the negotiating history of a subject through a number of negotiations may be necessary to ascertain the most reasonable meaning of the disputed provision.

That search may embrace evidence beyond the testimony, notes, and proposals that led to contract language. It may also embrace proposals not made, or proposals made and withdrawn, or letters of understanding that were developed when one or both of the parties wished to codify an understanding without incorporating it into the agreement. The search might also embrace earlier grievance settlements or arbitration decisions that stimulated one of the parties to initiate a proposal for new contract language to counteract the effect of that settlement or decision or to sanctify it by incorporating that result into the contract.

Regardless of how the arbitrator rules on such evidence, the presentation by each side of a chronology from the genesis of a proposal to the final incorporation of the disputed language into the parties' collective bargaining agreement is important to ensure that the arbitrator has full access to the steps taken by each side in moving toward that language. The arbitrator's examination of such documentation is essential to fulfil the obligation of ascertaining the meaning of the disputed language. Indeed, if the arbitrator is to fulfil the responsibility of interpreting and applying the parties' agreement, a detailed chronology may be the most crucial tool for reaching the arbitration goal of the parties—determining whose version of the meaning of contract language has greater credence.

Incorporation by Reference

The foregoing discussion is restricted to determinations of what the parties intended in language being interpreted by the arbitrator. But sometimes the parties, by agreeing to certain language, bring external elements into the parties' relationship and thereby impose upon the arbitrator the responsibility to apply such external standards. If they intended for external elements to be considered, the parties should embrace or at least expect the result. But the arbitrator, in ascertaining the result, has to undertake to determine what that external reference imposes on the parties.

Although the parties' collective bargaining agreement may be subject to the laws of the community in which it was negotiated, it has been generally accepted that the arbitrator's decision-making responsibility is limited to the interpretation and application of the contract terms without regard for the external law. But occasionally the parties' agreement collides with elements of the external law, thereby imposing on the arbitrator the responsibility to either stick to the contract and ignore the external law, or, alternatively, to reconcile the contract and the law, or, perhaps, to comply with the law even though it may impede upon the parties' contractual intent and language.

The procedure utilized by the arbitrator in such cases is first to ascertain from the parties' presentation whether the contract embraces any external law. If a collective bargaining agreement specifies that the employer agrees not to engage in racial or sexual discrimination, or that it commits itself to maintain a safe workplace, the arbitration is not therefore bound by EEO laws or by OSHA regulations when interpreting whether there had been discrimination or an unsafe working condition. If the parties had negotiated such standards, most arbitrators would look to internal negotiating history and to contract language to determine whether there had been discrimination or unsafe working conditions as the arbitrator would define those terms. Although the grievant may be dissatisfied with the arbitrator's finding or definitions and seek relief in a legal forum under EEO or OSHA laws, such scope of consideration would be beyond the arbitrator's jurisdiction, which most would hold is confined to the parties' agreement, without any specific reference to external law.

The problem becomes somewhat more difficult when the parties' agreement incorporates a reference to external law. Sometimes the reference is vague or indecisive, such as a nondiscrimination provision that reads: "The employer agrees to abide by all pertinent statutes and administrative rulings prohibiting discriminatory treatment."

In this instance, the arbitrator would try to determine whether the decision is to be based on the contract alone or whether it requires a ruling based upon external law. In this example, there is no guidance on which administrative rulings or law to follow. Is the arbitrator bound by state EEO administrative rulings, federal EEO administrative rulings, state or federal law, or state or federal judicial rulings? Some arbitrators may undertake to explore all of these forums as the scope of their mandate. Others would select federal law, as enforced by federal Supreme Court decisions, and follow those standards. Still others would avoid reliance on a specific jurisdiction or forum for fear that rulings in one area might be contradicted by rulings in another. Arbitrators in this group might simply interpret "the law" according to their individual understanding of it and leave to the losing party the option of challenging the arbitrator's decision in a later court proceeding.

The arbitrator's procedural quest is simpler if the contractual reference is to a specific law, such as: "The parties agree to conform to the rulings of the federal court in responding to charges of discriminatory treatment of employees."

A similar result may be imposed on the parties by the jurisdiction in question if the collective bargaining agreement is between a union and a community, state, or federal government. In the latter case, the advocates are generally quite sophisticated in informing the arbitrator about the intricacies and interrelationships of federal law and the collective bargaining agreement.

Once the appropriate legal forum has been identified, the arbitrator must next determine the pertinent external law. Should it be the statute, court rulings, or even the Supreme Court rulings? Most arbitrators adhere to the precept the parties should provide all the information necessary to the arbitrator's decision. When venturing into the area of the external law, all that information may not be forthcoming. One of the parties may be untutored in the law, or in that aspect of it. Indeed, only one or neither of the parties may be represented by a lawyer or knowledgeable layman. And even if the parties are equally expert, is the arbitrator bound by the legal information offered by them? What if that information is inaccurate, out of date, or wrong?

Arbitrators may undertake an independent investigation if so authorized by the parties, and that authorization would encompass investigations of the law or efforts to ascertain the thoroughness of the parties' input on legal requirements.

The next issue, procedurally speaking, is for the arbitrator to determine whether to undertake the independent legal inquiry. Even if the need for that step is not recognized during the hearing and the arbitrator subsequently decides that the legal issue has been inadequately presented, it is important for the arbitrator to secure the requisite authorization for independent investigation by a letter or by a phone call to the parties.

Once that permission is granted, or the arbitrator opts to investigate without specific authorization, the next procedural step is to read the legal cases presented and cited by the parties as well as any other rulings that the arbitrator deems appropriate in order to reach a conclusion based on the law, as the parties must have anticipated when they agreed to abide by that external law.

The final procedure for the arbitrator is to write findings in the requisite language, explaining why the result was what the parties had agreed to embrace when they negotiated the governing contract language.

Procedures in Deciding Discipline Cases

The procedures followed by the arbitrator in discipline cases are somewhat different from those followed in contract interpretation cases.

The two types of cases may present comparable threshold questions about arbitrability and about whether the contractual procedures and parties' practices have been adhered to in processing the case to arbitration, but if the case is to be resolved on the merits two distinctive sequential procedures apply.

The first is to determine whether or not there are even grounds for discipline. In receiving the evidence presented by the parties, the arbitrator must determine whether the behavior complained of was prohibited, whether the employee was aware of the prohibition, and then the crucial question of whether the grievant did commit the offense. It is incumbent upon the parties to provide the requisite evidence of company rules, testimony about the posting or delivery of such rules and the grievant's actual or constructive notice of the rules, and evidence about whether the grievant acted as charged. The latter evidence may be admitted by the grievant or may come from the testimony of witnesses so that the arbitrator must weigh some of the standards set forth previously for determining credibility.

Once the arbitrator has followed this procedure for determining whether or not there was just cause for any discipline, the subsequent procedure takes one of two tacks. If the arbitrator finds that the discipline was unjustified, or not for just cause, the arbitrator will order the employee to be returned to work with full reimbursement of losses suffered. But if the arbitrator finds that discipline was justified, the arbitrator must reexamine the parties' presentations to secure the evidence needed to impose the proper penalty for the infraction. Among the evidence that the parties should have provided for the arbitrator to make that determination are the standards of progressive discipline adhered to by the parties, the prior disciplinary penalties on the grievant's current record, the evidence of how similar situations were dealt with for employees in similar situations or with similar prior records, and any evidence about the employment or earnings of the grievant if he was suspended or terminated from employment.

Once an appropriate penalty is determined, the arbitrator has to handle the issue of remedy if the option is to reduce the penalty imposed on the grievant. If the employer has imposed an excessive penalty short of discharge, then it is relatively simple for the arbitrator to reduce the penalty to one deemed more appropriate and to make the employee whole for the difference, whether it be three weeks' back pay when reducing a four-week suspension to one week, or three days' back pay when reducing a three-day suspension to a letter of warning. Making the employee whole for lost earnings would not only create entitlement to the back pay, but should also entitle the grievant to reimbursement of that portion of overtime he or she would have earned but for the removal.

A more difficult implementation faces the arbitrator in reinstating a terminated grievant with a discipline less than removal. Clearly, if the grievant is innocent of the charges, then reinstatement with full back pay is appropriate. But if some measure of discipline was justified, but the arbitrator finds that termination was excessive, the arbitrator faces a dilemma in conforming to the traditional dictates of progressive escalated discipline. If the employee is warned of the increased risk of termination and granted substantial back pay windfall, that warning of risk will be washed away by the reward of a massive repayment of lost wages. Thus, if an employee was improperly terminated a year ago for a second offense of dozing on the job, an infraction for which the normal penalty has been a three-day suspension, reimbursement of a year's pay minus three days hardly seems an escalated penalty.

Some arbitrators balance the scales by reinstating the employee without back pay, so that the employer is not damaged by an excessive back pay award and the employee is given another chance. While such a baby-splitting approach may have value in a last-chance situation in which the employee's reinstatement is questionable, it does not meet the requirement of progressive discipline that the punishment should fit—but not exceed—the crime.

Some arbitrators believe that resolutions such as reinstatement without back pay will help maintain their acceptability to both parties. But some parties whose arbitrators rely on such palliatives report that both sides are hostile to outcomes in which neither side wins or loses. But many arbitrators reason that the employer took the termination action, that it had the authority to reinstate the employee at any time during the appeal procedure, and that it must bear the consequences if the arbitrator opts for a lesser penalty and conformity to the precepts of progressive discipline. Other arbitrators may grant the employer's right to have disciplined for what it viewed as a terminal offense when the action was apparently taken in good faith; thus, because the employee and employer both contributed to the extended suspension, these arbitrators will split the amount of the back pay.

The range of options is extensive in such situations, and the burden is upon the parties to spell out their respective remedies and to show why the arbitrator should embrace one rather than the other.

Quantum of Proof

As noted earlier, the burden of proof constantly shifts from one party to the other throughout the hearing as new evidence and testimony are introduced. But at the end of the hearing, when all the evidence is in, the arbitrator must make the final determination of whether the union has proven its allegations of contract violations or the employer has proven its allegation that discipline was imposed for just cause.

There have been numerous expositions about the extent of proof that must be provided for either of the parties to prevail. Advocates in courts of law devote considerable energy to determining the quantum of evidence required to prevail in civil and criminal actions. Although standards such as "preponderance of evidence," "clear and convincing," and even "beyond a reasonable doubt," or "beyond a shadow of a doubt" may be clear to those proclaiming them as appropriate standards of proof, there is no accepted definition of how much evidence is required to meet any one of those standards. Even if one were able to attach percentages of proof to those standards, it would be difficult to secure agreement on whether that standard had been met in any particular case. The judgments of whether these standards have been met are too subjective.

Fortunately, in labor arbitration, as opposed to the courts, there is no need to determine whether one standard rather than another is to control, let alone whether the evidence in the case meets that level. Although some arbitrators take the position that the tougher standard of proof beyond a reasonable doubt is required in discipline cases because they are comparable to criminal court proceedings, where that standard controls, discipline arbitrations do not entail the potential of death penalty, incarceration, or loss of freedom that drives the higher standards for criminal proceedings.

Most arbitrators continue to believe that, although termination may indeed be the "capital punishment of industrial relations," the proper standard is the one that controls civil, not criminal, cases. According to such reasoning, there is little profit in pursuing whether some objective threshold of proof—for example, "clear and convincing" or "preponderance"—has been reached because the controlling standard in arbitration is really no more than the ability to convince the arbitrator. No higher judicial review could overturn an arbitrator's decision as unsupported by proof of any quantum of evidence.

And if the arbitrator is one who holds that the decision should be written to convince the losing party that its case was not at all persuasive, that decision is unlikely to contain any of the handwringing that would enable the parties to claim that their proof came so close to meeting the quantum of legal proof as to raise doubts about whether or not the burden was met.

Reliance on the legal crutch of quantum of proof is not nearly as effective as "persuading the arbitrator" that the evidence supports a position on the claim in dispute.

Writing the Opinion and Decision

Arbitrators are usually wedded to a particular procedure when it comes to writing their decisions. Reading a number of decisions by different arbitrators will disclose their differences in opinion structure. Most arbitrators have thought out their conclusions before they begin the writing, and they write about elements they relied upon in analyzing the case and reaching their decisions. For some, the writing itself is the procedure they use to formulate their reasoning and articulate their justification for the decision. There is no correct decision-writing strategy. The career success of certain arbitrators over others testifies to the acceptability of the format of their opinions and the acceptability of their decisions.

The written opinion is used by arbitrators to convey their reasoning and its result to those who have presented and who have been awaiting the issuance of the award by which they will be bound. There are frequent debates about the audience for which the opinion is written. At one extreme are the arbitrators who write for publication in the reporting services. At the other extreme are the arbitrators who write shorthand opinions for the presenters, without much reference to the background of the case. Although arbitrators claim they write for the grievant, the level of language used is not always understandable by the grievant, particularly those with limited English. It appears that most arbitrators write for the presenters, particularly for the losing side, by explaining why each of the losing side's arguments was not acceptable, while dealing with and endorsing perhaps only one of the arguments of the winning side. The opinion is also written for company and union archives so that future management and union personnel reading the opinion will have the evidence and documentation on which the arbitrator relied in reaching the decision. Thus, the decision can have value for applying the precepts to subsequent disputes. It is usually considered to be up to the presenters, presumably those on the union side, to present and explain the opinion to the grievant.

In layout, the opinion usually begins with a short recital of the nature of the case, the names of the presenters, and the dates of the various presentations. Those details are usually followed by a listing of the issue to be arbitrated and a chronology of the facts that brought the case to arbitration, with the relevant documentary citations integrated into that litany. Thereafter, the positions of the parties are set forth, followed by the reasoning of the arbitrator in resolving the dispute and concluding with the actual arbitrator's decision.

The process of arbitration is presumed to be expeditious. Although it is clearly more expeditious than the procedures of the courts, arbitration is usually not as expeditious as the parties would like. The rules of the American Arbitration Association call for the rendering of an award within thirty days of the closing of the evidence. The Federal Mediation and Conciliation Service permits sixty days. Most arbitrators meet their deadlines, but some do not. That failure, in part, is because the parties flock to the busiest arbitrators to have their cases heard, regardless of delays in scheduling, rather than using other equally competent but lesser known arbitrators whose caseload would permit a more rapid issuance of the awards. The use of the busiest arbitrators may also be an effort by the spokespersons to protect themselves against criticism for using a neophyte if the case is lost. But the concentration of work among the busiest arbitrators imposes heavy workloads and, if the arbitrator is unable or unwilling to say no to new work, begets delays in the issuance of the awards. The party more adversely affected by the delay is reluctant to bother the arbitrator, let alone goad the arbitrator into a more rapid issuance of the award, for fear of antagonizing him or her. In many cases, the other side is less troubled by the delay and is content with the continuing status quo, even if the arbitrator's decision exceeds the time limits. In some cases, the parties jointly request the arbitrator to expedite the issuance of an overdue award, and some parties have been known to jointly advise the arbitrator that unless the award is issued within a certain number of days the case will be withdrawn from the arbitrator without compensation being paid, because the terms of the original contract calling for a decision within specified time limits or AAA rules were not met.

The arbitrator is bound by part 2J of the code:

Avoidance of Delay

1. It is a basic professional responsibility of an arbitrator to plan his or her work schedule so that present and future commitments will be fulfilled in a timely manner.

3. Once the case record has been closed, an arbitrator must adhere to the time limits for an award, as stipulated in the labor agreement or as provided by regulation of an administrative agency or as otherwise agreed.

The NAA Committee on Professional Responsibility and Grievances has dealt with the issue of arbitrators not rendering their awards in timely fashion. In cases brought to the committee by clients protesting the delay, the committee will investigate the charges utilizing the NAA internal appeal procedures and will suspend from active membership and directory listing for one year any members who have violated the prohibition against exceeding previously agreed-upon time limits. The FMCS and AAA, as co-sponsors of the code, have suspended guilty arbitrators from their lists for the period involved, thus enforcing the code while giving the penalized arbitrator the opportunity to catch up on overdue awards.

Retention of Jurisdiction

Although some arbitrators routinely retain jurisdiction over the implementation of their awards, regardless of whether they have been requested to do so, most do not. The latter reason that if one or both of the parties wish the arbitrator to retain jurisdiction, they would have so requested, so the arbitrator should not impose further services on parties who had the option but declined to ask for them. If implementation of the award is a problem for the parties, they still have the option of jointly asking the arbitrators to reopen the case, even though funtus officio. In any event, the union could file a new grievance protesting the employer's failure to implement the award it believes had been ordered by the arbitrator. Finally, most arbitrators are unwilling to retain jurisdiction without being requested to do so by at least one party for fear that it would be reviewed by the parties as an effort to create work.

Part 6.D1 of the NAA code provides: "No clarification or interpretation of an award is permissible without the consent of both parties." If the parties have a dispute over an issued award, they may jointly submit the question to the same arbitrator if they wish or, because the conflict creates a new issue and, potentially, a new grievance, they may mutually opt to send it to a different arbitrator. Many arbitrators feel that a losing party should not be forced to resubmit an issue of decision interpretation to an arbitrator with whom they may be unsatisfied.

However, besides interpretation of the award, there may be situations in which the arbitrators would need to reactivate jurisdiction after the award has been issued. One such case might occur when an obvious error has been called to the arbitrator's attention, such as a typographical or computational error in the decision portion of the document that is blatantly inconsistent with the reasoning and calculations set forth in the opinion section. Courts have held that it is appropriate for an arbitrator, even if jurisdiction had not been retained, to correct such errors.

On October 27, 1989, in opinion 20, the Committee on Professional Responsibility and Grievances declared:

> correction of the identity of one of the employees entitled to back pay and of the arithmetic error in calculation of the back pay awarded, or other corrections of similar evident clerical mistakes or computational errors, would not constitute "clarification or interpretation of an award" within the meaning of Part 6-D-1 . . . that kind of correction is not really "clarification or interpretation" but rather an attempt to rectify the arbitrator's carelessness in identifying grievants, making arithmetic calculations or proofreading the typewritten award.

... the common law rule of funtis officie does not bar correction of clerical mistakes or obvious computational errors.[14]

In a case of termination in which the employer presented no evidence during the hearing about the possibility of crafting a remedy, the reopening that could come as a consequence of the arbitrator having retained the requested jurisdiction would permit the introduction of evidence by both parties about interim earnings. The parties might also present evidence on efforts to secure employment, records of employment services on requests for or offers of work, consequential damages, or evidence on the obligation to mitigate damages by taking work of lesser pay, and so on. In addition, perhaps, evidence might be offered of the culpability of the respective parties for the delay in bringing the case to the reopened arbitration.

As noted earlier, errors of substance in an issued opinion and decision, or the discovery of new material evidence may trigger a request for the arbitrator to reopen the case. Usually, the request is initiated by one party, leading the arbitrator to react by declining the request or by forwarding it on to the other side. Arbitrators relieved of their authority usually would not reopen cases on their own, but they might encourage the parties to jointly request that the case be reopened if the subject matter is material, if it was not known of when the record was closed, and if, when received, it might make a difference in the outcome of the case.

Conclusion

This book has not been written to complicate the lives of the parties' representatives in preparing and presenting their cases to arbitration. Nor is it intended to increase the mystery of how arbitrators decide questions. Rather, this book has been written with the opposite goals in mind.

The adversarial legal system—out of which and in reaction to which arbitration was established—brought with it certain procedural requirements and obstacles that must be dealt with in order to ensure that justice is done in questions of contract interpretation and imposition of equitable discipline.

While some of the procedures may appear arcane or as impediments to labor–management conflict resolution, they do have the higher purpose of protecting the parties' and the grievant's rights to equitable and fair treatment under the collective bargaining agreement by which their relationship is governed. When understood and applied, these procedures also serve as effective guides to the arbitrator as the enforcer of those agreements.

Despite its detractors, and despite the zealous protestations that the procedure is overlegalized, arbitration appears to work. The extent to which nonunionized employers have embraced the system as a means of bringing stability to their employment relationships and of retaining the loyalty of their nonunion employees as an alternative to unionization underscores the effectiveness and the fairness of the process, even with its procedural baggage.

In the organized sphere, arbitration is relied upon by union and management alike as a device that permits ready resolution of those occasional disputes that might, in the absence of such an escape valve, bring serious disruption to the workplace in the form of work distractions, escalating antagonisms, and work disruptions, with the long-term scars that such traumas leave on the parties.

The issuance and ready acceptance of the overwhelming majority of arbitrator's opinions and the parties' return to the same arbitrators before whom they had previously lost cases testifies to the parties' faith in the arbitration process and to the commitment and integrity of its participants in utilizing this informal procedure as the preferred method of conflict resolution. It is a pity that other sectors of our litigious society have not undertaken the effort expended by labor unions and management in developing such an expeditious, equitable, and economical device for resolving their disputes.

Appendix
Code of Professional
Responsibility

OF THE
NATIONAL ACADEMY OF ARBITRATORS
AMERICAN ARBITRATION ASSOCIATION
FEDERAL MEDIATION AND CONCILIATION SERVICE

*As amended
and in effect
May 29, 1985*

Preamble

Background

Voluntary arbitration rests upon the mutual desire of management 1
and labor in each collective bargaining relationship to develop procedures
for dispute settlement which meet their own particular needs and obliga-
tions. No two voluntary systems, therefore, are likely to be identical in
practice. Words used to describe arbitrators (Arbitrator, Umpire, Impartial Chairman, Chairman of Arbitration Board, etc.) may suggest typical
approaches but actual differences within any general type of arrangement
may be as great as distinctions often made among the several types.

Some arbitration and related procedures, however, are not the prod- 2
uct of voluntary agreement. These procedures, primarily but not exclusively
applicable in the public sector, sometimes utilize other third party titles
(Fact Finder, Impasse Panel, Board of Inquiry, etc.). These procedures
range all the way from arbitration prescribed by statute to arrangements
substantially indistinguishable from voluntary procedures.

The standards of professional responsibility set forth in this Code 3
are designed to guide the impartial third party serving in these diverse labor-
management relationships.

Scope of Code

This Code is a privately developed set of standards of professional 4
behavior. It applies to voluntary arbitration of labor-management grievance disputes and of disputes concerning new or revised contract terms.
Both "ad hoc" and "permanent" varieties of voluntary arbitration, private
and public sector, are included. To the extent relevant in any specific case,
it also applies to advisory arbitration, impasse resolution panels, arbitration prescribed by statutes, fact-finding, and other special procedures.

The word "arbitrator," as used hereinafter in the Code, is intended 5
to apply to any impartial person, irrespective of specific title, who serves

in a labor-management dispute procedure in which there is conferred authority to decide issues or to make formal recommendations.

6   The Code is not designed to apply to mediation or conciliation, as distinguished from arbitration, nor to other procedures in which the third party is not authorized in advance to make decisions or recommendations. It does not apply to partisan representatives on tripartite boards. It does not apply to commercial arbitration or to other uses of arbitration outside the labor-management dispute area.

Format of Code

7   **Bold Face** type, sometimes including explanatory material, is used to set forth general principles. *Italics* are used for amplification of general principles. Ordinary type is used primarily for illustrative or explanatory comment.

Application of Code

8   Faithful adherence by an arbitrator to this Code is basic to professional responsibility.

9   The National Academy of Arbitrators will expect its members to be governed in their professional conduct by this Code and stands ready, through its Committee on Ethics and Grievances, to advise its members as to the Code's interpretation. The American Arbitration Association and the Federal Mediation and Conciliation Service will apply the Code to the arbitrators on their rosters in cases handled under their respective appointment or referral procedures. Other arbitrators and administrative agencies may, of course, voluntarily adopt the Code and be governed by it.

10   In interpreting the Code and applying it to charges of professional misconduct, under existing or revised procedures of the National Academy of Arbitrators and of the administrative agencies, it should be recognized that while some of its standards express ethical principles basic to the arbitration profession, others rest less on ethics than on considerations of good practice. Experience has shown the difficulty of drawing rigid lines of distinction between ethics and good practice and this Code does not attempt to do so. Rather, it leaves the gravity of alleged misconduct and the extent to which ethical standards have been violated to be assessed in the light of the facts and circumstances of each particular case.

1

Arbitrator's Qualifications and Responsibilities to the Profession

A. General Qualifications

1. Essential personal qualifications of an arbitrator include hones- 11 ty, integrity, impartiality and general competence in labor relations matters.

An arbitrator must demonstrate ability to exercise these personal 12 qualities faithfully and with good judgment, both in procedural matters and in substantive decisions.

a. Selection by mutual agreement of the parties or direct designa- 13 tion by an administrative agency are the effective methods of appraisal of this combination of an individual's potential and performance, rather than the fact of placement on a roster of an administrative agency or membership in a professional association of arbitrators.

2. An arbitrator must be as ready to rule for one party as for the 14 other on each issue, either in a single case or in a group of cases. Compromise by an arbitrator for the sake of attempting to achieve personal acceptability is unprofessional.

B. Qualifications for Special Cases

1. An arbitrator must decline appointment, withdraw, or request 15 technical assistance when he or she decides that a case is beyond his or her competence.

16   a. An arbitrator may be qualified generally but not for specialized assignments. Some types of incentive, work standard, job evaluation, welfare program, pension, or insurance cases may require specialized knowledge, experience or competence. Arbitration of contract terms also may require distinctive background and experience.

17   b. Effective appraisal by an administrative agency or by an arbitrator of the need for special qualifications requires that both parties make known the special nature of the case prior to appointment of the arbitrator.

C. Responsibilities to the Profession

18   **1. An arbitrator must uphold the dignity and integrity of the office and endeavor to provide effective service to the parties.**

19   a. To this end, an arbitrator should keep current with principles, practices and developments that are relevant to his or her own field of arbitration practice.

20   **2. An experienced arbitrator should cooperate in the training of new arbitrators.**

21   **3. An arbitrator must not advertise or solicit arbitration assignments.**

22   a. It is a matter of personal preference whether an arbitrator includes "Labor Arbitrator" or similar notation on letterheads, cards, or announcements. *It is inappropriate, however, to include memberships or offices held in professional societies or listings on rosters of administrative agencies.*

23   b. *Information provided for published biographical sketches, as well as that supplied to administrative agencies, must be accurate.* Such information may include membership in professional organizations (including reference to significant offices held), and listings on rosters of administrative agencies.

2

Responsibilities to the Parties

A. Recognition of Diversity in Arbitration Arrangements

1. An arbitrator should conscientiously endeavor to understand   24
and observe, to the extent consistent with professional responsibility,
the significant principles governing each arbitration system in which
he or she serves.

> a. Recognition of special features of a particular arbitration ar-   25
> rangement can be essential with respect to procedural matters and
> may influence other aspects of the arbitration process.

2. Such understanding does not relieve an arbitrator from a cor-   26
ollary responsibility to seek to discern and refuse to lend approval or
consent to any collusive attempt by the parties to use arbitration for
an improper purpose.

B. Required Disclosures

1. Before accepting an appointment, an arbitrator must disclose   27
directly or through the administrative agency involved, any current
or past managerial, representational, or consultative relationship with
any company or union involved in a proceeding in which he or she
is being considered for appointment or has been tentatively designated
to serve. Disclosure must also be made of any pertinent pecuniary
interest.

> a. The duty to disclose includes membership on a Board of   28
> Directors, full-time or part-time service as a representative or ad-
> vocate, consultation work for a fee, current stock or bond owner-

ship (other than mutual fund shares or appropriate trust arrangements) or any other pertinent form of managerial, financial or immediate family interest in the company or union involved.

29   **2. When an arbitrator is serving concurrently as an advocate for or representative of other companies or unions in labor relations matters, or has done so in recent years, he or she must disclose such activities before accepting appointment as an arbitrator.**

30   **An arbitrator must disclose such activities to an administrative agency if he or she is on that agency's active roster or seeks placement on a roster. Such disclosure then satisfies this requirement for cases handled under that agency's referral.**

31   a. It is not necessary to disclose names of clients or other specific details. It is necessary to indicate the general nature of the labor relations advocacy or representational work involved, whether for companies or unions or both, and a reasonable approximation of the extent of such activity.

32   b. *An arbitrator on an administrative agency's roster has a continuing obligation to notify the agency of any significant changes pertinent to this requirement.*

33   c. When an administrative agency is not involved, an arbitrator must make such disclosure directly unless he or she is certain that both parties to the case are fully aware of such activities.

34   **3. An arbitrator must not permit personal relationships to affect decision-making.**

35   **Prior to acceptance of an appointment, an arbitrator must disclose to the parties or to the administrative agency involved any close personal relationship or other circumstance, in addition to those specifically mentioned earlier in this section, which might reasonably raise a question as to the arbitrator's impartiality.**

36   a. Arbitrators establish personal relationships with many company and union representatives, with fellow arbitrators, and with fellow members of various professional associations. There should be no attempt to be secretive about such friendships or acquaintances but disclosure is not necessary unless some feature of a particular relationship might reasonably appear to impair impartiality.

4. If the circumstances requiring disclosure are not known to the 37
arbitrator prior to acceptance of appointment, disclosure must be made
when such circumstances become known to the arbitrator.

5. The burden of disclosure rests on the arbitrator. After appropri- 38
ate disclosure, the arbitrator may serve if both parties so desire. If the
arbitrator believes or perceives that there is a clear conflict of interest,
he or she should withdraw, irrespective of the expressed desires of the
parties.

C. Privacy of Arbitration

1. All significant aspects of an arbitration proceeding must be 39
treated by the arbitrator as confidential unless this requirement is waived
by both parties or disclosure is required or permitted by law.

a. Attendance at hearings by persons not representing the par- 40
ties or invited by either or both of them should be permitted only
when the parties agree or when an applicable law requires or permits. Occasionally, special circumstances may require that an arbitrator rule on such matters as attendance and degree of participation
of counsel selected by a grievant.

b. *Discussion of a case at any time by an arbitrator with per-* 41
sons not involved directly should be limited to situations where ad-
vance approval or consent of both parties is obtained or where the
identity of the parties and details of the case are sufficiently obscured
to eliminate any realistic probability of identification.

A commonly recognized exception is discussion of a problem 42
in a case with a fellow arbitrator. *Any such discussion does not relieve*
the arbitrator who is acting in the case from sole responsibility for
the decision and the discussion must be considered as confidential.

Discussion of aspects of a case in a classroom without prior 43
specific approval of the parties is not a violation provided the arbitrator is satisfied that there is no breach of essential confidentiality.

c. *It is a violation of professional responsibility for an arbitrator* 44
to make public an award without the consent of the parties.

An arbitrator may ask the parties whether they consent to the 45 *publication of the award either at the hearing or at the time the award is issued.*

46   (1) *If such question is asked at the hearing it should be asked in writing as follows:*

> *"Do you consent to the submission of the award in this matter for publication?*
>
> *( )*   *( )*
> YES   NO
>
> *If you consent you have the right to notify the arbitrator within 30 days after the date of the award that you revoke your consent."*

It is desirable but not required that the arbitrator remind the parties at the time of the issuance of the award of their right to withdraw their consent to publication.

47   (2) If the question of consent to the publication of the award is raised at the time the award is issued, the arbitrator may state in writing to each party that failure to answer the inquiry within 30 days will be considered an implied consent to publish.

48   d. It is not improper for an arbitrator to donate arbitration files to a library of a college, university or similar institution without prior consent of all the parties involved. When the circumstances permit, there should be deleted from such donations any cases concerning which one or both of the parties have expressed a desire for privacy. As an additional safeguard, an arbitrator may also decide to withhold recent cases or indicate to the donee a time interval before such cases can be made generally available.

49   e. *Applicable laws, regulations, or practices of the parties may permit or even require exceptions to the above noted principles of privacy.*

D. Personal Relationships with the Parties

50   **1. An arbitrator must make every reasonable effort to conform to arrangements required by an administrative agency or mutually desired by the parties regarding communications and personal relationships with the parties.**

a. *Only an "arm's-length" relationship may be acceptable to* 51
the parties in some arbitration arrangements or may be required by
the rules of an administrative agency. The arbitrator should then
have no contact of consequence with representatives of either party
while handling a case without the other party's presence or consent.

b. *In other situations, both parties may want communications* 52
and personal relationships to be less formal. It is then appropriate
for the arbitrator to respond accordingly.

E. Jurisdiction

1. An arbitrator must observe faithfully both the limitations and 53
inclusions of the jurisdiction conferred by an agreement or other sub-
mission under which he or she serves.

2. A direct settlement by the parties of some or all issues in a case, 54
at any stage of the proceedings, must be accepted by the arbitrator
as relieving him or her of further jurisdiction over such issues.

F. Mediation by an Arbitrator

1. When the parties wish at the outset to give an arbitrator authori- 55
ty both to mediate and to decide or submit recommendations regard-
ing residual issues, if any, they should so advise the arbitrator prior
to appointment. If the appointment is accepted, the arbitrator must
perform a mediation role consistent with the circumstances of the case.

a. Direct appointments, also, may require a dual role as media- 56
tor and arbitrator of residual issues. This is most likely to occur in
some public sector cases.

2. When a request to mediate is first made after appointment, the 57
arbitrator may either accept or decline a mediation role.

a. *Once arbitration has been invoked, either party normally has* 58
a right to insist that the process be continued to decision.

b. *If one party requests that the arbitrator mediate and the other* 59
party objects, the arbitrator should decline the request.

60   *c. An arbitrator is not precluded from making a suggestion that he or she mediate. To avoid the possibility of improper pressure, the arbitrator should not so suggest unless it can be discerned that both parties are likely to be receptive. In any event, the arbitrator's suggestion should not be pursued unless both parties readily agree.*

G. Reliance by an Arbitrator on Other Arbitration Awards or on Independent Research

61   **1. An arbitrator must assume full personal responsibility for the decision in each case decided.**

62   *a. The extent, if any, to which an arbitrator properly may rely on precedent, on guidance of other awards, or on independent research is dependent primarily on the policies of the parties on these matters, as expressed in the contract, or other agreement, or at the hearing.*

63   b. When the mutual desires of the parties are not known or when the parties express differing opinions or policies, the arbitrator may exercise discretion as to these matters, consistent with acceptance of full personal responsibility for the award.

H. Use of Assistants

64   **1. An arbitrator must not delegate any decision-making function to another person without consent of the parties.**

65   *a. Without prior consent of the parties, an arbitrator may use the services of an assistant for research, clerical duties, or preliminary drafting under the direction of the arbitrator, which does not involve the delegation of any decision-making function.*

66   *b. If an arbitrator is unable, because of time limitations or other reasons, to handle all decision-making aspects of a case, it is not a violation of professional responsibility to suggest to the parties an allocation of responsibility between the arbitrator and an assistant or associate. The arbitrator must not exert pressure on the parties to accept such a suggestion.*

I. Consent Awards

1. Prior to issuance of an award, the parties may jointly request 67
the arbitrator to include in the award certain agreements between them,
concerning some or all of the issues. If the arbitrator believes that a
suggested award is proper, fair, sound, and lawful, it is consistent with
professional responsibility to adopt it.

a. Before complying with such a request, an arbitrator must 68
be certain that he or she understands the suggested settlement ade-
quately in order to be able to appraise its terms. If it appears that
pertinent facts or circumstances may not have been disclosed, the ar-
bitrator should take the initiative to assure that all significant aspects
of the case are fully understood. To this end, the arbitrator may re-
quest additional specific information and may question witnesses at
a hearing.

J. Avoidance of Delay

1. It is a basic professional responsibility of an arbitrator to plan 69
his or her work schedule so that present and future commitments will
be fulfilled in a timely manner.

a. When planning is upset for reasons beyond the control of 70
the arbitrator, he or she, nevertheless, should exert every reasonable
effort to fulfill all commitments. If this is not possible, prompt notice
at the arbitrator's initiative should be given to all parties affected.
Such notices should include reasonably accurate estimates of any
additional time required. To the extent possible, priority should be
given to cases in process so that other parties may make alternative
arbitration arrangements.

2. An arbitrator must cooperate with the parties and with any ad- 71
ministrative agency involved in avoiding delays.

a. An arbitrator on the active roster of an administrative agen- 72
cy must take the initiative in advising the agency of any scheduling
difficulties that he or she can foresee.

b. Requests for services, whether received directly or through 73
an administrative agency, should be declined if the arbitrator is una-
ble to schedule a hearing as soon as the parties wish. If the parties,

nevertheless, jointly desire to obtain the services of the arbitrator and the arbitrator agrees, arrangements should be made by agreement that the arbitrator confidently expects to fulfill.

74   *c. An arbitrator may properly seek to persuade the parties to alter or eliminate arbitration procedures or tactics that cause unnecessary delay.*

75   **3. Once the case record has been closed, an arbitrator must adhere to the time limits for an award, as stipulated in the labor agreement or as provided by regulation of an administrative agency or as otherwise agreed.**

76   *a. If an appropriate award cannot be rendered within the required time, it is incumbent on the arbitrator to seek an extension of time from the parties.*

77   b. If the parties have agreed upon abnormally short time limits for an award after a case is closed, the arbitrator should be so advised by the parties or by the administrative agency involved, prior to acceptance of appointment.

K. Fees and Expenses

78   **1. An arbitrator occupies a position of trust in respect to the parties and the administrative agencies. In charging for services and expenses, the arbitrator must be governed by the same high standards of honor and integrity that apply to all other phases of his or her work.**

79   **An arbitrator must endeavor to keep total charges for services and expenses reasonable and consistent with the nature of the case or cases decided.**

80   **Prior to appointment, the parties should be aware of or be able readily to determine all significant aspects of an arbitrator's bases for charges for fees and expenses.**

    a. Services Not Primarily Chargeable on a Per Diem Basis

81   By agreement with the parties, the financial aspects of many "permanent" arbitration assignments, of some interest disputes, and of some "ad hoc" grievance assignments do not include a per diem fee for services as a primary part of the total understanding. *In such*

situations, the arbitrator must adhere faithfully to all agreed-upon arrangements governing fees and expenses.

b. Per Diem Basis for Charges for Services

(1) When an arbitrator's charges for services are determined 82 primarily by a stipulated per diem fee, the arbitrator should establish in advance his or her bases for application of such per diem fee and for determination of reimbursable expenses.

Practices established by an arbitrator should include the basis 83 for charges, if any, for:

(a) hearing time, including the application of the stipulated basic per diem hearing fee to hearing days of varying lengths;

(b) study time;

(c) necessary travel time when not included in charges for hearing time;

(d) postponement or cancellation of hearings by the parties and the circumstances in which such charges will normally be assessed or waived;

(e) office overhead expenses (secretarial, telephone, postage, etc.);

(f) the work of paid assistants or associates.

(2) Each arbitrator should be guided by the following general 84 principles:

(a) Per diem charges for a hearing should not be in excess 85 of actual time spent or allocated for the hearing.

(b) Per diem charges for study time should not be in excess 86 of actual time spent.

(c) Any fixed ratio of study days to hearing days, not agreed 87 to specifically by the parties, is inconsistent with the per diem method of charges for services.

(d) Charges for expenses must not be in excess of actual ex- 88 penses normally reimbursable and incurred in connection with the case or cases involved.

(e) When time or expense charges are involved for two or 89 more sets of parties on the same day or trip, such time or expense charges should be appropriately prorated.

90   (f) *An arbitrator may stipulate in advance a minimum charge for a hearing without violation of (a) or (e) above.*

91   (3) *An arbitrator on the active roster of an administrative agency must file with the agency his or her individual bases for determination of fees and expenses if the agency so requires. Thereafter, it is the responsibility of each such arbitrator to advise the agency promptly of any change in any basis for charges.*

92   Such filing may be in the form of answers to a questionnaire devised by an agency or by any other method adopted by or approved by an agency.

93   *Having supplied an administrative agency with the information noted above, an arbitrator's professional responsibility of disclosure under this Code with respect to fees and expenses has been satisfied for cases referred by that agency.*

94   (4) *If an administrative agency promulgates specific standards with respect to any of these matters which are in addition to or more restrictive than an individual arbitrator's standards, an arbitrator on its active roster must observe the agency standards for cases handled under the auspices of that agency, or decline to serve.*

95   (5) *When an arbitrator is contacted directly by the parties for a case or cases, the arbitrator has a professional responsibility to respond to questions by submitting his or her bases for charges for fees and charges.*

96   (6) *When it is known to the arbitrator that one or both of the parties cannot afford normal charges, it is consistent with professional responsibility to charge lesser amounts to both parties or to one of the parties if the other party is made aware of the difference and agrees.*

97   (7) *If an arbitrator concludes that the total of charges derived from his or her normal basis of calculation is not compatible with the case decided, it is consistent with professional responsibility to charge lesser amounts to both parties.*

98   **2. An arbitrator must maintain adequate records to support charges for services and expenses and must make an accounting to the parties or to an involved administrative agency on request.**

3
Responsibilities to Administrative Agencies

A. General Responsibilities

1. An arbitrator must be candid, accurate, and fully responsive to an administrative agency concerning his or her qualifications, availability, and all other pertinent matters.   99

2. An arbitrator must observe policies and rules of an administrative agency in cases referred by that agency.   100

3. An arbitrator must not seek to influence an administrative agency by any improper means, including gifts or other inducements to agency personnel.   101

a. It is not improper for a person seeking placement on a roster to request references from individuals having knowledge of the applicant's experience and qualifications.   102

b. Arbitrators should recognize that the primary responsibility of an administrative agency is to serve the parties.   103

4
Prehearing Conduct

104 **1. All prehearing matters must be handled in a manner that fosters complete impartiality by the arbitrator.**

105 a. The primary purpose of prehearing discussions involving the arbitrator is to obtain agreement on procedural matters so that the hearing can proceed without unnecessary obstacles. If differences of opinion should arise during such discussions and, particularly, if such differences appear to impinge on substantive matters, the circumstances will suggest whether the matter can be resolved informally or may require a prehearing conference or, more rarely, a formal preliminary hearing. When an administrative agency handles some or all aspects of the arrangements prior to a hearing, the arbitrator will become involved only if differences of some substance arise.

106 b. *Copies of any prehearing correspondence between the arbitrator and either party must be made available to both parties.*

5
Hearing Conduct

A. General Principles

1. An arbitrator must provide a fair and adequate hearing which assures that both parties have sufficient opportunity to present their respective evidence and argument.   107

    a. *Within the limits of this responsibility, an arbitrator should conform to the various types of hearing procedures desired by the parties.*   108

    b. An arbitrator may: encourage stipulations of fact; restate the substance of issues or arguments to promote or verify understanding; question the parties' representatives or witnesses, when necessary or advisable, to obtain additional pertinent information; and request that the parties submit additional evidence, either at the hearing or by subsequent filing.   109

    c. *An arbitrator should not intrude into a party's presentation so as to prevent that party from putting forward its case fairly and adequately.*   110

B. Transcripts or Recordings

1. Mutual agreement of the parties as to use or non-use of a transcript must be respected by the arbitrator.   111

    a. *A transcript is the official record of a hearing only when both parties agree to a transcript or an applicable law or regulation so provides.*   112

    b. An arbitrator may seek to persuade the parties to avoid use of a transcript, or to use a transcript if the nature of the case appears   113 to require one. *However, if an arbitrator intends to make his or her appointment to a case contingent on mutual agreement to a transcript, that requirement must be made known to both parties prior to appointment.*

114   c. If the parties do not agree to a transcript, an arbitrator may permit one party to take a transcript at its own cost. The arbitrator may also make appropriate arrangements under which the other party may have access to a copy, if a copy is provided to the arbitrator.

115   d. Without prior approval, an arbitrator may seek to use his or her own tape recorder to supplement note taking. The arbitrator should not insist on such a tape recording if either or both parties object.

C. Ex Parte Hearings

116   **1. In determining whether to conduct an ex parte hearing, an arbitrator must consider relevant legal, contractual, and other pertinent circumstances.**

117   **2. An arbitrator must be certain, before proceeding ex parte, that the party refusing or failing to attend the hearing has been given adequate notice of the time, place, and purposes of the hearing.**

D. Plant Visits

118   **1. An arbitrator should comply with a request of any party that he or she visit a work area pertinent to the dispute prior to, during, or after a hearing. An arbitrator may also initiate such a request.**

119   *a. Procedures for such visits should be agreed to by the parties in consultation with the arbitrator.*

E. Bench Decisions or Expedited Awards

120   **1. When an arbitrator understands, prior to acceptance of appointment, that a bench decision is expected at the conclusion of the hearing, the arbitrator must comply with the understanding unless both parties agree otherwise.**

a. *If notice of the parties' desire for a bench decision is not given prior to the arbitrator's acceptance of the case, issuance of such a bench decision is discretionary.* 121

b. *When only one party makes the request and the other objects, the arbitrator should not render a bench decision except under most unusual circumstances.* 122

2. When an arbitrator understands, prior to acceptance of appointment, that a concise written award is expected within a stated time period after the hearing, the arbitrator must comply with the understanding unless both parties agree otherwise. 123

6
Post Hearing Conduct

A. Post Hearing Briefs and Submissions

124   **1. An arbitrator must comply with mutual agreements in respect to the filing or nonfiling of post hearing briefs or submissions.**

125   a. An arbitrator, in his or her discretion, may either suggest the filing of post hearing briefs or other submissions or suggest that none be filed.

126   b. When the parties disagree as to the need for briefs, an arbitrator may permit filing but may determine a reasonable time limitation.

127   **2. An arbitrator must not consider a post hearing brief or submission that has not been provided to the other party.**

B. Disclosure of Terms of Award

128   **1. An arbitrator must not disclose a prospective award to either party prior to its simultaneous issuance to both parties or explore possible alternative awards unilaterally with one party, unless both parties so agree.**

129   a. Partisan members of tripartite boards may know prospective terms of an award in advance of its issuance. Similar situations may exist in other less formal arrangements mutually agreed to by the parties. In any such situation, the arbitrator should determine and observe the mutually desired degree of confidentiality.

C. Awards and Opinions

1. The award should be definite, certain, and as concise as possible.   130

    a. When an opinion is required, factors to be considered by an   131
arbitrator include: desirability of brevity, consistent with the nature
of the case and any expressed desires of the parties; need to use a
style and form that is understandable to responsible representatives
of the parties, to the grievant and supervisors, and to others in the
collective bargaining relationship; necessity of meeting the significant
issues; forthrightness to an extent not harmful to the relationship of
the parties; and avoidance of gratuitous advice or discourse not essential to disposition of the issues.

D. Clarification or Interpretation of Awards

1. No clarification or interpretation of an award is permissible   132
without the consent of both parties.

2. Under agreements which permit or require clarification or inter-   133
pretation of an award, an arbitrator must afford both parties an oppor-
tunity to be heard.

E. Enforcement of Award

1. The arbitrator's responsibility does not extend to the enforce-   134
ment of an award.

2. In view of the professional and confidential nature of the arbitra-   135
tion relationship, an arbitrator should not voluntarily participate in legal
enforcement proceedings.

References

1. Taylor, George W., Effectuating the labor contrct through arbitration. *The Profession of Arbitration.* (Washington, D.C.: Bureau of National Affairs, 1957).
2. Mittenthal, Richard, Whither arbitration?, *Arbitration 1990, The Changing Face of Arbitration in Theory and Practice* (Washington, D.C.: Bureau of National Affairs, 1992).
3. *Code of Professional Responsibility for Arbitration of Labor Management Disputes,* National Academy of Arbitrators, 1985.
4. Voluntary Labor Arbitration Rules, American Arbitration Association, 1988.
5. Ibid.
6. Ibid.
7. Ibid.
8. Advisory opinion #13, National Academy of Arbitrators formal advisory opinions, 1992.
9. Advisory opinion #2, *Formal Advisory Opinion,* op. cit.
10. Voluntary Labor Arbitration Rules, op. cit.
11. Howlett, Robert G., Metzler, Bernard D., Ruminations About Ideology, law and labor arbitrations. *The Arbitrator, the NLRB and the Courts* (Washington, D.C.; BNA, 1967).
12. Loftus, Elizabeth F., Memory and searching for truth, *Arbitration 1987, The Academy at Forty* (Washington, D.C.: BNA, 1988).
13. Advisory opinion #8, *Formal Advisory Opinion,* op. cit.
14. Advisory opinion #20, Formal Advisory Opinion, op. cit.

Index

About the Author

Arnold Zack is a graduate of Tufts College, Yale Law School, and the Harvard Graduate School of Public Administration. He has been an arbitrator and mediator in the labor relations field for the past thirty years. He has served as arbitrator under many collective bargaining agreements and has issued several thousand awards. In addition he served as the director of the Labor Management Institute of the American Arbitration Association in 1966 to 1968, exploring the adaptability of the private labor management model into the then-new field of public sector collective bargaining. Zack has served as a member of the Board of Governors, a vice president of the National Academy of Arbitrators, and for five years he was chairman of its continuing education program. He has served as a member of two presidential emergency boards. He has been a consultant to the International Labor Office establishing and evaluating mediator and arbitrator training programs and training in Australia, Greece, Ethiopia, Malaysia, the Philippines, South Africa, Spain, Zimbabwe, and elsewhere. This is his tenth book on labor relations. He is the recipient of the Whitney North Seymour medal of the American Arbitration Assoication (1980), the Cushing-Gavin Award of the Archdiocese of Boston, (1986), and the Distinguished Service Award of the American Arbitration Association, (1989). He is also twice recipient of the Mildred Spaulding Award of the Duke County Agricultural Society for the years' outstanding vegetable and fruit preserves. He is married to Dr. Norma W. Zack, a physician in Boston, and they have two children, Jonathan and Rachel.